Magnus Edizioni wishes to thank
the Direction of the Pontifical Monuments,
Museums and Galleries - Vatican City,
the Vatican Apostolic Library - Vatican City,
the Istituto Geografico De Agostini
Photographic Archive - Novara,
and the Nippon Television Network - Tokyo
for the kind assistance in the preparation
of this book.

ISBN 88-7057-140-8

Printed in Italy by Grafiche Lema - Maniago Pn

THE VATICAN

history and treasures

Text by
CLAUDIO RENDINA

English translation by
DANIELA PERESSINI

MAGNUS

The Vatican, or more precisely the Vatican City, is a State whose sovereign is the Pope, Bishop of Rome, Vicar of Christ, successor to the Prince of the Apostles, Sovereign Pontiff of the Universal Church, Patriarch of the West, Primate of Italy, Bishop and Metropolitan of the Diocese of Rome. However this State is not in effect a sovereign state; the sovereignty is retained by the Holy See which is inseparable from the very person of the Sovereign Pontiff, who remains the head of the Universal Church, albeit as "servant of the servants of God" in keeping with the designation inherited from Pope Gregory the Great who so defined himself.
The Vatican City as we know it today was born on 11 February 1929 with the signing of the Lateran Pact between Italy and the Holy See. This Pact resolved the so-called "Roman question" which had remained open since 20 September 1870 when the breaching of Porta Pia sealed Rome's passage from capital of the Papal State to capital of the unified Italy. Having risen as an *enclave* in the middle of Rome, the Vatican (as we will call it from now on) or Holy See cannot be demarcated solely on the basis of "so much territory", as Pius XI put it, because its enormous religious and moral influence reaches out all over the world and because of the Catholic presence on every continent.
The Vatican's history is not, however, limited to the period from 1929 onwards. These years are connected in one instance with over a thousand years of temporal events of the Papal State, and in another with the spiritual events initiated by Christ's foundation of the Church. The Vatican is, in fact, 2,000 years old and has lived this period within Rome always as an enclave in an urban and ideological ambiguity. This ambiguity, expressed successively on either side of the city-walls and the Tiber, has bound Peter's tomb and his basilica with the city to such an extent as to identify them with Rome itself. To narrate the history and "treasures" of the Vatican means, therefore, retracing the origins and events of the Papacy within those bastioned town-walls raised in defence of the tomb of the Prince of the Apostles, immortal symbol of its very raison d'être.
At the beginning there is a "field", the ager or *campus Vaticanus,* at the foot of the *montes Vaticani,* the range of hills stretching from Mount Mario to Janiculum. It has a sacred nature which determines its name already in pagan times. Aulus Gellius tells us the name comes from the vaticinii, or prophecies, which have demonstrated the power and divine inspiration present in that territory. It is an area outside the Servian and Aurelian walls, rendered marshy and malaria infested by the Tiber's frequent floods. At the outset of the Empire the "field" is reclaimed and so villas and gardens take form, such as Vipsania Agrippina's (Germanicus' wife), extending from the *montes Vaticani* to the Tiber. Her son, the Emperor Caligula, in the year 33 A.D. constructs a circus there within which he has an obelisk raised, the same red granite obelisk which is now in the centre of St Peter's Square. The scene is thereby set for the events destined to render the Vatican sacred, this time in the Christian sense. The players are the martyrs and their executioner is Nero. The fateful date is 19 July of the year 64 A.D. when in the area of the Circus Maximus that famous fire breaks out. It is to flare for a week, destroying two thirds of the city. The voice of the populace accuses the Emperor who, in turn, indicates the guilty parties as "men hated for their wicked rites, commonly called Christians", writes Tacitus; "they are cruelly condemned to death and some, covered with pitch and resin, are slowly burned alive on tree trunks in order to serve as torches to illuminate the games in the circus". They die in their hundreds, but many remain imprisoned for long periods and in some cases the sentences are carried out years after the fire. This is true for St Paul and St Peter, martyrs together, according to tradition, in the year 67. Paul is decapitated at *Aquas Salvias* in the place today known as Three Fountains (Tre Fontane) and buried in the Ostiense burial ground where the basilica dedicated to him will rise. Peter is crucified in the Vatican Circus, but asks to be hung head-down, retaining himself unfit to die in the same manner as Christ. He is buried in a grave in the burial ground beneath the Circus which was used between the first and fourth centuries by pagans and Christians alike, the so-called Vatican Necropolis which today opens up on the two sides of the Holy Grottoes.

Peter's tomb

The roots of the sacred Vatican lie here. Along the route flanked by mausoleums you can breathe the beginning of Christianity, not only due to the presence of the first Pope's tomb, but by the very fact that those Christian tombs restore to us intact the truly mystical spirit of the faith in Christ which lies at the origins of the Church in Rome. At the spot in the Basilica where the present altar of the Confession rises there is an unpretentious place labelled "field P" by archeologists, bounded by the so-called "red wall". Nearby is a simple monument made up of two niches, one above the other, and separated by a slab of marble supported by two small columns. This is a funerary aedicule of the second century, embellished in the third, and marks the original burial place of Peter. Amongst the numerous graffiti inscriptions traced by the early faithfull there is one in Greek: *Petr(os)eni*, that is "Peter is here". This is the tomb of the Prince of the Apostles.
The necropolis takes us back to the Holy See's primitive age, the "pre-catacomb" period of the Church of Rome. At that time the community was mainly made up of faithful of humble social status, many of Hebrew origin and certainly not landowners, who buried their dead in graves shared with the pagans. The Milan Edict of 313 brings the Church of Rome out of the catacombs and grants it citizenship rights. Constantine perceives the new religion's potential spiritual power compared to that of the pagans as a possible backup for the shaky imperial structures. As a result he uses "state" funds to finance the public practice of the Christian cult. He donates his wife's house, the *domus Faustae,* to the Laterans, to Sylvester I in order to give the Pope a decent residence. This will become the episcopal seat and will remain such until our time. The basilica which will rise there, St John's, will be Rome's Cathedral. Constantine saves the

greatest attention for Peter's tomb, symbol of the Bishop of Rome's preeminence. For this reason he commits himself personally to its glorification by constructing a basilica and an altar. He intervenes with authority in the hollowing out of the Vatican hill, he levels and canalizes the surrounding swampy area, he fortifies it with protective walls and even has the necropolis desecrated in order to isolate the Apostle's grave.
The year 320 sees the laying of the first stone. According to the *Liber pontificalis*, Constantine himself digs the foundations and has Peter's bones buried in a bronze sarcophagus in an underground room above which a ciborium, or bronze canopy, is erected, supported by four columns. The ciborium is in the middle of the grand building which Constantine's son, Constants, will complete in 349. The finished basilica has five aisles. The nave will be 91 metres long, illuminated by numerous windows up to the triumphal arch at the entrance and separated from the smaller aisles by a double file of architraved pillars. Outside is the huge atrium known as "Paradise" ("il paradiso"), a quadriporticoed courtyard in the centre of which will later be built a nympheum with the water springing from a bronze pinecone. The pinecone will later be moved to the Court of the Pinecone (or Pigna) in the present-day Vatican. Peter's tomb therefore has a magnificent situation which will be made more sumptuous by precious gifts from sovereigns and pilgrims and embellished with gold and silver by the Popes themselves in a true celebration of the Church of Rome, identifying in the tomb of the Prince of the Apostles the affirmation of its primate over other churches as the only Holy See. In this way the Pope can impose his authority in dogmatic disputes from the time of Leo I (440-461) onwards. He is the first to exalt the primate of Peter's seat and of his descendants, subjecting the bishops of Gaul, calling the Council of Chalcedonia and asserting his authority in the dispute with the Alexandrian patriarch on the nature of Christ.
The Holy See, born as a community of believers with solely spiritual aims, once drawn into the state context soon comes into conflict with imperial power.
The Pope enjoys an authority equal to that of a "caesar" initially only in religious matters. Politics and imperialism slowly take hold in its upper hierarchy and temporal events become more and more intertwined with spiritual matters. With the Barbarian invasions, the Pope's authority substitutes that of the timorous and inept emperors. He becomes *defensor urbis* and, even if powerless against the Goths of Alaric in 410 and the Vandals of Genseric in 456, manages to have St Peter's and St Paul's spared during the pillage. Leo I also manages to stop Attila, the "scourge of God", with his Huns on the Mincio in 453. According to tradition this is a miracle, but it is a miracle that brings with it a commitment to pay a huge gold tribute, emptying the Papal coffers.
With the fall of the Western Empire the city finds in the Pope the bulwark of its culture. The Byzantine emperor is weak and distant and in 564 the Bishop of Rome obtains a real jurisdiction over territories and cities that becomes concrete under Pelagius (556-561) with the delimitation and organization of several estates, forming the so-called Patrimony of St Peter. This estate spreads out in the *ager Romanus* to cover the Sabine and Tuscia areas under Gregory the Great, a Pope unique for his integrity as *consul Dei*. In a city lacking a civil authority the Pope tackles and resolves social and administrative problems, offering to the needy the funds raised from "the estates of the Apostle Peter" whose tomb continues to be the object of veneration. By now the Holy See must deal with the powers that be of the European kingdoms as a true sovereign kingdom, and the concern of ensuring their support increases from this point onwards.

The birth of a city

The "Dark Ages", as the period up to the constitution of the Holy Roman Empire will be known, pass by. This event is evocatively represented in the setting of Peter's tomb: Charlemagne, on the large porphyry disk in the Vatican basilica (conserved to this day in the pavement of the Basilica's nave), is proclaimed "anointed by God" as "Augustus crowned by God" by Leo III. The Emperor commits himself to defending the heritage of St Peter (even if he will not always do so) and the Pope renounces every pretension to imperial power. In truth, the Pope believes he will exercise such power indirectly: this is the beginning of the conflicts between Church and Empire which characterize at least five centuries of history.
The defence of the "heritage" means, firstly, the defence of the Basilica and St Peter's tomb, both continuously at risk. The surrounding area is made up of wooden buildings, easy prey for fires which tradition says were subdued by miracle. Paschal I (817-824) walks barefoot through the flames which are overcoming the Basilica's portico and the fire dies down immediately. In 848 Leo IV need only make the sign of the cross to quell an even more devastating fire. In 846, however, the Saracens manage to sack the Basilica, a sign that the Emperor is no sure guarantee of security. It is at this stage that Leo IV comes up with the idea of erecting a type of barricade around St Peter's. As a result in 852 the *Civitas Leonina* is born and a bastioned wall delineates the *enclave* inside a city over which the Popes want to exercise their own direct power.
So that Rome may become "papal" the Popes are forced to undertake civil wars within the city. This is the urban environment of the Middle Ages, a combination of ecclesiastic, imperial and baronial forces pointing the way to anarchy in the clash between factions controlled by local aristocratic families or indirectly by foreign sovereigns who are in any case incapable of asserting themselves and leaving a lasting trace. This is the city of the feuds between towers and fortresses built on ancient monumental buildings. It is here that the Teofilatto, Crescenzi, Frangipane and Conti families tear themselves apart, siding in turn with the popes of convenience imposed by dubious and unscrupulous figures such as Teodora and Marozia, and on the wings of the fanciful restauratio imperii of Otto III, in "sacred harmony" with Pope Sylvester II (999-1003). Rome is also the city of *renovatio Senatus*, from Arnaldo da Brescia's

mystic vision to Brancaleone degli Andal 's ferocity in flattening the urban towers. These were the breeding ground for the feuds and conspiracies which rendered the Pope's position insecure, especially since his defence was entrusted to fortuitous mercenary forces. Lucius II (1144-1145) dies due to a blow with a stone during the attack on the Capitol (Campidoglio), while the Lateran cathedral, seat of the Bishop of Rome, is often the stage for raging battles.
The payoff lies in the *Dictatus papae* of Gregory VII (1073-1085), the dogmatic affirmation of Papal sovereignty over Church and State, with Innocent III's (1198-1216) ensuing attempt to establish a theocratic state within which claim is laid to the Pope's absolute power over the spiritual and material, over the ecclesiastic and lay worlds, even if all remains a utopia. In the meantime the idea of a residence in the form of a fortress within the Civitas Leonina to function as a physical safeguard for the Pope gains momentum. Eugenius III (1145-1153) lays the foundations of a building in the area to the north of the Basilica. Work continues under his successors Clement III and Celestine III, but it is Innocence III who gives it more ample dimensions by adding an imposing tower. This is the original building nucleus upon which the eastern wing of the present Sala Ducale will rise. The combination palace-fortress is completed under Nicholas III (1277-1280), the first Pope to reside permanently in the Vatican. It takes up a quadrangular arrangement and a second tower is added. It is also protected from the outside with an addition to the boundary-wall towards the Tiber which is connected to Castel Sant'Angelo via the Borgo passage ("passetto"). In 1302 Boniface VIII (1294-1303) in the *Unam Sanctam* Papal bull declares that both the spiritual and temporal are based on the authority of the Church. The former is exercised by the Church itself by hand of the priest, the latter on behalf of the Church by the king, but always according to the priest's will. This is the theory refused by the European rulers, causing the Pope's transfer to Avignon (1305-1371) and the subsequent schism of the West, with the revolt of the French cardinals followed by the Pope's return to Rome. This schism will provoke the nomination of the antipope. The moral stature and authority of Urban VI (1378-1389), the first Pope elected after the Avignon period, will restore strength and prestige to the Holy See. It is also with him that the Vicar of Christ, in the clashes with national States, discovers a new payoff in the figure of the "sovereign" Pontiff: the Pope-King.
At the beginning of the 15th century the Pope asserts himself authoritatively in this capacity within the Rome controlled by barons, with a new strength springing from a conception of power defined in the Papal State's reconstruction carried out by very steadfast cardinals such as Giovanni Vitelleschi and Egidio Albornoz. The Pope takes the place of the emperor and the commune. The ancient noble familes are reorganized and must come to terms with the newcomers which arrive in the retinues of the Papal families. During the 16th century they are the Borgia, Della Rovere, Medici, Farnese, Boncompagni and Peretti; in the 17th century the Borghese, Ludovisi, Barberini, Pamphilj, Chigi, Rospigliosi, Altieri and Odescalchi. It will be the triumph of authority but also, unfortunately, of nepotism - the "power within the power" authorized in every sense as a guarantee of the reigning "sovereign". This is a true renouncement of the State, rewarded with the construction of palaces, churches and fountains within the framework of an urban redesigning of Rome which is to become the capital of a modern State reflecting the image of the Pope-King.
This image is not damaged by episodes of immorality and even murders during the pontificate of Innocent VIII (1484-1492) and Alexander VI (1492-1503), nor by the sale of indulgences and Luther's invectives against Julius II (1503-1512) and Leo X (1513-1521) or Clement VII's (1523-1534) political errors which lead to the pillage by the Lansquenets in 1527.
Opposition to the revolutionary antipapal Reformation is posed by the reactionary Counter-Reformation which seeks to reinforce the Papal primate invoked as an assurance of the Pope-King's total immunity within the national and international context. Rome is the "holy city" of Pius V (1566-1572) and Sixtus V (1585-1590), a piece of propaganda for the Counter-Reformation in exalting Catholicism's renewed *caput mundi*. Rome is the Baroque "city-stage" of Urban VIII (1623-1644), Innocent X (1644-1655) and Alexander VII (1655-1667), with a magnificence which must transmit to the world the exaltation of the Papal image. Spectacular liturgies and ceremonies elevating religious ideology distinguish a period punctutated by the Jubilees, and not only every 25 years considering the numerous extraordinary Jubilees called for special festivities and exceptional holy anniversaries. In this way Rome is reconstructed and restructured to mirror itself in an urban architecture which goes so far as to become an exasperating search for "wonders", beginning with the construction of the new Vatican and the new St Peter's Basilica.
Speaking in terms of royal palaces, the Apostolic Palaces take form with Nicholas V (1447-1455) who restructures Nicholas III's building, enriching it with frescoed rooms by a succession of artists from Fra Angelico to Pinturicchio and Raphael. Another addition is the complex of Sixtus IV's (1471-1484) chapel, which will be named after him and will be resplendent with Michelangelo's frescoes and Alexander VI's Borgia Tower. In the meantime, however, external protection is not overlooked, and the boundary-walls are fortified with circular turrets according to Leon Battista Alberti's plan.
It is with Sixtus IV's successor, Pope Innocent VIII, that the Vatican complex is extended beyond its original area. Uphill from the gardens rises the small Belvedere Palace which under Julius II will be connected to the palace of Bramante by two parallel corridors, creating in the small valley in between a huge courtyard of descending terraces. This spectacular space was destined for entertainments, festivities and tournaments throughout the 1500s, until the courtyard is divided into two by the transverse library "wing" and later into three during the 1800s with the building of the "new wing" of the Chiaramonti Museum.
Under Leo X, again with Bramante, the Court of St Damasus takes shape. The courtyard is destined to become the heart of the Apostolic Palaces, next to the arched loggias erected to disguise the building's

medieval appearance. The work on the loggias is supervised by Raphael who also frescoes them almost completely, so much so that they will be named after him. Under Paul III the Sala Ducale, Royal Hall and another chapel, the Pauline, open towards the Sistine Chapel. The Pauline Chapel is frescoed by Michelangelo, veteran of the enormous toil of the Sistine. The present bastioned wall also rises, and the definitive barricading within the Vatican is effected after the Lansquenet pillage.
Gregory XIII adds a new wing to the loggias, while with Sixtus V the "third wing" of the Court of St Damasus is created. In fact, this is a separate palace facing St Peter's Square. Clement VIII (1592-1605) will raise it by one storey with the rooms of the modern Papal Apartment, although he will never live there, preferring the palace which Gregory XIII had built at the Quirinal. The same is true of his successors until 1870. The Apostolic Palaces become the official Papal seat and acquire the final touch of splendour with the Royal Staircase requested by Urban VIII and completed by Alexander VII.

The monumental complex of St Peter's

The complex of St Peter's proceeds in parallel, from the point when Julius II adopts Nicholas V's idea of radically renovating the basilica which means the destruction of half of the ancient construction. The project is executed by Mastro Ruinante, better known as Donato Bramante. The plan is in the form of a Greek cross surmounted by a huge dome. The intention is "to put the Pantheon on the vault of the Temple of Peace", as Maxentius' basilica was known at the time. The first stone is laid on 18 April 1506 and work will proceed slowly, tied to the noteworthy cost involved. To meet expenses, with the *Salvator Noster* Papal bull the famous sale of indulgences is introduced from 12 February 1507. That same sale will greatly damage the Church, practically sparking Luther's revolt. Michelangelo designs the dome, but will not survive to see it finished. With his death, work will stop at the drum. The curved section will be executed by Giacomo Della Porta under Sixtus V. In the meanwhile the Square with its obelisk, erected in 1586, and the façade of the Basilica gain definition. The Basilica is lengthened in transforming it from a Greek cross plan to a Latin one with three aisles. The work is carried out, under Paul V (1605-1621), by Carlo Maderno. What still remains of the ancient basilica below, between the atrium and the five aisles, is then pulled down. Only Peter's tomb is saved, with the new altar wanted by Clement VIII laid on top of the previous ones. Above this rises Bernini's bronze canopy. The incomparable spectacle of the Square is completed between 1656 and 1675 with Bernini's colonnade centred on the obelisk, reference point for the entire complex.
St Peter's and the Vatican, symbols of the Papacy, are by now defined. The details will only increase the demonstration of triumph and spectacle, from the Basilica's magnificent internal arrangement to the Sacristy erected in 1748 by Carlo Marchionni, from the gardens enriched by kiosks and fountains to the museums that proliferate like ramifications of the Apostolic Palaces in a mix of patronage, propaganda and ambition.

The decline of temporal power

With the Westphalia Treaty of 1648 the Papal State begins the gradual process of ceasing to be a player on the international political scene, and from the 18th century the figure of the Pope-King also diminishes notably. His power becomes more and more isolated and he finds himself in economic difficulties. European culture moves towards the layman and is pervaded by anticlericalism. The Church of Rome is not able to propose idelogical alternatives, but rather settles back on a century's emptiness, amongst pleasure-loving abbots and prelates and the last spasms of an increasingly pathetic and provincial nepotism, from Clement XI's (1700-1721) Albani family to Pius VI's (1775-1799) Braschi family. It does not stand up to the rhythm of renewal dictated by the French Revolution and Napoleon. The painful experience of the exile of Pius VI and Pius VII (1800-1823) automatically brings with it a reactionary policy, in the midst of abuse of administrative and judicial power. Paraphrasing Gioachino Belli's words, the "holy city" becomes a cesspit as a consequence of the civil decadence into which the centre of Christianity has fallen. This is the Rome of Gregory XVI (1831-1846) where religion has become a formality, an external rite which is all staging of pontificals surrounded by hypocrisy and superstition. The figure of the Pope-King becomes unsteady. It poses as liberal with Pius IX (1846-1878), who, after the flicker of Mazzini and Garibaldi's Roman Republic, returns to a hard, reactionary regime aimed at maintaining a temporal power which no longer has any future. The loss of the territories of Bologna, Romagna, Marches and Umbria, annexed to the kingdom of Sardinia in 1860, does not inspire Pope Mastai to change his mind and he becomes more and more intransigent. He excommunicates the "usurpers" and in the *Sillabo* of 1864 confirms the impossibility of reconciliation "with progress, with liberalism, with modern society". The First Vatican Council, which opens on 8 December 1869, confirms the Pope's primate over the entire Church and his infallibility in *ex cathedra* definitions regarding the doctrines on faith and morality. The Council is suspended on 20 October 1870 to a date to be set, although Rome has become Italian one month earlier and the Pope's temporal power has effectively ceased. Pius IX considers himself a prisoner inside the Vatican and the Holy See rejects the "law of guarantee" aimed at ensuring to the Pope the qualities necessary solely for the exercise of spiritual authority.
In this way Pius IX's three successors live as "prisoners" in the Vatican, each with a different interpretation of the new power to exercise. Leo XIII (1878-1903) marks a clamorous change with the social opening up of the *Rerum Novarum*. Pius X (1903-1914) takes up an even more intransigent position, hurling invectives against modernism. Benedict XV (1914-1922) breaks with Pius IX's *Non expedit*, accepting the initiative of a popular Catholic party without blessing or condemning it.

Pius XI is aware of the change that must now take place in the Papacy's mission in Italy and the world. An able politician, he is not willing to remain a "prisoner"in the Vatican. With the Lateran Treaty in 1929 he manages to bring about the "conciliation" which reconstitutes, albeit on a smaller territory, the Papal State, while a "concordat" establishes the powers of the religious and the qualities of ecclesiastical properties in Italy. He is the great founder of the "Vatican City" with its new constructions, and with him the Papacy rediscovers its own universal image in the *Civitas Leonina*. Pius XII (1939-1958) proceeds on this course, with all the charisma needed to repropose the figure of the Pope as "pastor angelicus". He tries in vain to make himself heard amongst the belligerent powers of the World War and labours as "*defensor urbis*" in Rome, the "open city", making the Vatican a refuge for many politically persecuted persons.
Again during the period following the War he is the Pope that exalts religion's worldwide supremacy, a thoroughly political commitment working towards a "better world".
It is with John XXIII (1958-1963), however, that the Vatican's barriers are overcome once and for all. He is the Pope who visits the sick in the Roman hospitals and the prisoners in the Regina Coeli prisons. In affirming that "the head of the Church is Christ, not the Pope" he brings the Papal charisma to an everyday level. This is the boost towards a Christian community centred on the oppressed, the discriminated and the powerless in accordance with a principle which becomes concrete with the Second Vatican Council. Paul VI (1963-1978) endows this "revolutionary" political change in Papal policy with a pastoral concern open to the contradictions of the modern world. His travels are evidence of the Church stripping itself of royal pretensions and becoming a "pilgrim on earth" as a messenger of peace. The few weeks of John Paul I's papacy cannot have any historical weight, but John Paul II (from December 1978) shows himself to be a real innovator of the Holy See. His personality permits a true leap in quality of the Pope's image, bringing it right to the heart of world problems. He is a true leader who takes a firm stand on the devious plots of international power along the lines of a resolute Apostolic mission, restirring the purer voice of the Church of Rome's social commitment.
The Vatican reproposes itself in this way with a renewed religious purpose, liberating itself from all the past ambiguities. It offers itself candidly to the world with all its spiritual values, and the world continues to look towards the great dome with renewed faith in tomorrow. The continuous tide of faithful and tourists in St Peter's Square is evidence of this and constitutes a powerful invitation to admire the Vatican City's "treasures" in order to rediscover its immortal artistic masterpieces.

The Square and Basilica

The spectacle of the Vatican mirabilia opens on the majestic stage of the Square, a huge ellipse measuring 240 metres in width and surrounded by the two hemicycles of the colonnade, closed off at the bottom by the Basilica's façade which is dominated by the huge dome. A design attributed to Bernini symbolically depicts the architectural spectacle as a human being face down with the head representing the dome and the open arms representing the colonnade. This is the square that is to welcome all humanity with a profoundly apostolic message. It is also, however, the Baroque stage for unusual illusionary effects: the 284 columns each 16 metres high arranged in four files with the balustrade crowned by 140 statues of saints determine an infinite number of groupings, depending on the observation point. In this way, viewed from one of the two marble disks in the pavement (which coincide with the ellipse's two focal points) - the one which reads "centre of the colonnade" - the three external files of columns disappear behind the innermost file as if by magic. The secret lies in the gradual increase in diameter of the columns working from the inner to the outer files so as to maintain the reciprocal distances constant. This interpretation of space is capable of offering the spectator new horizons, with the symbolical reference point being the compass card inscribed on the pavement around the mythical centre of the Square, the obelisk.
This is the monolith which Caligula had transported from Alexandria for his circus. It is the monolith which testifies to Nero's martyrs. It is the medieval *aguglia* whose bronze globe was believed to hold Caesar's ashes. The obelisk remained standing to the left of the Basilica until Sixtus V ordered its removal to the centre of the Square in 1586. It was the event of the century given the daring of the enterprise, directed by Domenico Fontana and employing 800 workers with 140 horses. A "suspended road" transported the monolith horizontally, 40 winches hauled it up and a "wooden castle" secured it to the ground. The effort came complete with legendary anecdotes: from the "wet the ropes" shouted by the worker who realized that the support cords were about to snap, to the horses made ready by Fontana so as to escape Pope Peretti's anger should the obelisk have collapsed. All went well, however, and after five months of incredible work it was on its new base with the bronze cross on its peak by September.
The twin fountains of three overlaid basins were placed at its sides by Maderno and Bernini between 1613 and 1675. With their never-ending water effects they offer a natural sound animation to the imposing architectural space, contributing further to enlivening the charm of the spectacle. On a large, three-levelled stairway with the two colossal statues of St Peter and St Paul at the sides, one's gaze is instinctively drawn to the loggia in the middle of the façade erected by Maderno from 1607 to 1614. It is here that the Pope appears during important festivities to give the *Urbi et Orbi* benediction and where the election of a new Pope is announced. The Basilica through its consecration to St Peter is obviously the church of the Prince of the Apostles, but it is also that of all his descendants. It is therefore the "church of the Pope". In any case, it is the temple of Papal catechism, amongst religious ceremonies and audiences which gravitate inside it and in the Square in the charismatic spirit that each Pope has always given to this place. It should essentially be seen, however, as the "mother of all churches", that is

the "Mother Church" which rose on the rock of Peter, *Mater Ecclesia* patently reflected in Peter's glory. Everything refers to him in a symbolic key, beginning with the famous mosaic of the *Little Boat* (Navicella) at the central entrance of the portico, a 17th century remake of Giotto's original which decorated the quadriportico of the ancient basilica. The "little boat" is Peter's fishing vessel on the lake at Tiberiad, but represents the Church crossing the seas of the Earth. The equestrian statues of Constantine by Bernini (1670) and Charlemagne by Cornacchini (1725), respectively to the right and left of the atrium, represent *Mater Ecclesia's* "secular arm" according to medieval ideology.
The bass-reliefs of the bronze doors which decorate the five entrances are, however, all based on the same old apostolic spirit, from the ancient one in the middle executed by Filarete between 1440 and 1445 to the modern ones. These are: on the left by Luciano Minguzzi in 1977 dedicated to the theme of Good and Evil and by Giacomo Manzù in 1964 known as "of Death"; on the right by Venanzio Crocetti in 1964 inspired by the Sacraments and Vico Consorti in 1950. This last one is the "Holy Door" which is opened only on the occasion of the Jubilee.
Inside, right at the beginning of the nave one already remains fascinated by the structure's majesty, immediately drawing the gaze towards the vital centre of the Basilica - the Papal altar which faces onto the area of the "Confession" constructed by Maderno with its 99 perennially burning lamps. Here Bernini's bronze canopy is most imposing, while in the background of the apse the *Throne of Peter* stands out against the *Glory* by the same artist. This is a triumph of angels amidst clouds illuminated by the light of an oval window of white and yellow stained glass upon which the dove of the Holy Spirit is striking.
There, in the Baroque apotheosis, the *Mater Ecclesia* is re-echoed in the words inscribed on the frieze of the dome's pediment (*Tu es Petrus...*), the words with which Christ instituted the Church. In the end it matters little that this episcopal chair never belonged to the first Pope, being in truth a royal throne given by Charles the Bald to John VIII in 875. The "glory" of Peter's primate remains equally immortalized in the artistic splendours seen as a "face" of this power, at the same time spiritual and temporal. So, in the white marble of Carrara of the four bases supporting the columns of the canopy, amongst the eight gigantic bearings of Pope Urban VIII, Borromini has not exalted the Barberini bees, but the "Mother Church" through seven female faces depicted during the various phases of conception and birth, up to the last smiling face of the newborn child.
This is an extraordinary work that may seem "profane", but which actually goes right to the heart of the "sacred" nature of the Papacy and its preeminence, or, in other words, of the *Sedes Apostolica Romana*, the "Mother" of all the other episcopal sites generated by her.
The exaltation of the holiness of the "Catholic" Church is furthered by the large statues of the founders of religious orders in the niches carved out of the columns of the nave, the transept and the apse, as well as the medallions on the pilasters portraying 56 canonized Popes. These images seem to crown the bronze statue of St Peter, in front of the last pilaster to the right. The thousand year long veneration for this church is transferred to him, as can be seen by the right foot, worn by the kisses and touches of the faithful. No likeness of his successors can equal him. Although masterpieces, the Papal tombs have never been the centre of a devotion comparable to that paid to the ancient bronze of the Prince of the Apostles. On the contrary, these have often been the "altars" of velenous attacks through disrespectful epitaphs. The tombs, rather, turn the Basilica into a true museum of funerary art - the most splendid collection of mausoleums in the world by a list of artists such as Pollaiolo, Della Porta, Bernini, Algardi, Canova and Thorvaldsen.
Paul III's monument is by Della Porta and is on the left of St Peter's Throne. Two striking figures representing Prudence and Justice are part of this work. Tradition wants that these be the likenesses respectively of Giovannella Caetani, the Pope's mother, and the beautiful Giulia Farnese, his sister who had managed to win him the cardinal's cap as Alexander VI Borgia's "favourite". Originally sculpted nude to be covered later by an ample mantle, this remains in any case an image that evokes profane memories contrasting with the holiness of the place.
The only statue that can stand comparison with the bronze of St Peter is without doubt Michelangelo's *Pietà*. This can be seen in the first chapel in the right aisle, standing behind protective glass after its brutal mutilation by hammer blows at the hands of a madman on 21 May 1972. It illuminates the Basilica with a "female touch". The Basilica is, in fact, unique in reserving a place of honour for no less than three "lay-women": Matilda of Canossa (1046-1115), Christine of Sweden (1626-1689) and Maria Clementina Sobieski Stuart (1702-1735). All three earned this special honour by their contributions to the Church of Rome's prestige: Matilda in defending the Pope from Emperor Henry IV's overbearing manner, Christina (whose true grave is in the Holy Grottoes) in her conversion to Catholicism and Maria Clementina in giving a Catholic education to her firstborn, Charles, although detrimental to every right to a possible reconquest of the English throne. The Basilica is also a huge "reliquary" which pivots on St Peter's tomb with a series of sacred objects and miraculous images that have always been venerated and are therefore particularly well conserved. We can begin with the recesses made by Bernini above the niches carved into the pilasters supporting the dome. A fragment of the lance with which the centurion Longinus pierced Christ on the Cross, given to Innocence VIII by Bajazet, the son of Sultan Mohammed II, is in the recess above the statue of the Roman soldier, the "Holy Visage" is above the statue of St Veronica and there are some fragments of the Holy Cross above the statue of St Helen. In the fourth recess above St Andrew's statue the Saint's head was conserved until 1964 when Paul VI returned the precious relic to the Patriarch of the Orthodox Church so that it could be held at Patras where the Saint is believed to have been martyred.

The Holy Grottoes

Access to the tomb of the Prince of the Apostles is via a small passage at the base of the pillar of St Longinus. This passage also leads to the Holy Grottoes, a type of underground church made in the interspace formed between the levels of the present and the ancient basilica after the demolition of Constantine's construction. The first area, organized as soon as the new works began, is the "New Grottoes". The "New Grottoes" are arranged in a semicircle around the Chapel of St Peter erected on his grave by Clement VIII around the original crypt of Gregory the Great, with an internal ambulatory and three low aisles. Through a glass partition, the base of the "Confession", where the relics of St Peter lie, appears in all its splendour together with the Niche of the Palliums (Nicchia dei Pallii). Here the stoles for the newly-ordained metropolitans are held behind the bronze grate dating from the era of Innocent III (1198-1216), and illuminated by a 9th century mosaic of the Saviour on its back wall.
In this way even today, although in a less mysterious spirit than in the past, the veneration of the *Sepulcrum Sancti Petri Apostoli* (as the marble scroll flanked by two Gothic angels at the entrance announces) is proposed to the faithful. This area is surrounded by 10 chapels in a radial arrangement, four of them being carved from the bases of the piers corresponding to the dome's pillars. These four are dedicated to Saints Longinus, Helen, Veronica and Andrew. The last leads to the "Old Grottoes" which unfold in the area beneath the Basilica's central nave, branching out into the Pre-Constantinian Necropolis. The huge funerary museum continues with the tombs of Popes and Cardinals, together with great lay-persons, so that this place has rightly been defined a true compendium of European history. Leaving aside the Papal tombs, which alone recall the events of a millennium from Gregory V (996-999), Adrian IV (1154-1159) to Boniface VIII (1294-1303) and from Innocent VII (1404-1406) to the present-day John XXIII (1958-1963), Paul VI (1963-1978) and John Paul I (1978), most imposing are the tombs of Emperor Otto III (955-983), Queen Charlotte of Savoy-Lusignan (1442-1487), Christine of Sweden (1626-1689) and of the last of the Stuarts. All constitute a testament to the involvement of Peter's seat in temporal events.

The Treasury

St Peter's museum environment becomes a true treasury of works of art and precious pieces in the Sacristy constructed by Carlo Marchionni between 1766 and 1784, with its entrance from the funerary monument to Pius VIII at the end of the left aisle of the church. This building is an addition to the Basilica, but housed in these adjoining rooms is what seems to be a collection of true wonders. The Treasure of St Peter lies here, tracing the Basilica's history amongst oddities and masterpieces in a collection of objects from various eras and made of various materials. On the subject of oddities, the display commences with a gigantic wardrobe unique in the world due to its size (seven and a half metres high) and its internal spiral staircase giving access to the shelves. These nine rooms hold the finest gifts from sovereigns and personages devoted to the Prince of Apostles spanning a thousand years, despite the fact that part was plundered by the Lansquenets and Napoleon. The silver and crystalware, bronzes and gold pieces with lapis lazuli, crosses, candelabra, monstrances, vases, chalices and pyx together with holy vestments, reliquaries and embroideries alone constitute a patrimony of inestimable value. The immense Triple Crown in silver and gold with gems and pearls dating from the 18th century is splendid. It is used to crown the bronze statue of St Peter each year on 29 June. The so-called *Dalmatic of Charlemagne* is beautiful. Traditionally believed to have been worn by the Frankish king on the night of his coronation, it is in fact a Byzantine patriarchal saccos from the 14th century decorated with sacred figures. In addition: the *Crux Vaticana* given to the city of Rome by the Eastern Emperor Justin II in 578, ivory fragments of Byzantine diptychs, odd and precious at the same time is the *Rooster* dating from the 8th century in gilt metal which was once on the bell tower of the ancient Basilica and recalls Peter's triple denial of Christ, and finally two beautiful candelabra attibuted to Benvenuto Cellini. The great relics follow, including the miraculous *Madonna della Febbre* (Madonna of the Fever), once a widely venerated image, and the Holy Column on which Jesus is believed to have leaned in Solomon's temple in Jerusalem, although it is really a 4th century Roman column. It is also called the "Column of the Possessed" because, amongst other supernatural powers, it was supposed to exorcise simply upon touch. And, finally, there is Donatello's marble tabernacle produced during his stay in Rome in 1432, Pollaiolo's grand funeral monument to Sixtus IV and the ancient sarcophagus of the *praefectus urbis* Giunio Basso who converted to Christianity in 359. With the Treasury of St Peter's we have already entered the Vatican's "artistic" world - the other face of the apostolic seat. The splendour of the Basilica, aimed at glorifying the religion and the "image" of the "Mother of all Churches", moved into the Apostolic Palaces from their conception as the royal palace of a sovereign, finally constituting a patrimony which must now be managed as true museums.

The Sacred Palaces

The famous Bronze Gate at the beginnning of the right-hand colonnade leads to the "House of the Pope". In times gone by solemn processions began here, with the Pope beneath the canopy on the gestatorial chair amidst flabella and trumpet blares, with a cortege of noble guards and prelates in great style. Having passed the Gate and crossed the ambulatory of "Constantine's Wing", named after the equestrian statue in the portico of the Basilica to which it is connected, the famous Royal Stairway opens up. Gian Lorenzo Bernini's masterpiece leads to the Royal Hall, commenced by Antonio da Sangallo for Paul III in 1538 and not finished until 1573.
The spendid room, which was once the reception hall for private audiences with sovereigns, displays an

exceptional iconographic device specially contrived to influence the guests. In depicting the Pope's "victories", each fresco was intended to remind the visiting monarchs of the Roman Pontiff's preeminence over temporal sovereignty. The result is the *Submission of Barbarossa to Alexander III* by Francesco Salviati, the *Return of the Provinces* by Orazio Samacchini, the *Offering of Peter of Aaragon to Eugenius III* by Livio Agresti and the *Donation of Ravenna* by Sermoneta, as well as the victories over the Turks such as the *Capture of Tunis* by Taddeo and Federico Zuccari and the *Battle of Lepanto* by Giorgio Vasari. This room displays the "face of power" par excellence, recalling the times of the Pope-King's dominance over sovereigns expressed as an earthly apotheosis and only partly mitigated by the *Benediction of Gregory XIII* by Federico Zuccari. Today, diplomats accredited to the Holy See are received here. From the Royal Hall one passes to the Sala Ducale where princes and minor sovereigns were once received for audiences. The Sala Ducale was created by Gian Lorenzo Bernini, joining two rooms through the device of a marble curtain supported by two angels. The grottesques by Marco da Siena on the vault and the landscapes by Paul Brill on the walls are of decorative intent and transmit a bucolic and poetic atmosphere, much different to the "political" spirit of the Royal Hall which leads to the Pauline and Sistine Chapels.

The Sistine Chapel

The Pauline Chapel was also erected by Sangallo for Paul III, in 1540, and contains a collection of Michelangelo's last dramatic frescoes: the *Conversion of St Paul* and the *Martydom of St Peter* which the artist created after having finished the cycle in the nearby Sistine Chapel. Although the Sistine is now included in the tour of the Vatican Museums, it was originally the Papal chapel wanted by Sixtus IV, after whom it is named. Designed by Giovannino de' Dolci, it was commenced in 1475 and completed in 1481. It was decorated in four different periods: the walls up to the window arches between 1481 and 1483 by various artists including Perugino, Pinturicchio, Botticelli, Ghirlandaio and Signorelli; the vault and large lunettes above the windows between 1508 and 1512 by Michelangelo; on the wall behind the altar is Michelangelo's great *Last Judgement* executed between 1536 and 1541; the entrance wall between 1571 and 1572 by Hendrick van der Boreck and Matteo da Lecce. The *Last Judgement* is the masterpiece that scandalized Pius IV (1560-1565) with its nudity. In order to remedy the situation, the Pope commissioned Daniele da Volterra to cover the "shame" in some way. The famous "braghe" draping the figures were the result, giving the artist his nickname of Braghettone. The lengthy restoration of Michelangelo's work, commenced in 1980 and completed in 1994 (work on the 15th century frescoes continues), has rightly been defined the "restoration job of the century". The coat of smoke and the animal-based glues has disappeared and the whole Chapel can be seen in a new, dazzling light. Above all, the additions made during the 18th century to disguise the nudity have been removed, so as return the work to its original condition. The Sistine is also known as the site of the Conclave, that is the assembly of Cardinals which meets after the death of one Pontiff to elect his successor. The Popes of our century from Pius X to John Paul II were all proclaimed here, even if during the last elections the area set aside for the Conclave was extended to other parts of the Apostolic Palaces. This is the temple of the Holy Spirit, called on to illuminate the Cardinals. This is the polling station with the table in the middle of the Chapel at which each Cardinal sits in turn to vote on a card which is then dropped into the large chalice on the altar. Today the benches are no longer constructed for the elections because the area is not large enough to accommodate all the Cardinals, their number having been increased from the original 70 by the recent Popes. A stove is used to burn the voting cards, once with the addition of damp straw, but today with the addition of chemical products to produce black smoke and let the faithfull waiting in St Peter's Square know that the new Pope has not yet been elected. Alternatively, the cards are burned alone, producing white smoke, to announce the election of the new Pope.

The Stanze

The Royal Hall opens onto other rooms that, although now part of the Museums, were originally part of the Ancient Papal Apartments. Accordingly, the present Sala dei Paramenti, where the Pope dons his sacred vestments before functions in St Peter's, used to be the room of Nicholas V, later used by Sixtus IV and Innocent VIII. The same is true of the Borgia Apartment which precedes it, used by Alexander VI and lived in by Julius II until 1507 when he moved to the next storey, using the rooms frescoed by Raphael together with the Loggias of the three storeys of the more ancient Apostolic Palace. Each room has its own story intimately tied to the Popes who lived within it and should not be visited in the same spirit as any cold art gallery, but rather within the context of the personal, historical and artistic motivations at its origin.

The Borgia Apartment unfolds over six rooms, three within the Borgia Tower and the rest in Nicholas V's building. These rooms recall a turbid era for the Papacy, with Alexander VI and his children Juan, Cesare, Lucretia and Jofr, as well as his women, Vannozza de' Cattanei and Giulia Farnese, along with an entourage of courtesans, mercenaries and hired killers. The Apartment was, at the time, the breeding ground for corruption and crime. Numerous books have been written on the topic which, although containing fictional digressions, are based on truth from Lucretia's three magnificent wedding ceremonies to the assassination of Juan, Duke of Gandia and Alfonso, Duke of Bisceglie and Lucretia's second husband.

It is difficult, therefore, to recognize the participants in such deeds in the celestial personages supposedly painted in their likeness in Pinturicchio's frescoes within these rooms. The Pope is in Papal robes in the *Resurrection* lunette in the Room of the Mysteries of the Faith. The "lustful" Jofr, is unconvincing as the young, downhearted man in armour, like grim Cesare in the kneeling personage. Vannozza, mother of the Pope's four children, is shamelessly portrayed in the *Annunciation*, like Giulia Farnese in the *Madonna and Child* on the door of the Room of the Saints. This latter work seems a blasphemous characterization of her nickname, "Christ's bride" as the Pope's concubine. Similarly, in the *Dispute of St Catherine of Alexandria with the Philosopers*, apart from Juan who is fairly true to life in the youth on horseback in oriental dress given his love for outlandish costumes, a 14 year old Lucretia is not at all convincing in the role of the saint. At that stage the Pope's daughter had already been through a first, ill-omened matrimony and was perhaps the willing victim of her brother Cesare's wickedness.

The rooms of the Papal Apartment overhead were used by the Popes resident in the Vatican from Julius II to Pius V. They tried to suit the residence to their own nature, reflecting in the rooms their personal idea of the Papacy up to the point of seeing themselves in the characters of the frescoes, in line with the same narcissistic instinct displayed, after all, by Alexander VI. In this way an apartment made-to-measure for the Popes was evolving within the Apostolic Palaces encompassing, under Julius II, an area from the so-called Raphael's Stanze to the Room of the Swiss Guards for the guard corps, the Room of the Palafrenieri for the grooms, the Nicholine Chapel (where, as a matter of fact, Fra Angelico had already portrayed Nicholas V in the figure of Sixtus II) and the Loggias.

The four true "Stanze" were arranged in a very functional manner. The dining room was in the Room of the Fire in Borgo which Leo X, however, adapted to a music room.

The study and library were in the Stanza della Segnatura, so named when it was assigned to this ecclesiastical Court. The Room of Heliodorus was used as the waiting room. The Hall of Constantine was a reception and ceremonial area. To the west of this apartment Pius V constructed his own, made up of two rooms, as well as the present Sobieski Room and a chapel at the far end of a gallery.

This chapel was situated directly above two others on the two floors below. As a result, of a total of six rooms there were no less than three chapels, one on each floor, in accordance with this Pope's profoundly religious convictions.

The subjects of the frescoes are extremely significant. Julius II wanted Raphael to reflect his policy of restoration. *Gregory IX Receiving the Decretals* in the Stanza della Segnatura demonstrates an extremely harsh conception of justice. The *Miracle of Bolsena* in the Room of Heliodorus recalls the miracle that gave rise to the institution of the *Corpus Domini*. Here Julius II is depicted kneeling before the altar, alluding to the vow he made during his first trip to Bologna when he paused in prayer at the Cathedral of Orvieto in adoration of Christ in the Eucharist. The *Expulsion of Heliodorus* recalls Julius II's crusade against foreigners who were to be expelled from Italy.

Taking up the apartment when work was already underway, Leo X adapted himself to his predecessor and was not lesser than him. He had himself exalted in the *Liberation of St Peter* in the Room Of Heliodorus, alluding to his release from prison after the Battle of Ravenna when he was Cardinal. He appears twice in the *Meeting of Attila and Leo the Great*, since it was already planned to include his portrait prior to his succession to the Papacy. The Medici Pope was also able to have himself immortalized in the Room of the Fire in Borgo in the faces of the Popes bearing his same name, Leo III and IV. In the *Coronation of Charlemagne* he was depicted, probably by Giulio Romano, in the figure of Leo III, while Francis I is depicted in the figure of the Emperor, thereby recalling the concordat between the Church and France reached in Bologna in 1515. Similarly, the *Oath of Leo III* (also by Giulio Romano) depicts the Pope in St Peter's defending himself against the slander of the nephews of Adrian I. This is an allusion to the Lateran Council of 1516 on the conflict between the Papacy and the Lutheran theories which were cropping up. Again, in the *Battle of Ostia* the celebration of the victory over the Saracens refers to the crusade against the Turks called by the Medici Pope, portrayed in the figure of Leo IV. The glorification of Clement VII follows in the Hall of Constantine, conceived as iconographic propoganda aimed at the exaltation of the Church through two false arrases frescoed by Giovanni Francesco Penni. These are the *Baptism of Constantine*, who was really baptized by an Aryan bishop a few days prior to his death, and the *Donation of Constantine*, scene for the *Constitutum Constantini*.

The Loggias, on three storeys facing the Court of St Damasus which at the same time separates and connects the Apostolic Palace with the Sistine, are today behind glass installed in the 19th century to protect the fresco decoration. Raphael finished the architectural work in 1519, completing the job undertaken by Bramante. The loggias were frescoed in three phases. First, the second storey onto which faces the apartment of Julius II and Leo X, executed by Raphael with an army of helpers, painters and stucco-workers. The vaults made up of thirteen bays were frescoed with biblical scenes, the intrados of the arches were decorated with stucco-work, while in the lunettes, pillars and pilasters grotesque designs appeared, inspired by the decorations discovered at that time in the "grottoes" of Nero's *Domus Aurea*.

The same type of decoration appears in the loggia on the first storey, corresponding to the Borgia Apartment, completed after 1519 by Giovanni da Udine. Between 1560 and 1564, this same artist, with assistants, saw to the ornamentation of the small vaults of the loggia on the third storey where the offices of the Secreteriat of State are presently located. This is known as the Cosmography Loggia after the cartographic frescoes on the walls by Antonio Vanosino based on cartoons by Etienne Dupérac, a true rarity for that era.

Connected to this ancient complex of Papal apartments in the direction of the Court of St Damasus is the present Palace of Sixtus V which began with the new factory corps wanted by Gregory XIII, the so-called "second wing" completed by Martino Longhi the Elder, joining up on its eastern side with the "third wing" begun by Ottaviano Mascherino. This work was finished by Domenico Fontana between 1589 and 1590 with the construction of the quadrilateral building ordered by Pope Peretti and completed under Clement VIII. This is the building that opens onto the Square: the Pope resides on the last storey, and it is here that he appears every Sunday at the second last window from the corner. On the second floor is the Noble Apartment, the Pope's formal apartments. This is a "flight" of 13 rooms, from the majestic and sumptuously decorated Clementine Room entirely frescoed by Giovanni and Cherubino Alberti, to the Room of the Consistory reserved for the meetings of the Sacred College of Cardinals and frescoed by Giovanni Alberti and Matthijs Brill. The ceiling of this room is famous for the beauty of its very fine golden inlay work. The Library is furnished in an austere fashion, with splendid landscape frescoes on the higher part of the walls. The Throne Room is also austere, today no longer lavish as it once was, but with a simple chair and statues of the Apostles Peter and Paul.

The Museums

The Vatican's most precious art "treasures" are naturally to be found in the Museums, born from the Popes' typically Renaissance enthusiasm for the collection of art works, spurring them to its patronage. The collections were conserved in specially constructed buildings, so much so as to change the Apostolic Palaces, except for the real "home of the Pope", into an enormous gallery. The Vatican Museums today constitute a historical-artistic complex unique in the world. The entrance is in Viale Vaticano. Via the so-called Atrium of the Four Gates, situated in a Neoclassical building, one enters a series of imposing rooms dedicatd to ancient Roman constructions and holding thousands of ancient sculptures, many of which are of exceptional interest. Conserved here are: the famous *Belvedere Torso* signed by the Athenian Apollonius and discovered at the beginning of the 15th century, the *Belvedere Apollo*, probably by Leochares and brought to light at the end of the 15th century at San Pietro in Vincoli, and the large marble group of the *Laocoön*, a first century copy of an original Hellenic bronze excavated in the Domus Aurea in 1506. In the Pio-Clementine Museum complex, which takes its name from the two Pontiffs responsible for its construction, Clement XIV (1769-1774) and Pius VI (1775-1799), other reknowned scultpures can be seen. Amongst these are: the *Apoxyomenos* from an original bronze by Lysippus discovered at Trastevere in 1849; the *Hermes* known as the "Belvedere Antinoo", a second century A.D. copy of an original from the 4th century B.C. by the School of Praxiteles; the *Meleager* with dog and head of the dead boar, second century A.D. copy of a 4th century B.C. original by Skopas; the *Venus of Cnido*, copy of the famous Aphrodite by Praxiteles; the *Jupiter of Otricoli*, Roman copy of a 4th century B.C. Greek original; *Hercules*, the colossal gilded bronze discovered near Pompey's theatre.
More statues and busts are below in the Chiaramonti Museum, named after the family of Pius VII (1800-1823).
This Pope was also responsible for the "New Wing" where the following works can be viewed: the beautiful *Augustus of Prima Porta*, a copy of a bronze statue erected in honour of Augustus discovered in 1863 in the "ad Gallinas Albas" excavations at Saxa Rubra; the *Nile*, a first century work from a Hellenistic original found in 1513 near the church of Santa Maria Sopra Minerva together with the *Tiber*, now held at the Louvre. Another famous statue is the *Todi Mars* held in the Etruscan Museum founded by Gregory XVI in 1837. It is a life-size bronze from the late 5th century B.C. and stands out amongst the precious archeological exhibits, the majority of which is the fruit of excavations effected in the first half of the 19th century in southern Etruria. These include the well-known tomb of Regolini Galassi of Cerveteri which was brought to light intact in 1836. Objects in gold, silver, gilded and embossed silver, bucchero (a local clay), fibulas, breast pieces, cups as well as tripods, plates, spits and a bronze bed, a cart and the remains of a biga. The important Guglielmi Collection, which comes mainly from Vulci and was donated in 1937 to Pius XI by Marquis Benedetto Guglielmi, has recently been completed with the pieces which had remained with the family. The Gallery of Tapestries is precious. On display here are the large tapestries woven in Brussels by Peter van Aelst from cartoons by Raphael, along with others from the Barberini workshop with scenes from the life of Urban VIII. Particularly spectacular is the following Gallery of Maps which Gregory XIII had decorated with maps of all the Italian regions painted by Antonio Danti (1580-1583) from drawings by his brother, the Domenican Egnazio who was the greatest geographer of his time.
At the end of the Gallery is the Tower of the Winds, specially erected as an astronomical observatory.
On the tower there was a sundial made of a revolving arm which transmitted its movement, via an ingenious mechanism invented by Egnazio Danti, to an indicator below the vault of the main room, later know as the Meridian Room, in this way showing the wind direction. We are in the momentous places which gave rise to the reform of the calendar in 1582.
From here one can pass on to the Room of the Aldobrandini Wedding, containing the large Roman fresco discovered in 1605 at Galieno's Arch on the Esquiline and depicting Alexander the Great's wedding with Roxane. Property of the Aldobrandini family who conserved it in their villa in Largo Magnanapoli, it was sold to Pius VII in 1818 for 10,000 scudi, an incredible amount at the time.

The Vatican Apostolic Library

The museums of the Vatican Apostolic Library are of great effect. The Library was founded by Nicholas V in 1451, but officially institutionalized by Sixtus IV in 1475. Its rooms stretch from the Gallery of Urban VIII, housing the earlist known planispheres, including that belonging to Giovanni da Verrazzano dating from 1529 and bearing the first depiction of the New World, to the two Sistine Rooms. On display here are the gifts received by the Pontiffs. Then there is the Salone Sistino, a grand, two-aisled hall constructed in 1589 by Domenico Fontana. It is frescoed with scenes of ancient libraries on one side and the Ecumenic Councils on the other. In the lunettes above the windows are scenes depicting the most important events in the pontificate of Sixtus V. The sources of donations to the Library are many, from the most ancient such as the Palatine in 1622 and Federico da

Montefeltro in 1658, to Christine of Sweden, the Capponi and Ottoboni to the modern acquisitions such as the Borghese, Barberini, Chigi (donated by the Italian State in 1933) and De Luca in 1975.
A patrimony presently based on over 75,000 manuscript volumes, 70,000 archivist volumes, 100,000 autographed documents, 8,200 incunabula, 100,000 engravings and maps, and a million printed volumes.

The Pinacoteca

Finally, the pictorial art "treasury", which holds additional extraordinary wonders, is brought together in the Vatican Pinacoteca (or picture gallery). The Pinacoteca was instituted by Pius VI and holds a collection which has passed through various sites ending with the present palace erected by Pius XI in 1932 from a plan by Luca Beltrami and facing the so-called "Square Garden" at the far end of the Vatican Gardens. The evolution of Italian painting from the 11th to the 18th centuries is illustrated here, with inestimable masterpieces such as Giotto's *Stefaneschi triptych*, Leonardo da Vinci's *St Jerome*, Melozzo da Forlì's *Sixtus IV Nominates Platina Prefect of the Vatican*, Caravaggio's *Deposition* and a series of works by Raphael. This series is composed of: the *Coronation of the Virgin*, the *Transfiguration* which the artist from Urbino began and which Giulio Romano and Giovanni Franceso Penni completed, the *Madonna of Foligno* and the 10 famous tapestries displayed for the first time in 1519 in the Sistine Chapel. Fra Angelico, Gentile da Fabriano, Crivelli, Filippo Lippi, Giovanni Bellini, Titian, Veronese, Guercino, Guido Reni and Poussin are present with absolute masterpieces. The Pinacoteca, however, is not the last of the Vatican Museums' buildings due to the ever-present need for new rooms to house the constantly increasing collections. For this reason, in 1968 a new palace arose behind the Pinacoteca to house the pieces previously in the Lateran Palace. The new palace houses the Gregorian Profane Museum, the Pio Christian Museum instituted by Pius IX and the Missionary-Ethnological Museum founded by Pius XI. Opened to the public in 1970, amongst its most precious exhibits are fragments from the sculptures of the Parthenon.

The Gardens

The proliferation of the Museums has put the existence of the Vatican Gardens in danger, although they had already been reduced in the area behind the Belvedere during the urbanization of the new city-state. The ancient *mons Vaticanus* has no more space available on the surface so it is planned to expand its buildings underground. In 1973, then, the Historical Museum was constructed under the Square Garden. The Museum houses the means of transport used by the Popes from the sedan chairs to the carriages and antique automobiles. In 1982 a vast building under the Court of the "Pinecone" in turn takes shape to allow room for the Secret Archive. In 1985 a similar construction is completed in order to satisfy the needs of the Apostolic Library, again under the Court of the "Pinecone". These underground premises are the salvation of the Gardens, much too dear to the Pontiffs, especially those of our century, to contemplate submerging them with constructions. For them this piece of green is a "corner of paradise" within easy reach, a spiritual refuge, a space for dreaming in a kind of "lure of faraway places". One senses this yearning upon passing under the Arch of the Bells and seeing two large green areas: the cypresses beside the Teutonic Cemetery and the garden of holm-oaks and magnolias beside the Basilica.
Once beyond the wider area in front of the railway station, the fountain of the *Conchiglia* (shell), encircled by geometric borders of evergreens, marks the entrance to the Gardens. Meanwhile, on the slope in front of the Government Palace, the floral coat of arms of the reigning Pope, composed of various botanic species, shows that we are in the heart of the Vatican Gardens. The Gardens stretch between the Pinacoteca and the Ethiopian College in an "Italian garden" arrangement with the characteristic box hedges. Close to the walls ranges a glade of platinums and pines with hanging orchards. In a secret garden the vegetables, bay leaves and thyme for the Pope are still cultivated. There are also splended fountains fed by an ancient and ingenious irrigation system. Amongst these is the *Fountain of the Galley*, conceived by Maderno and positioned at the foot of the Belvedere Palace. In addition there are the two by Giovanni Vasanzio, namely the *Fountain of the Eagle*, named after the large eagle sculpted at the top of the rocks above the basin, and the other imposing fountain positioned against the Leonine Wall, with jets of water arranged so as to take the shape of candles in front of a monstrance and therefore called the *Fountain of the Sacrament*.
The Gardens certainly no longer have the same appearance or luxurious varieties they once possessed. After all, the vegetation survives as best it can amidst the asphalted avenues and in small open spaces. As the great Vatican expert Silvio Negro said, they remain "something between garden and park, between a convent's shady promenade due to the many chapels and statues, and the florid embankment of a fortress due to the solid ramparts all around". As a result it sometimes happens that certain precious constructions within the Gardens are lost in the wider architectural context which they accompany. This is the case of the "Casina" of Pius IV, designed by Pirro Logorio for Paul IV Carafa who wanted somewhere to spend his leisure time in the woods, since the Belvedere Palace was no longer suitable. Work proceeded slowly and it was Pius IV who could finally enjoy its benefits in 1561. Presently the headquarters for the Pontifical Academy of Sciences, it is the classic example of a building created as a place of mystic evasion, able to give the illusion of being elsewhere because of the serenity it still offers today with its nympheum and a type of Mannerist architecture.
The Gardens, then, can be considered a fitting frame for that which the Popes, artists and time have contributed to producing - a complex unique in the political and artistic history of humanity.

Claudio Rendina

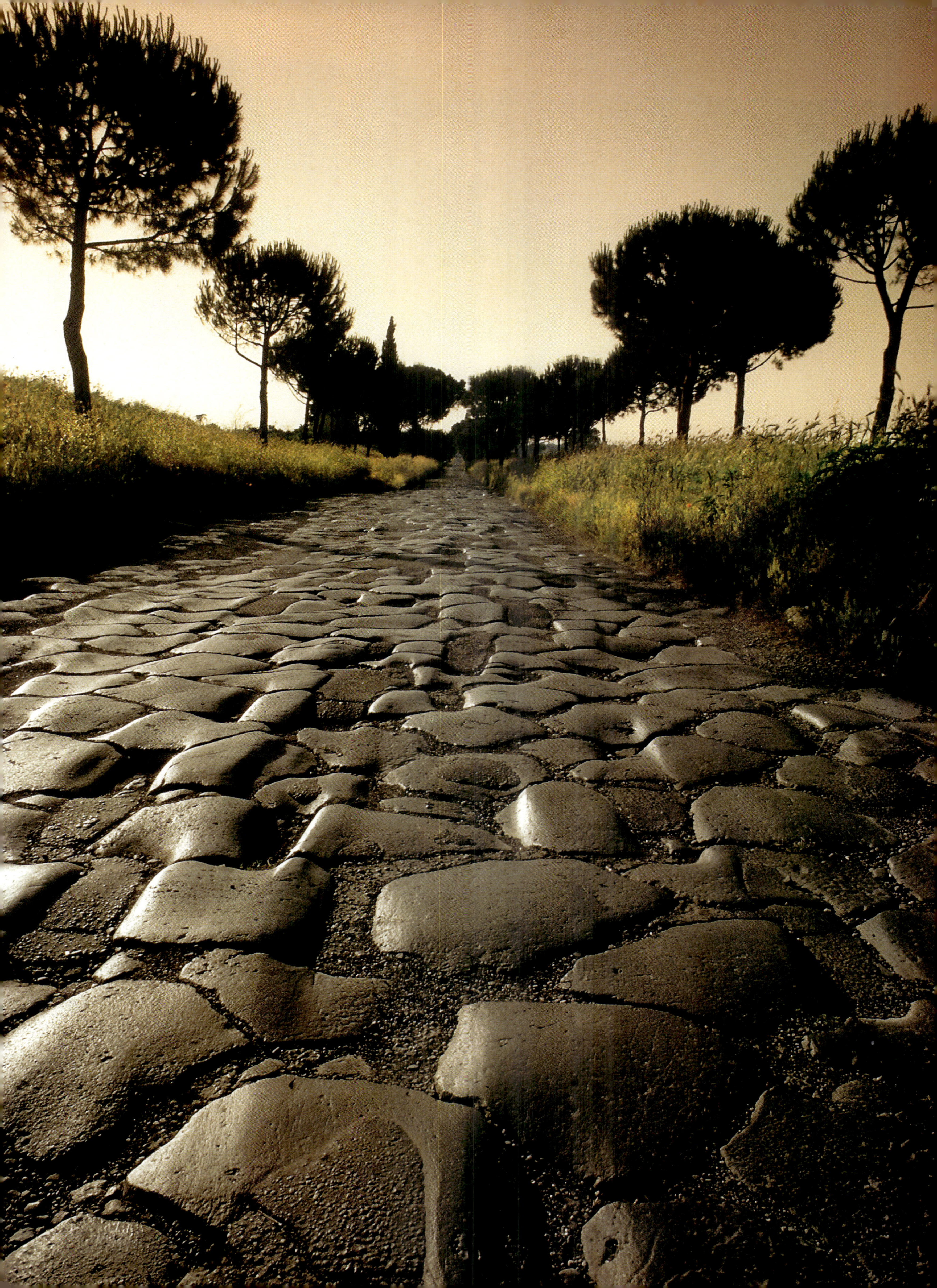

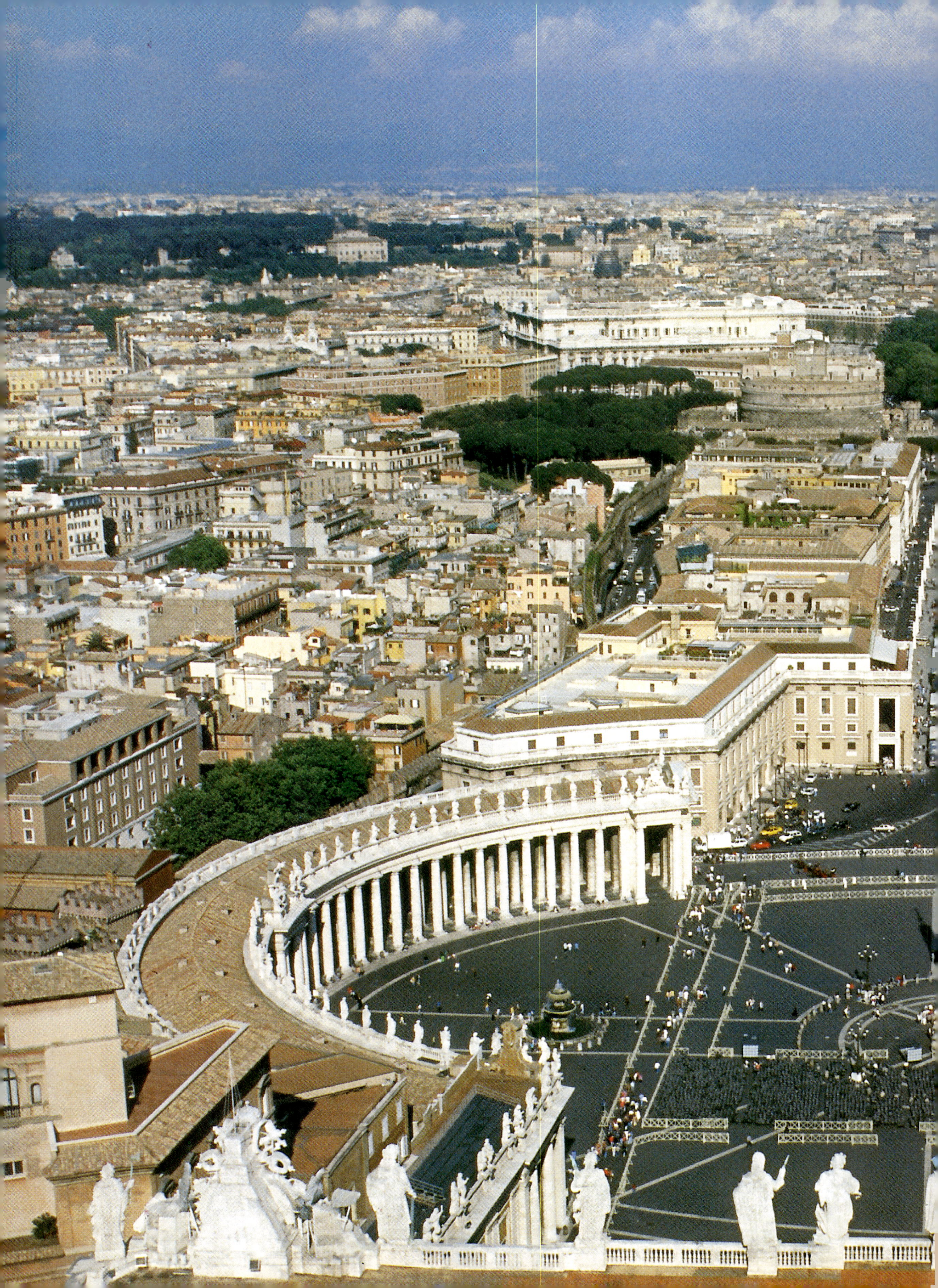

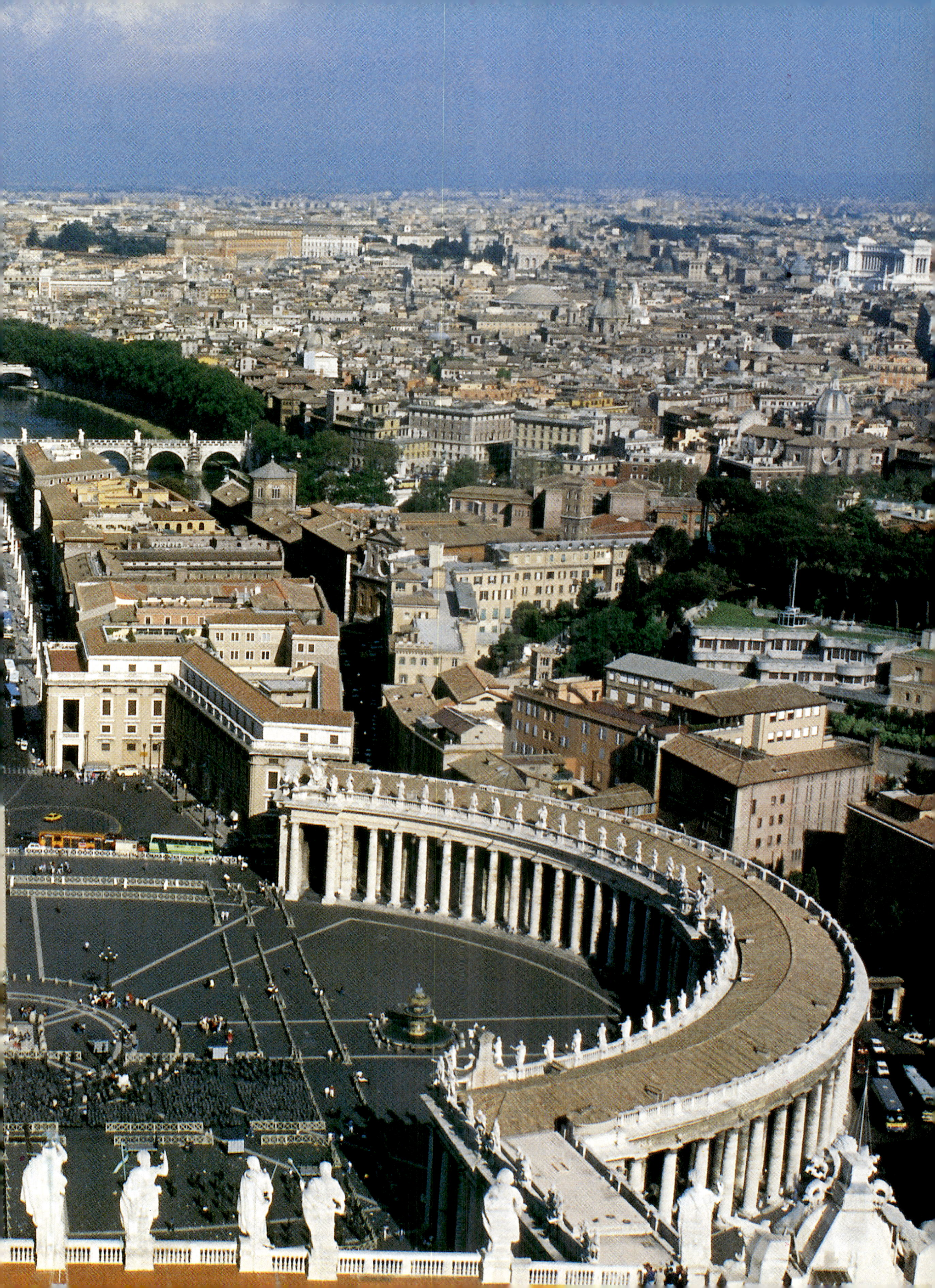

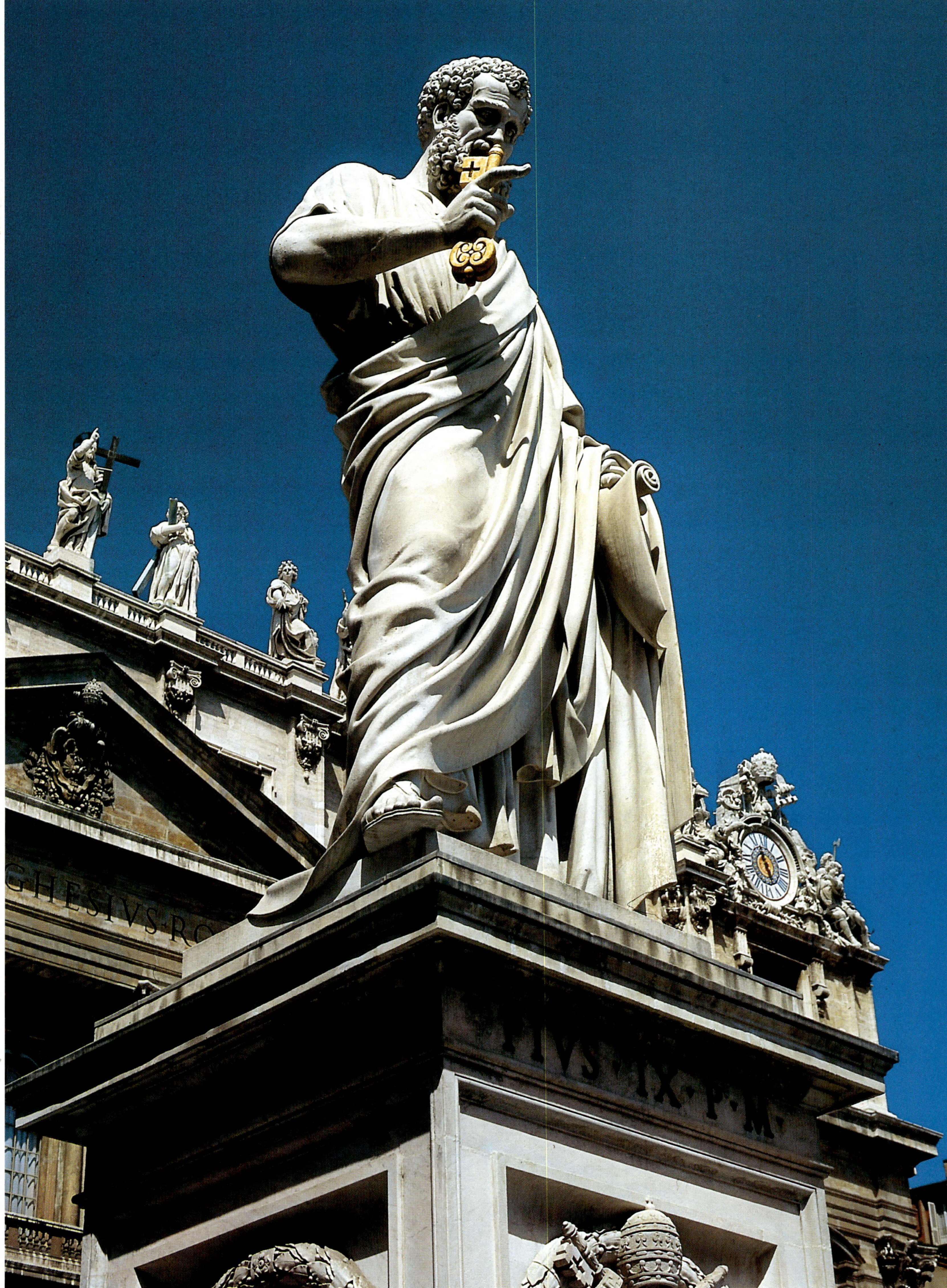
PIVS·IX·P·M

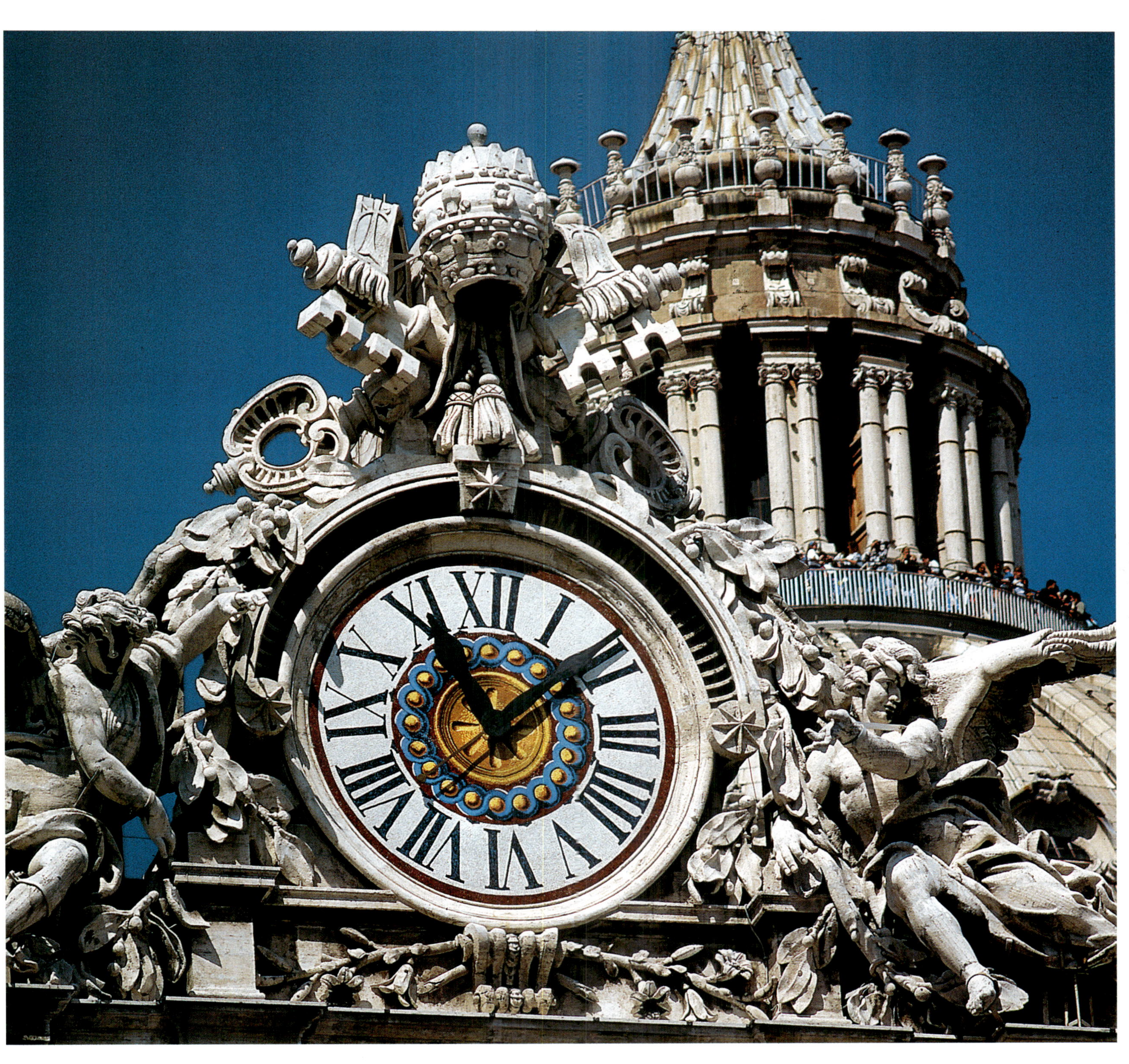

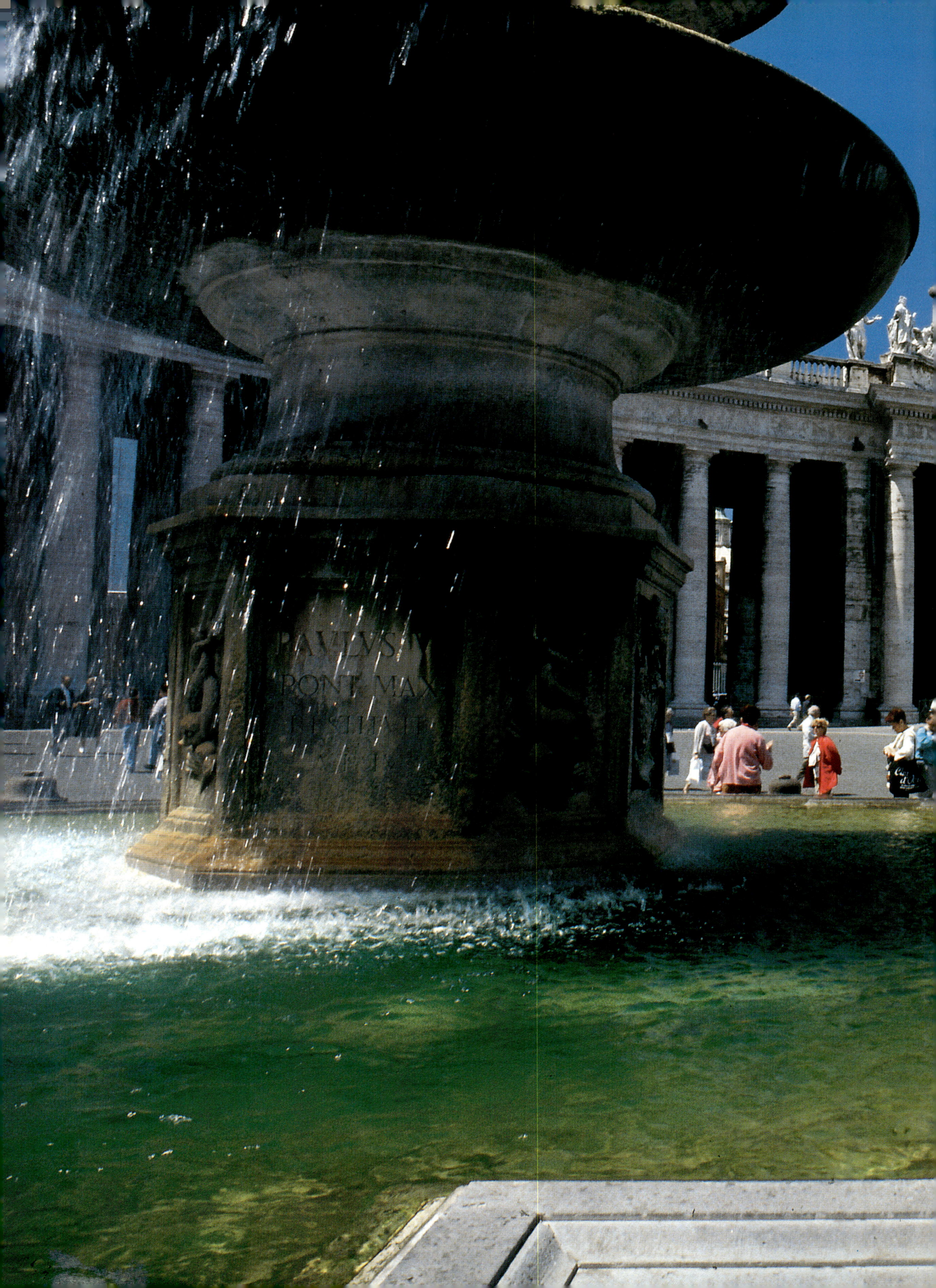
PAVLVS
PONT MAX

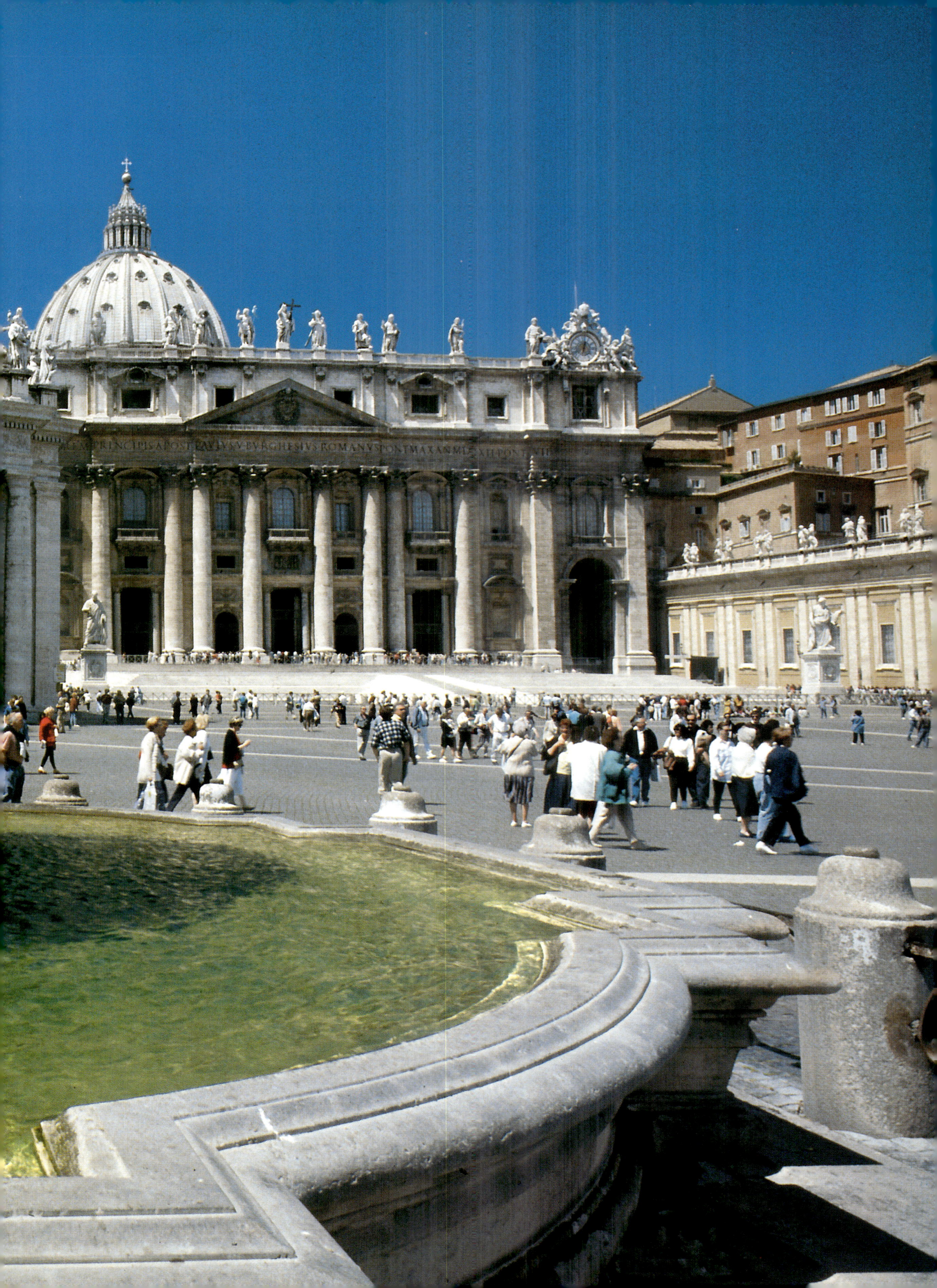

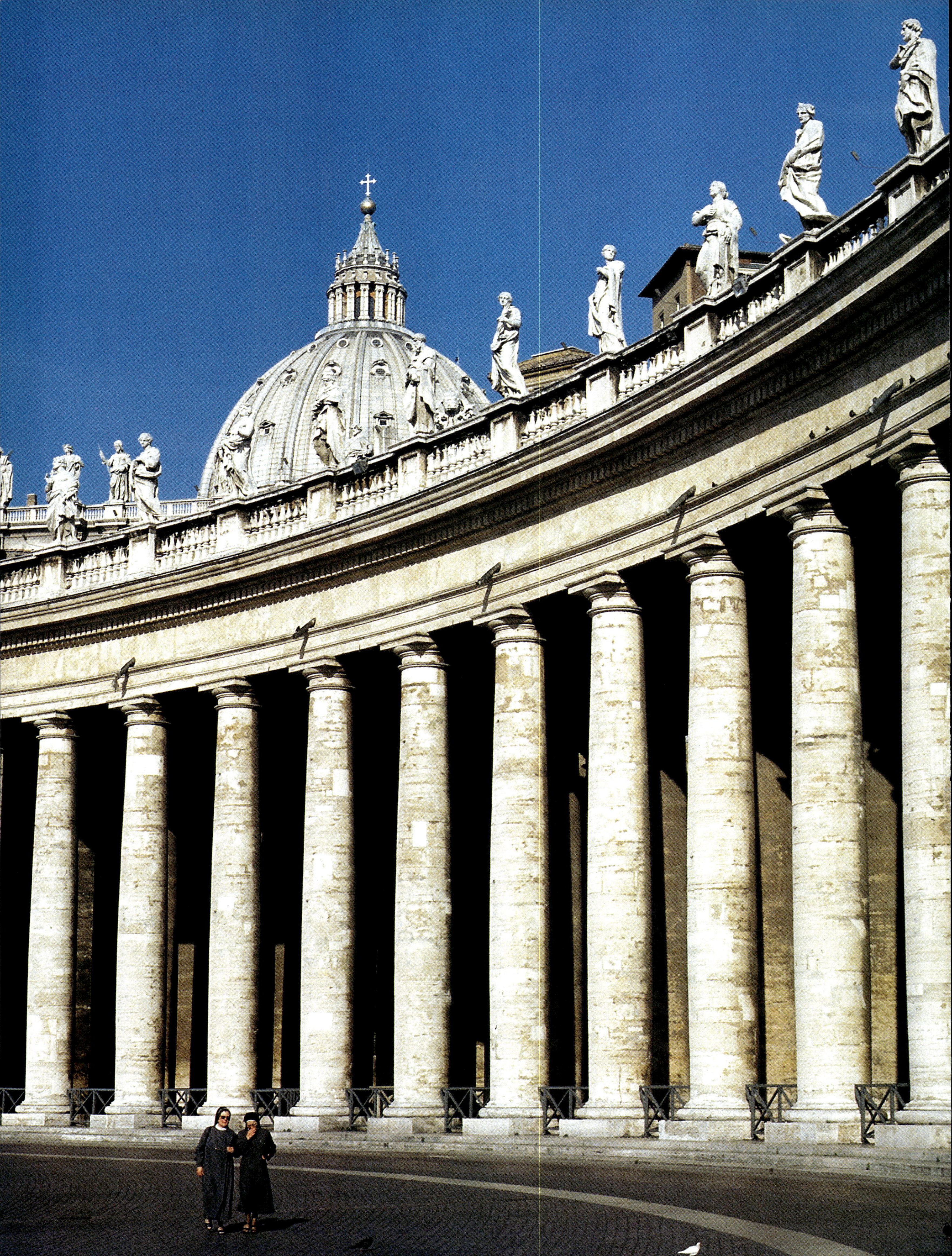

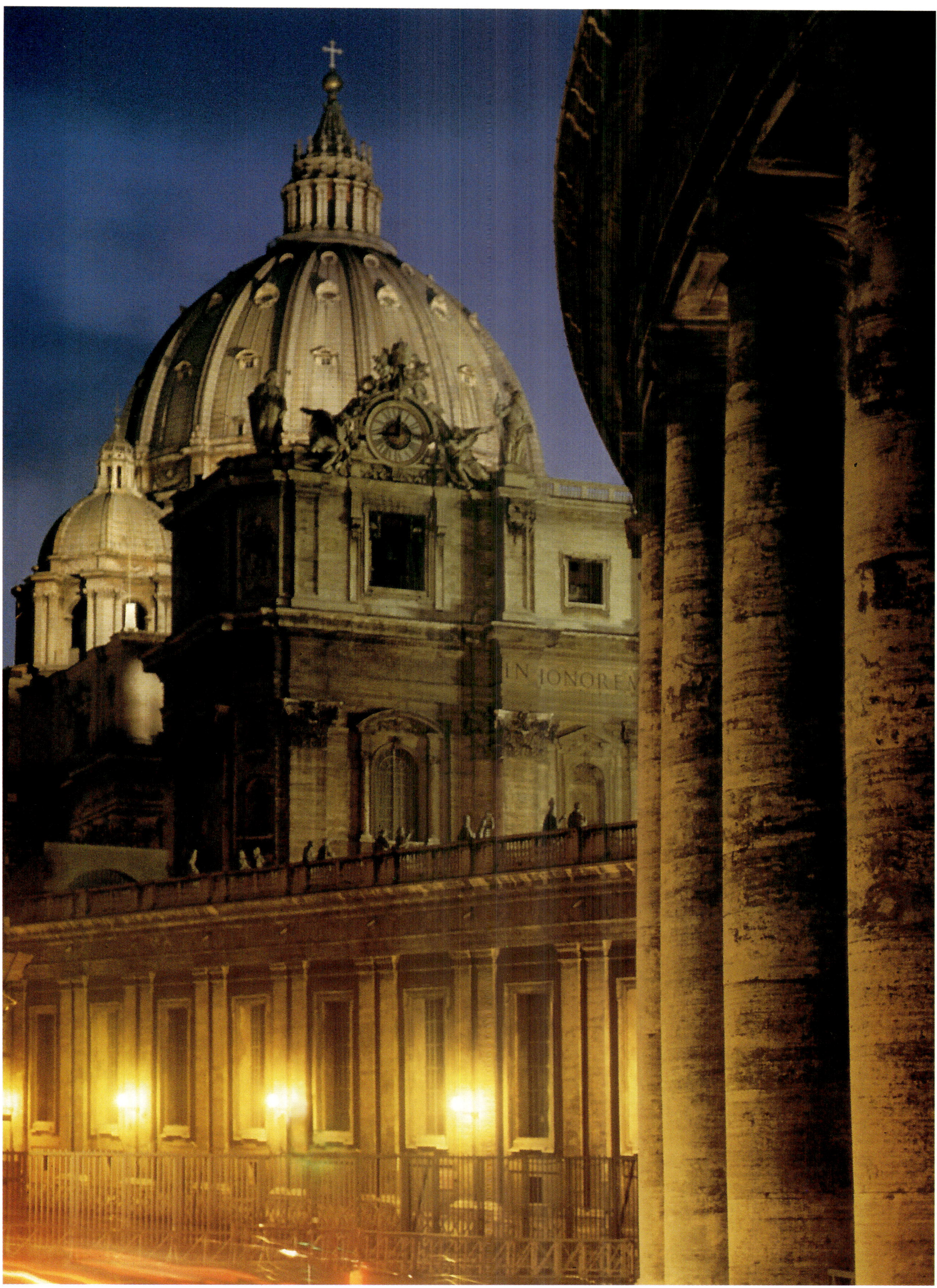

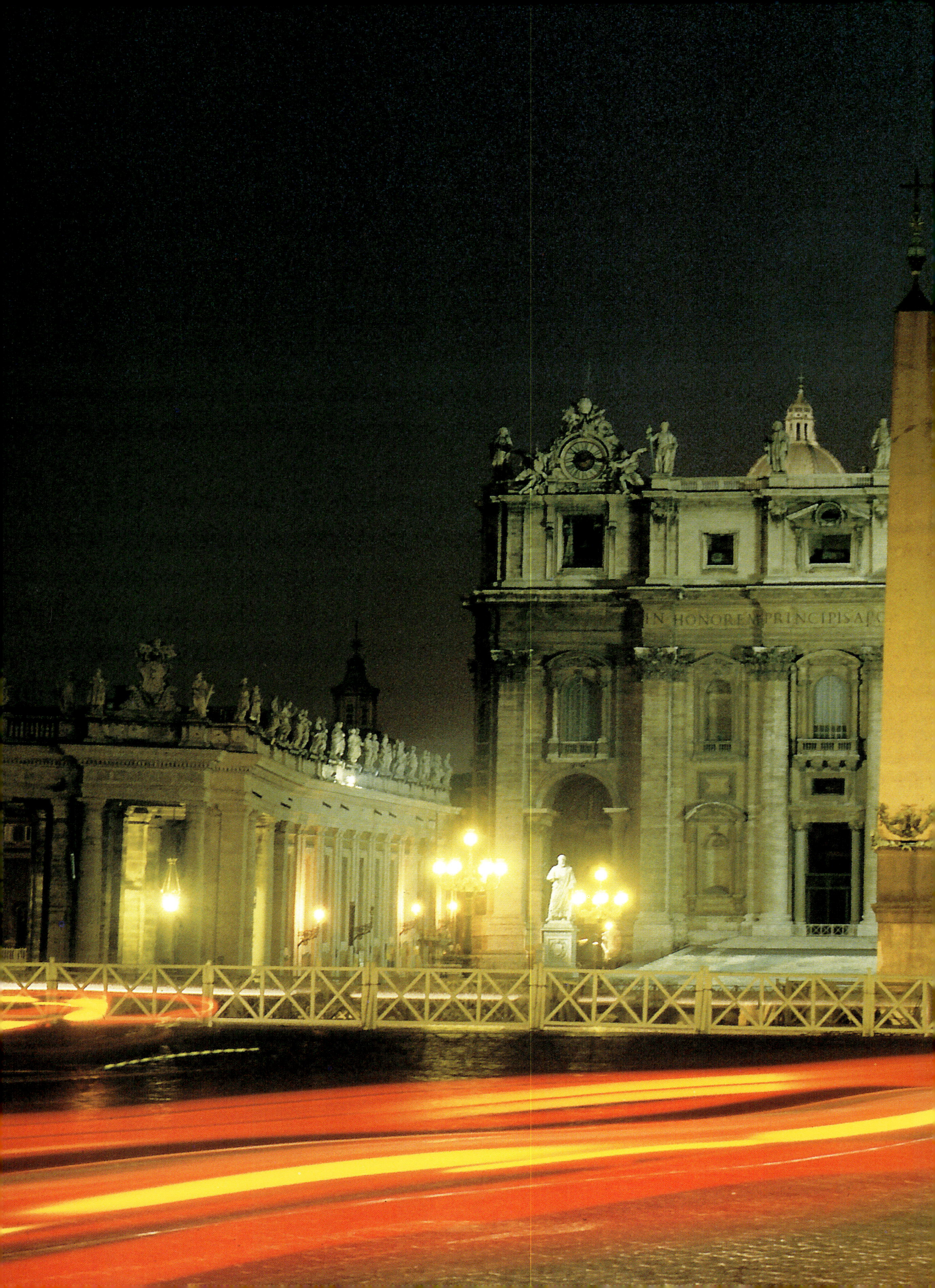
IN HONOREM PRINCIPIS

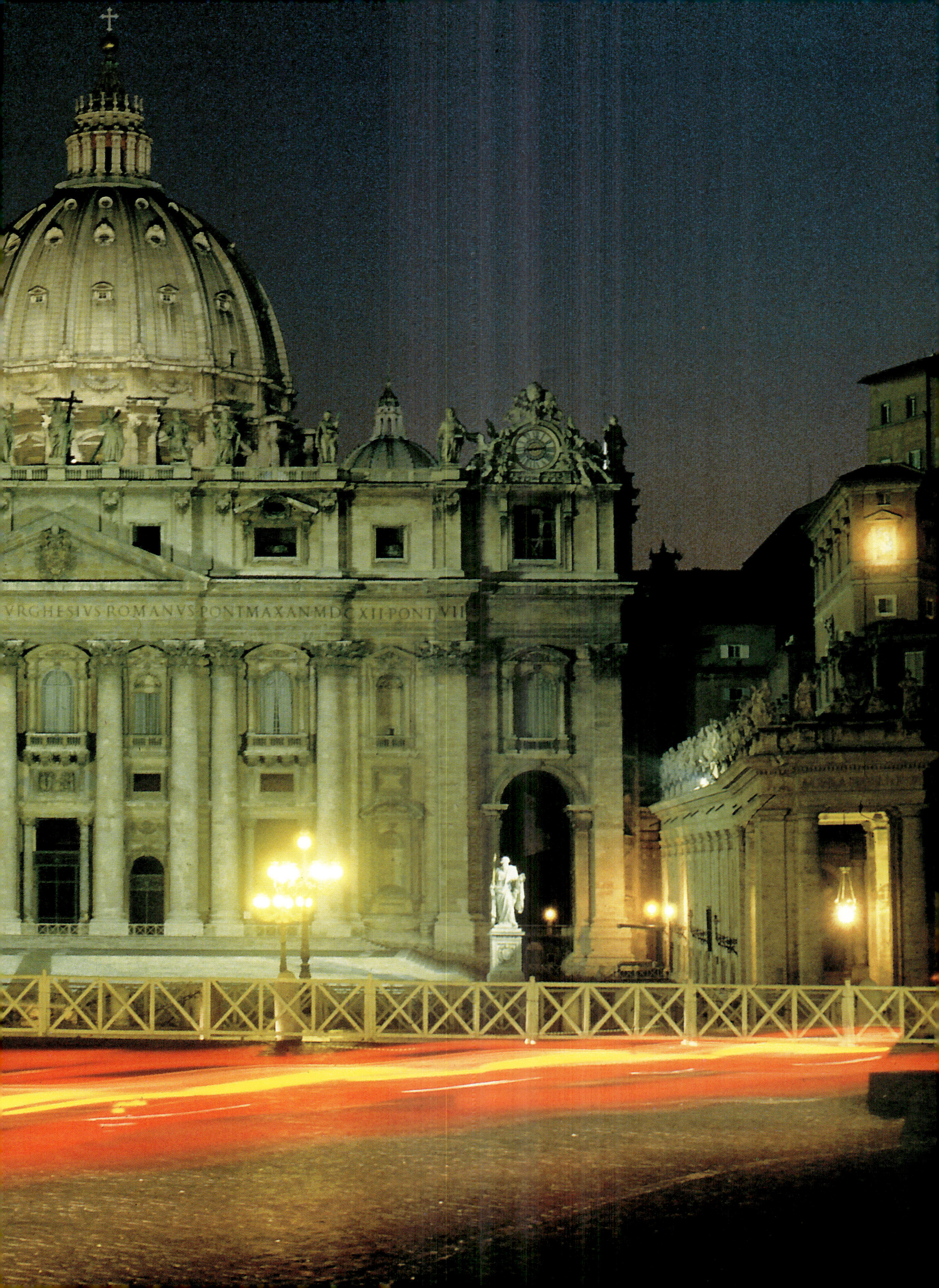
VRGHESIVS ROMANVS PONT MAX AN MDCXII PONT VII

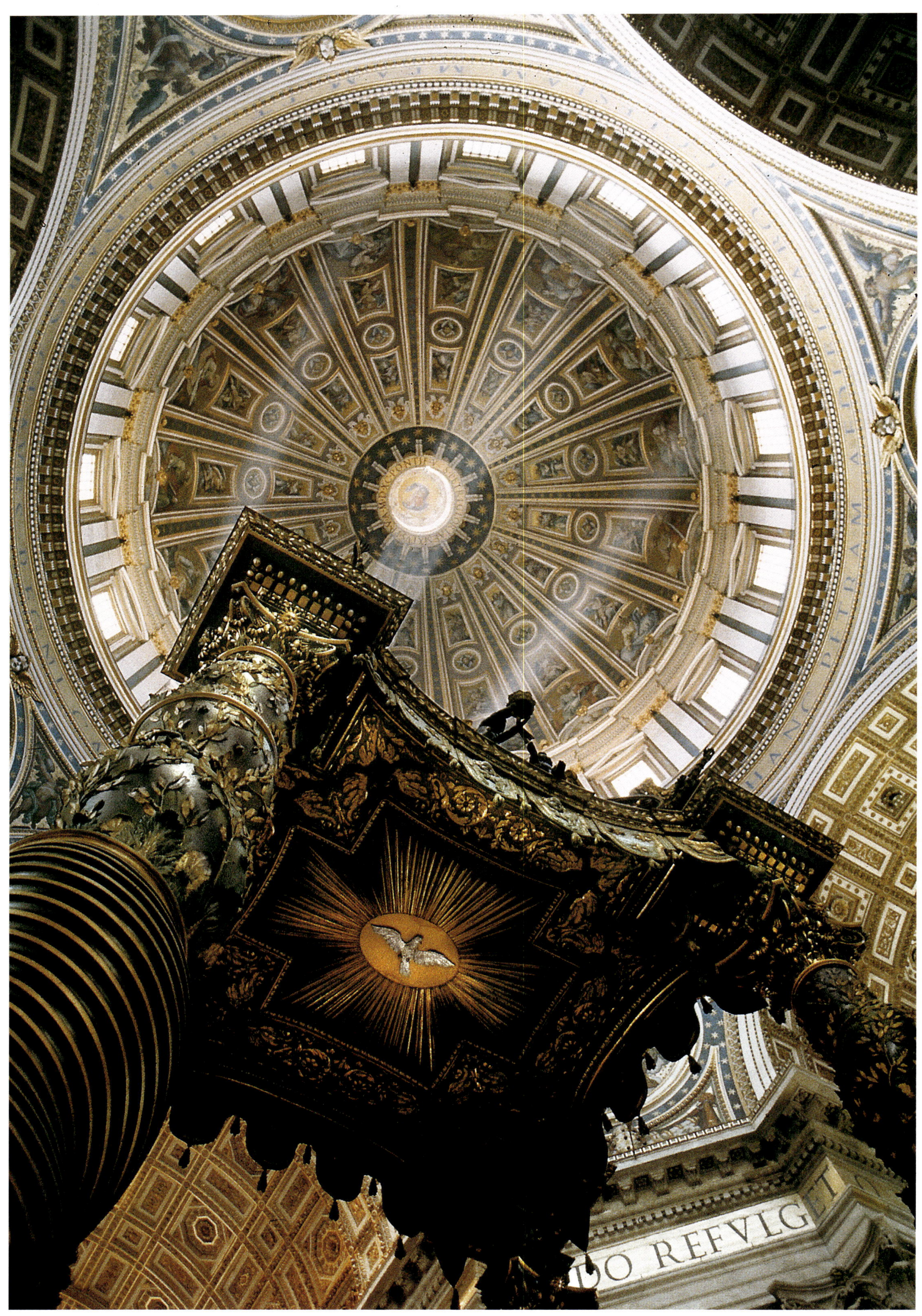
DO REFVLGET

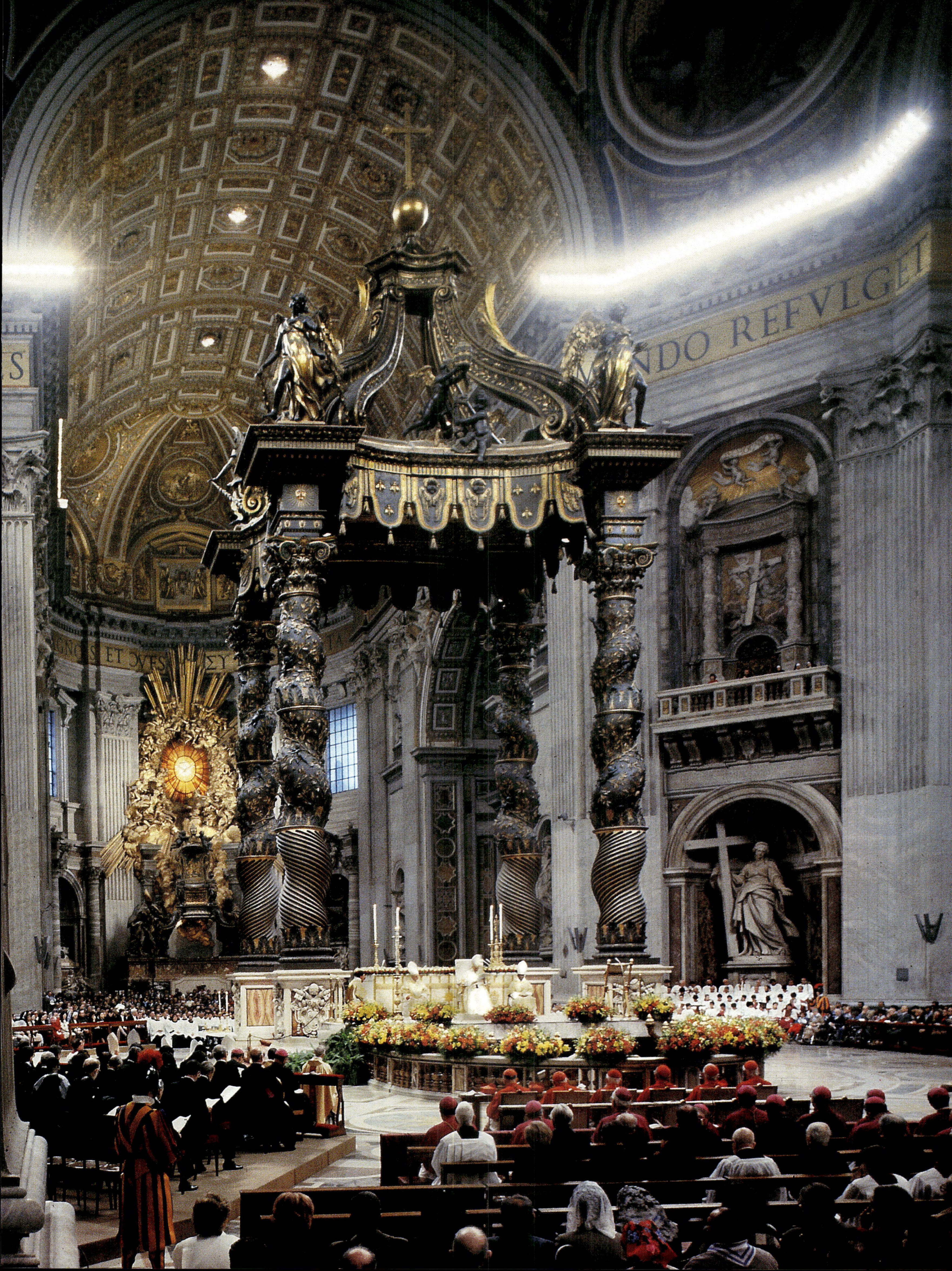
NDO REFVLGET

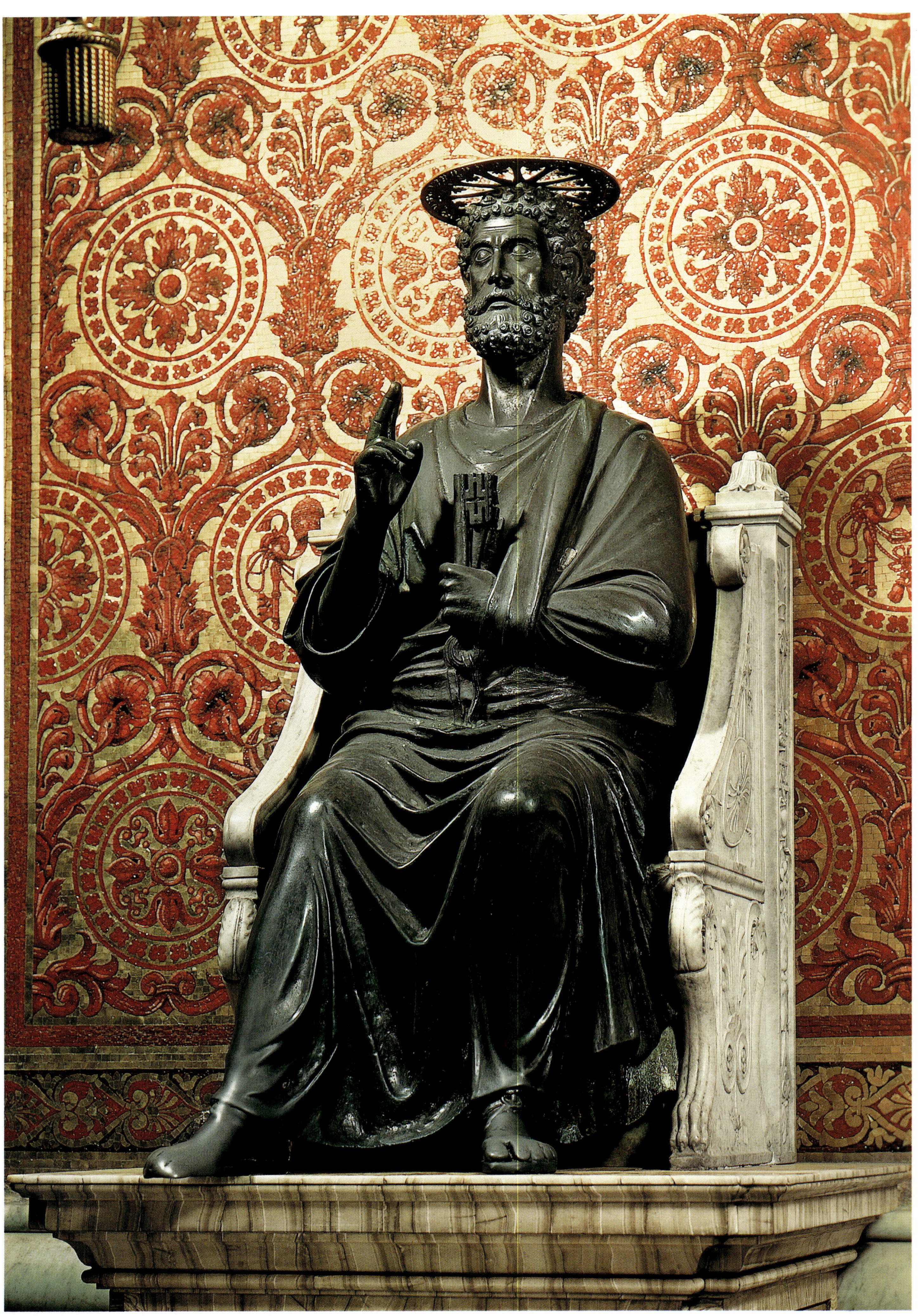

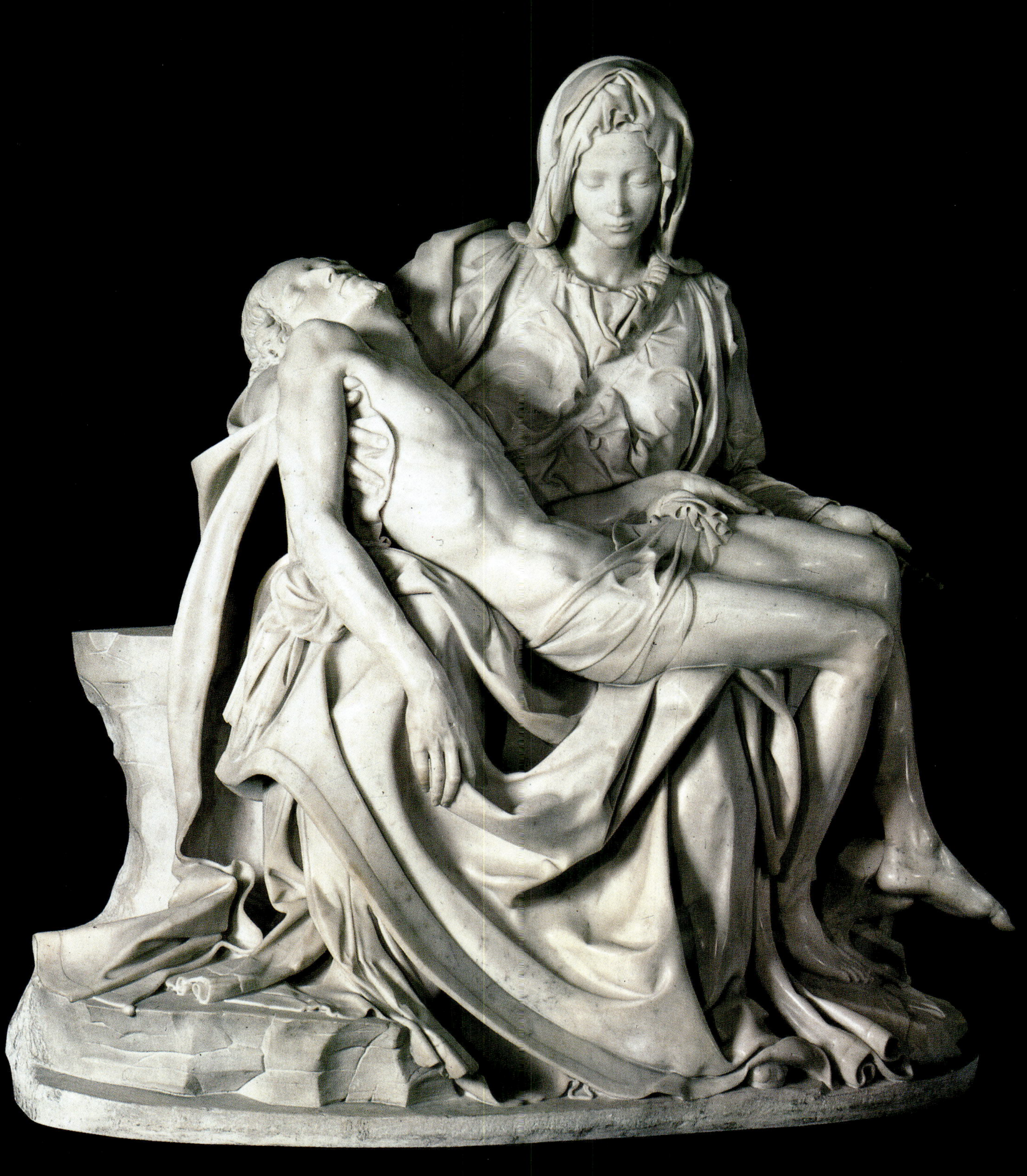

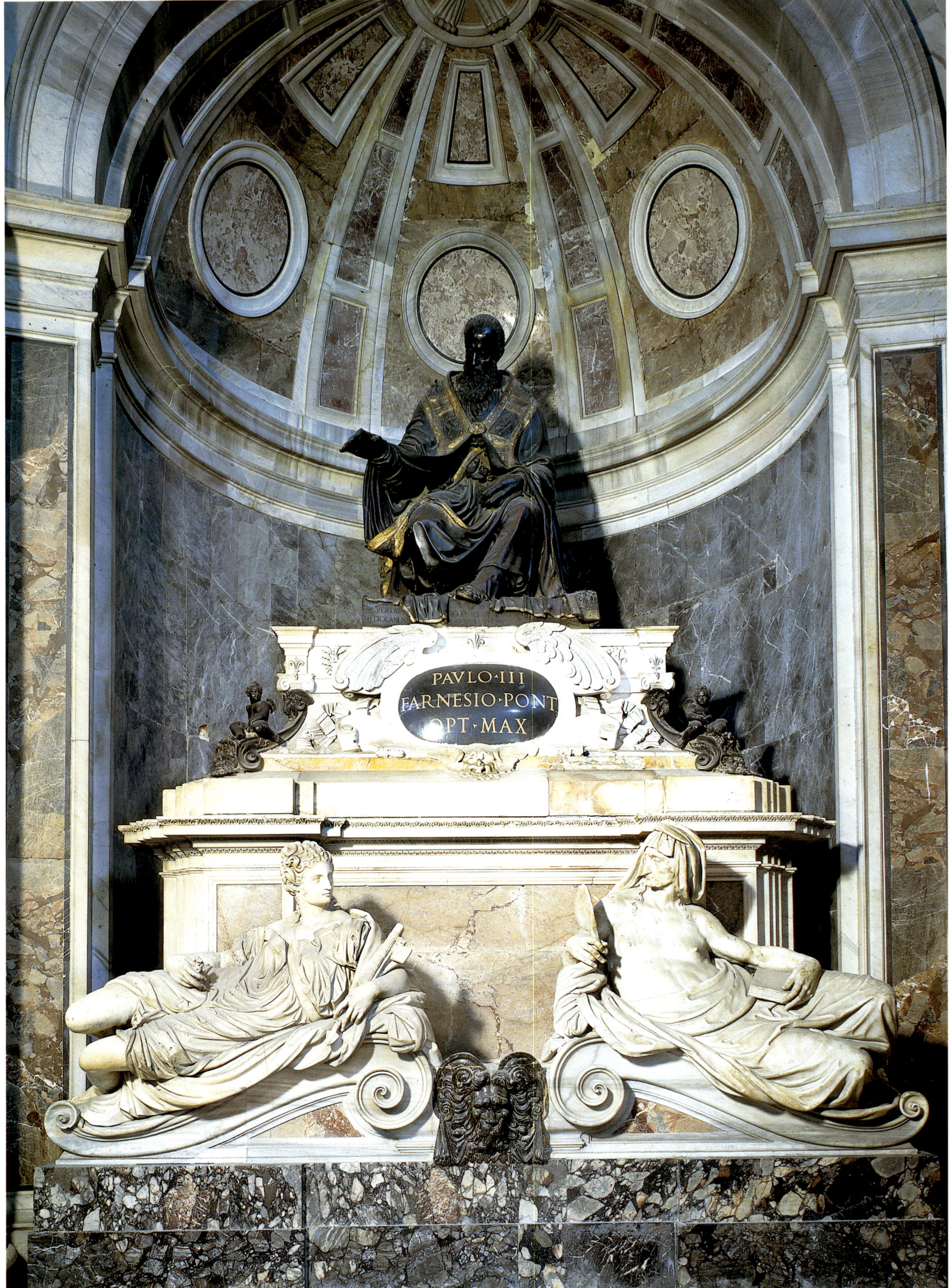
PAVLO·III
FARNESIO·PONT
OPT·MAX

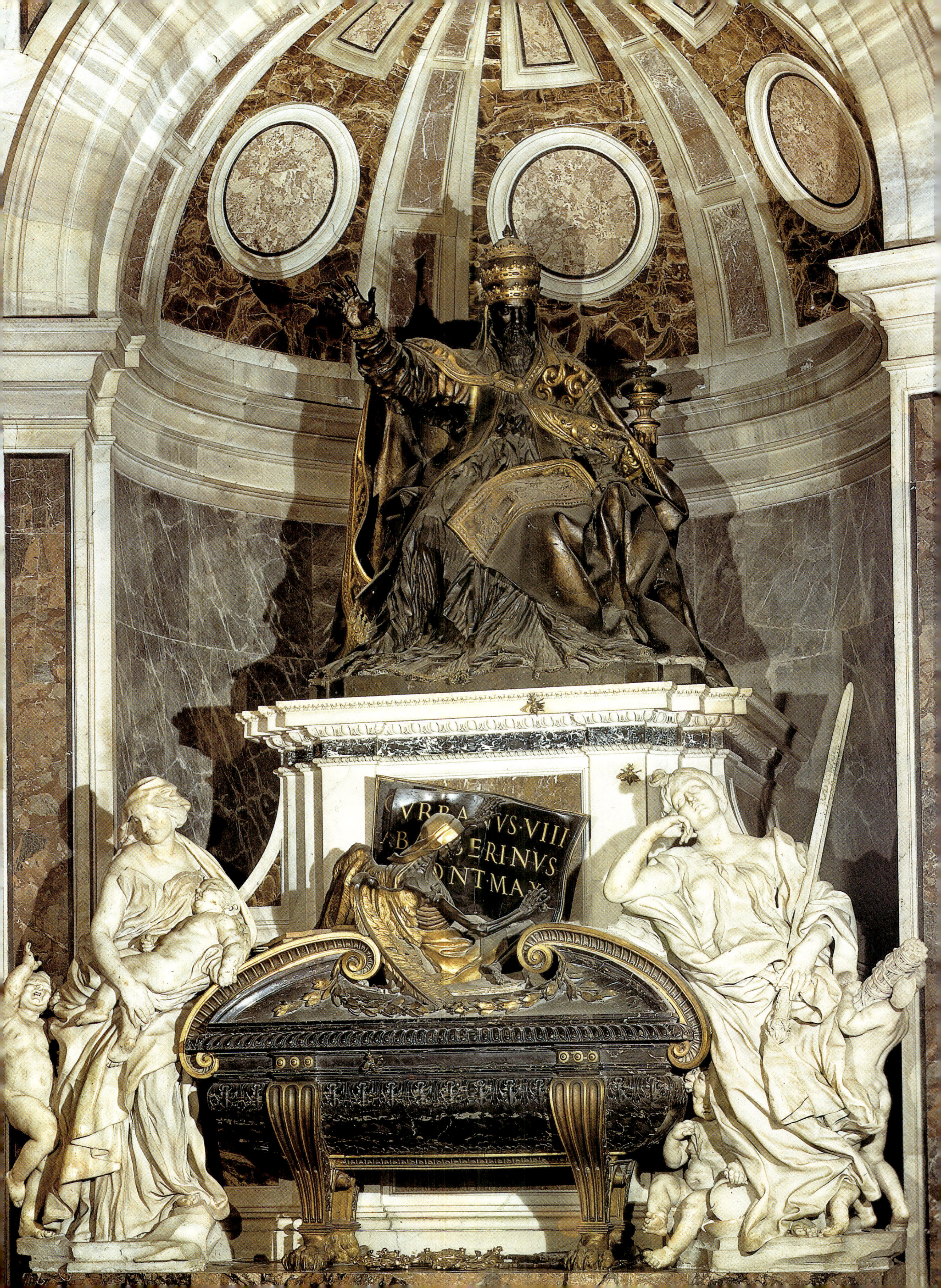
VRBA NVS·VIII
BA BERI·NVS
ONT·MAX

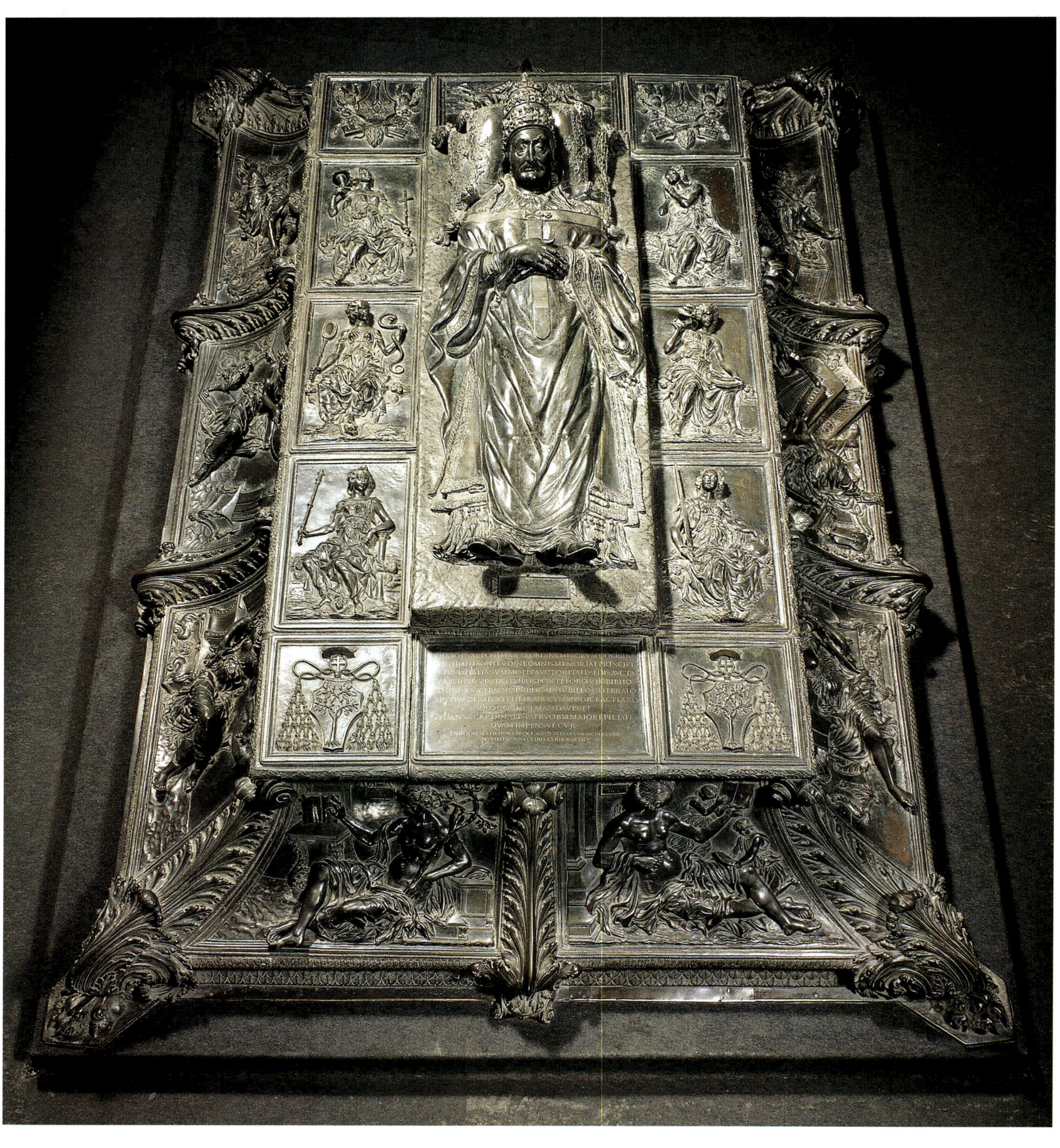

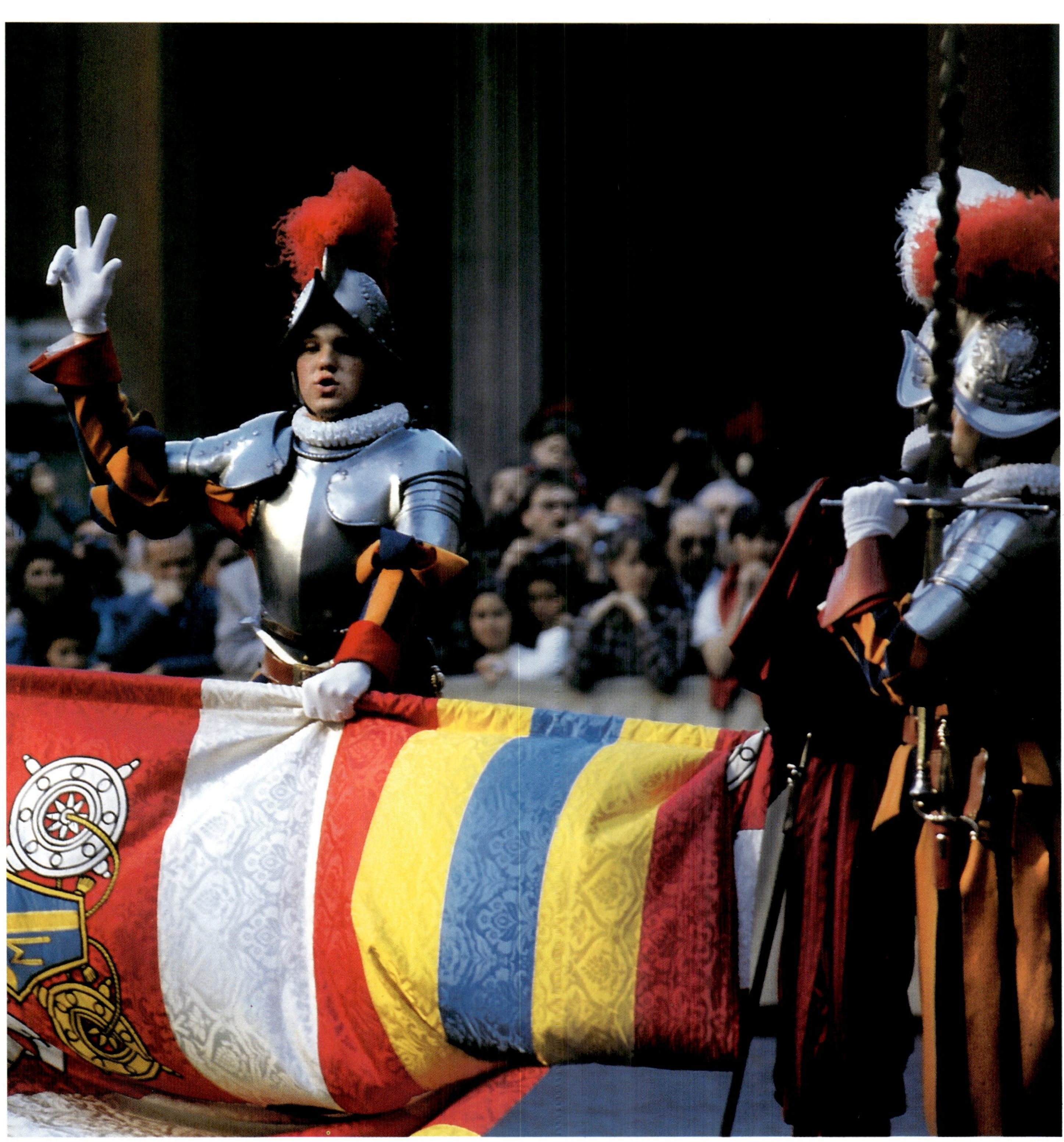

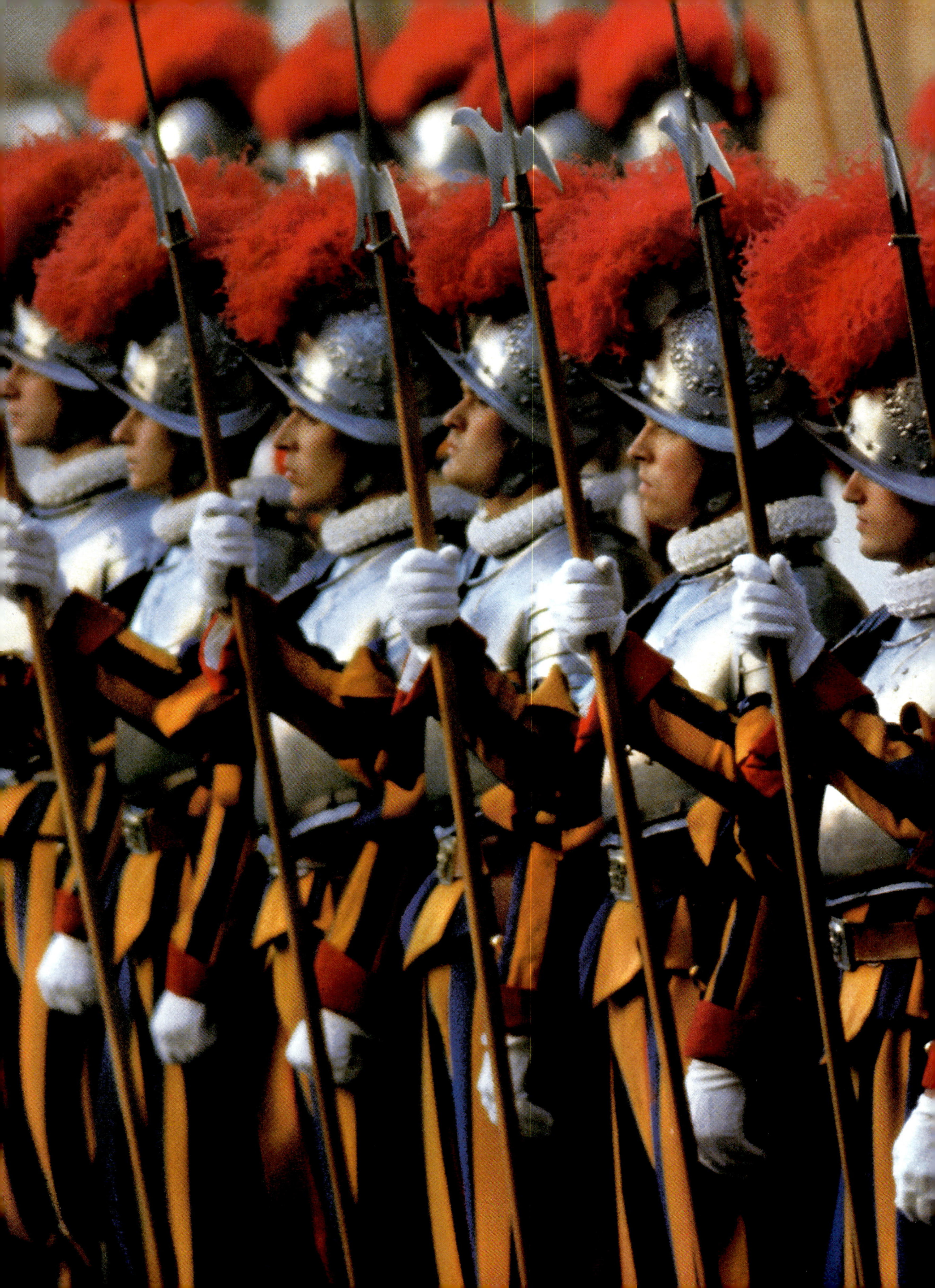

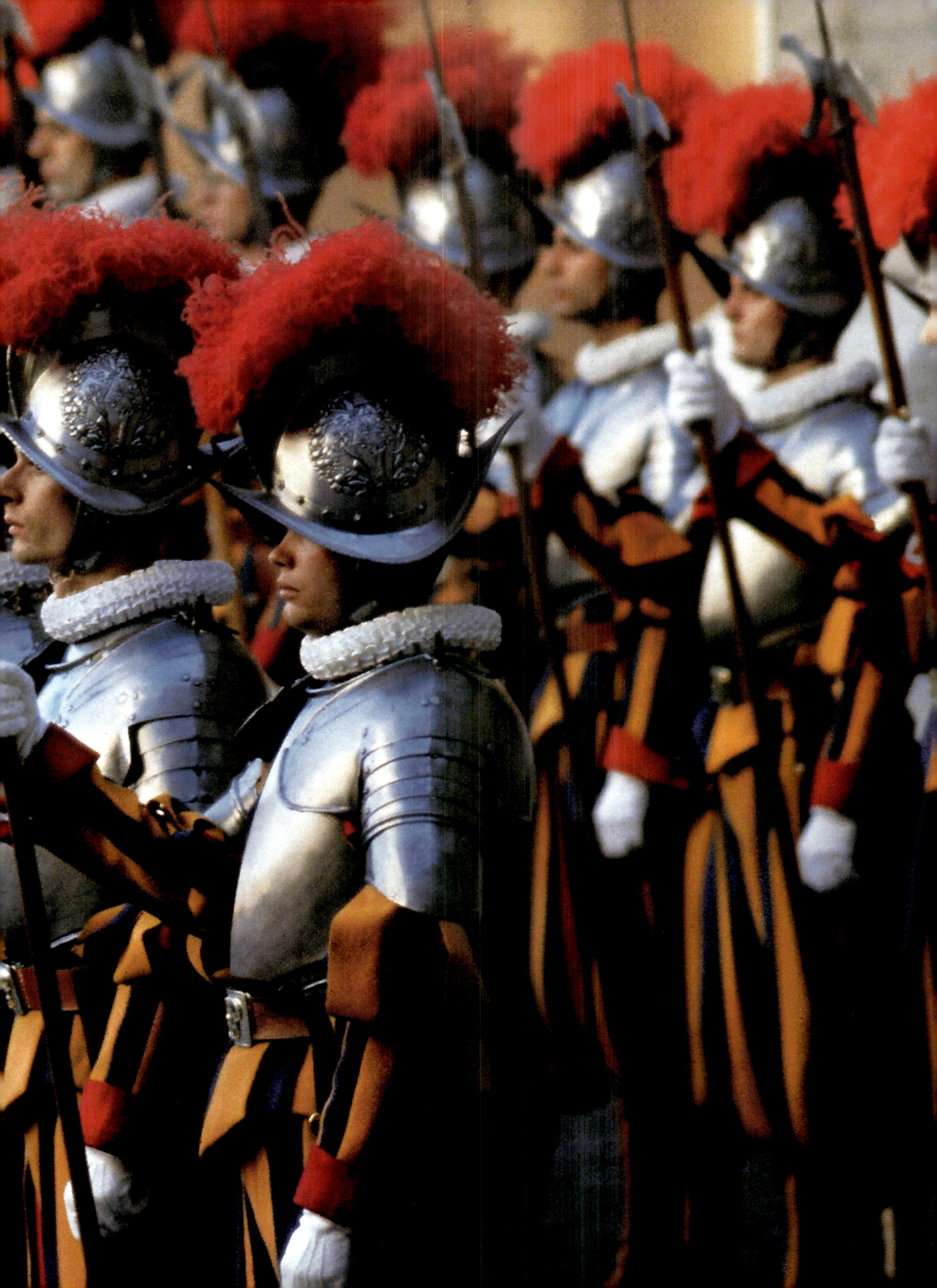

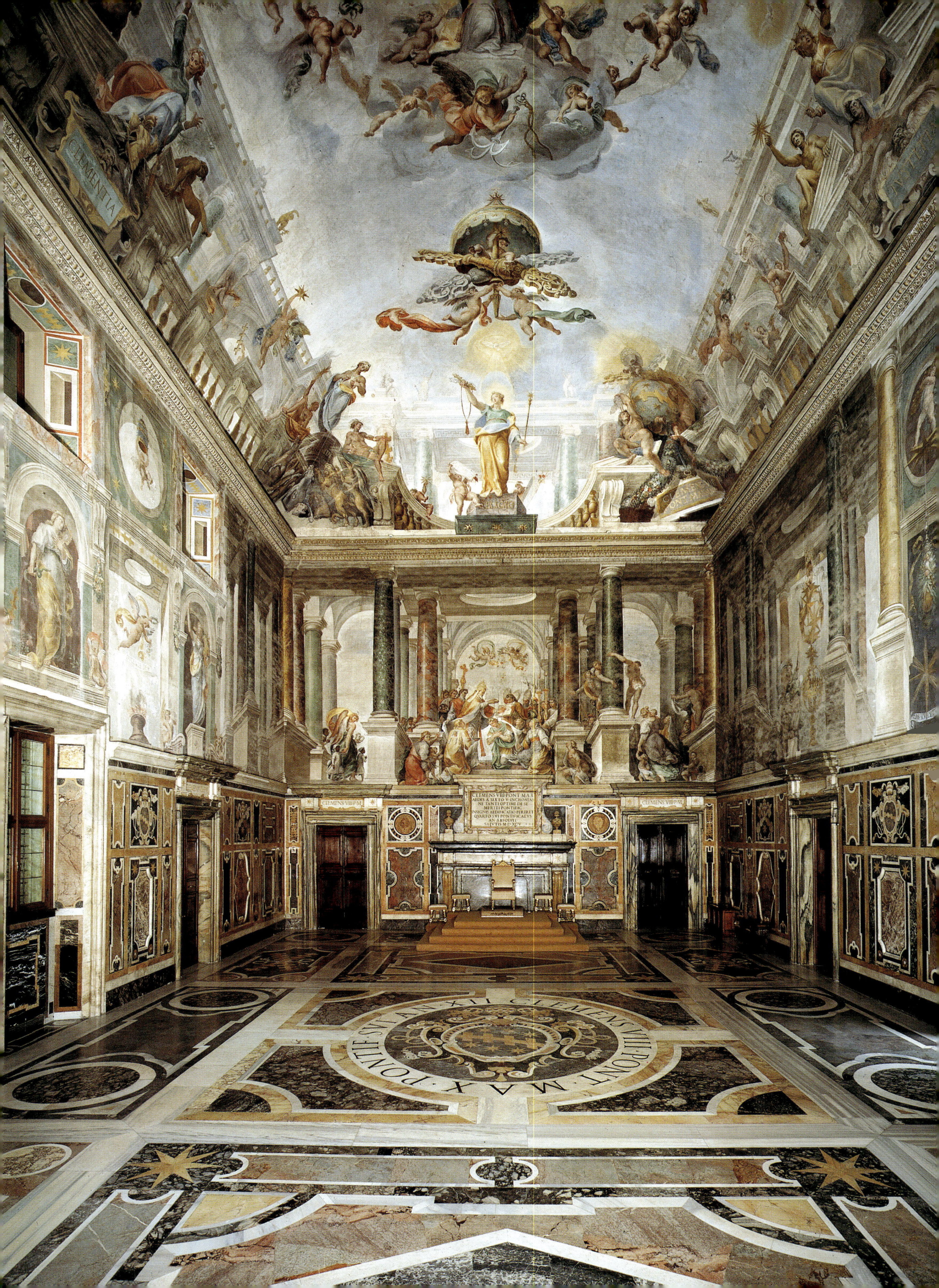
CLEMENS VIII PONT MAX PONTIF SVI AN XII

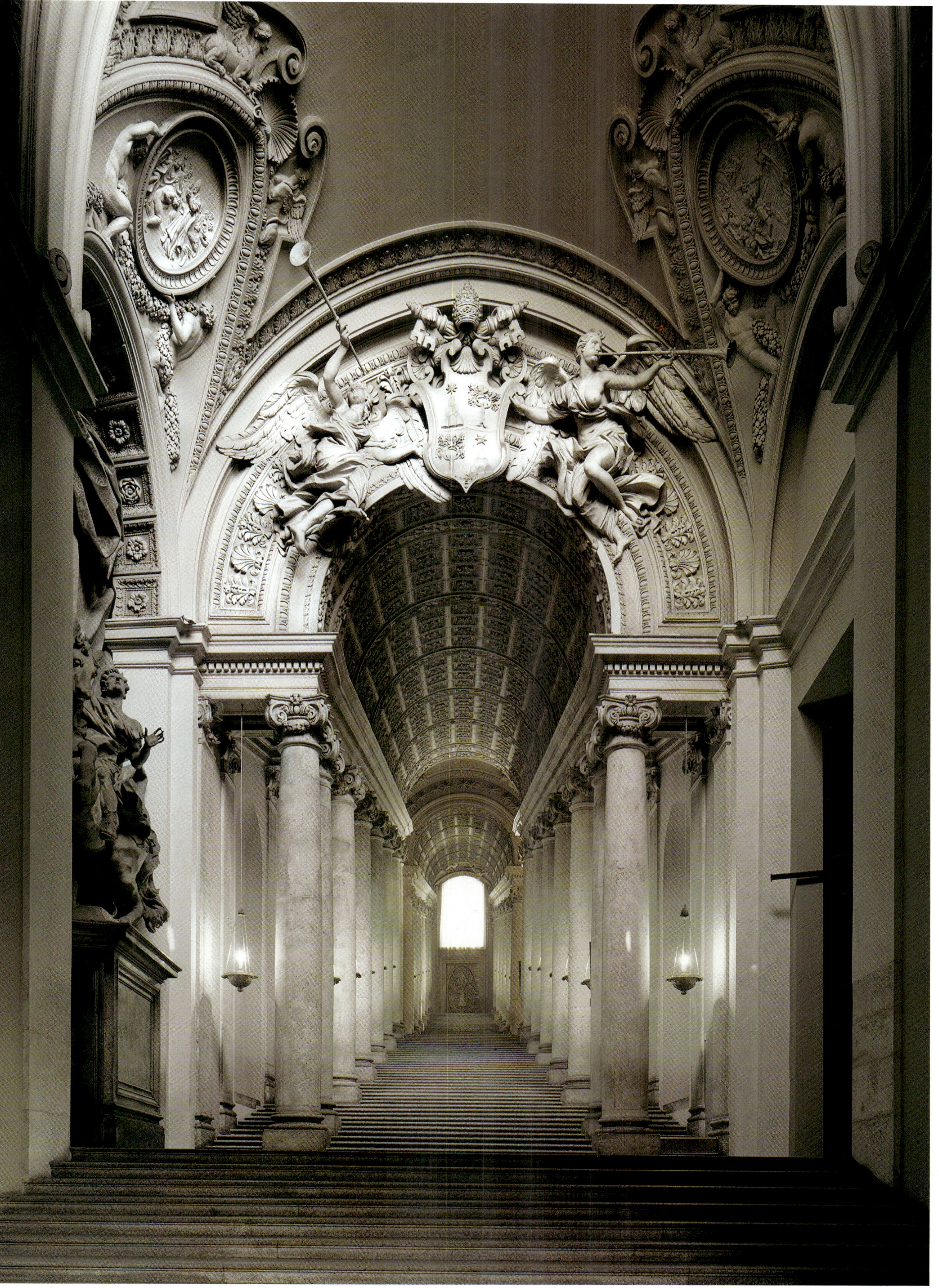

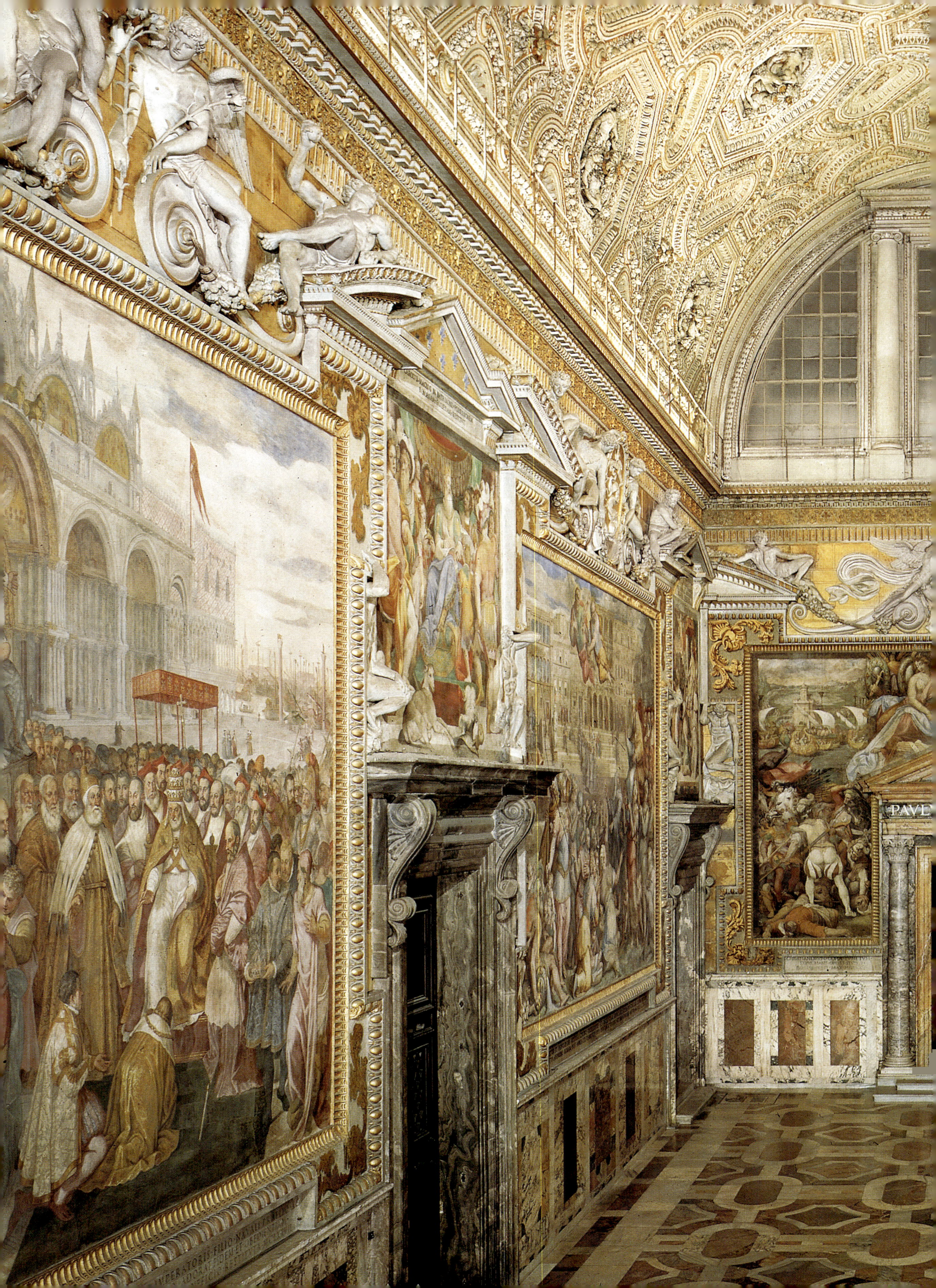
PAVE

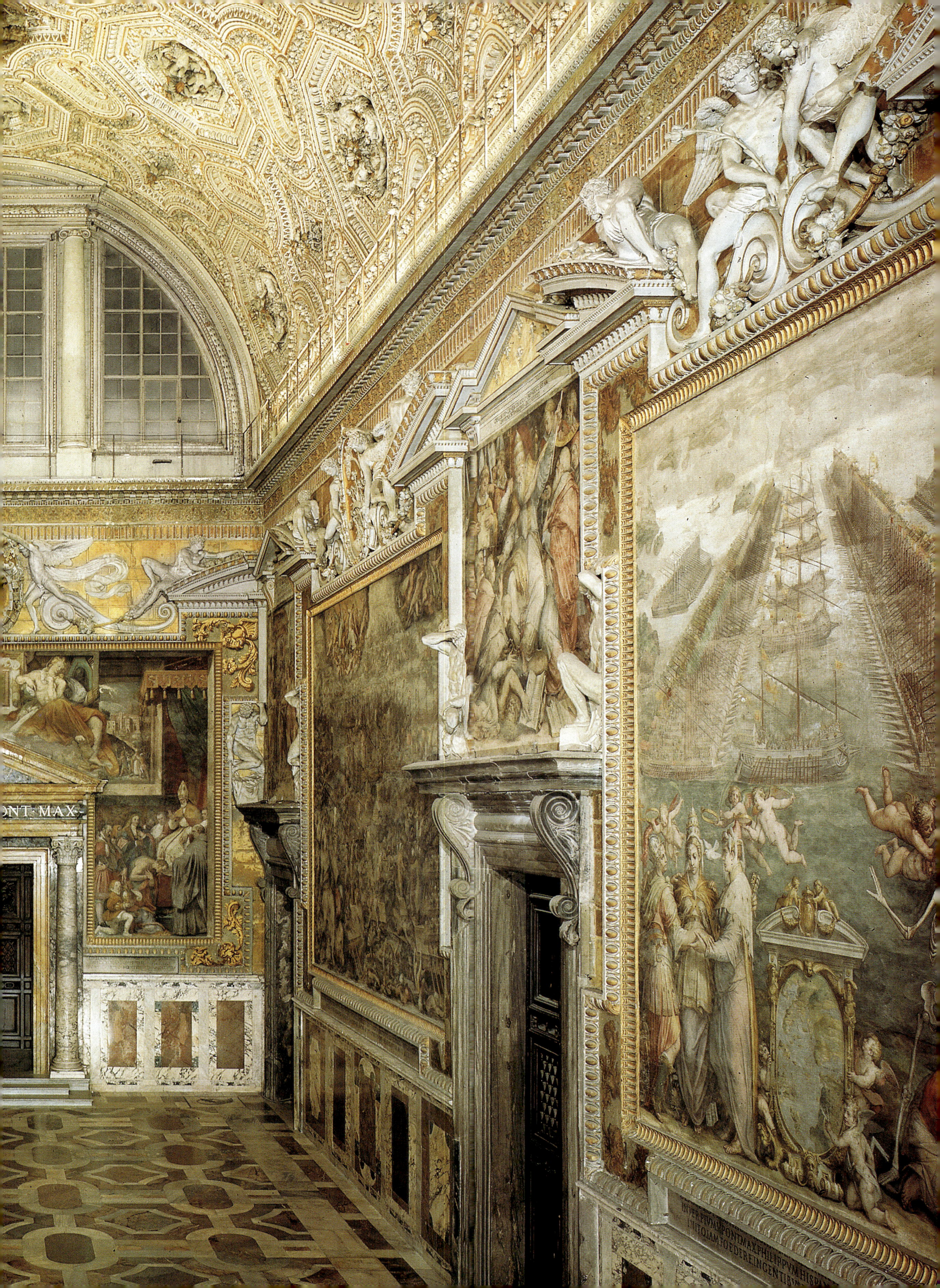
ONT. MAX
INTER PIVM PONT MAX PHILIPPVM HISP
INITO IAM FOEDERE INGENTIBVS

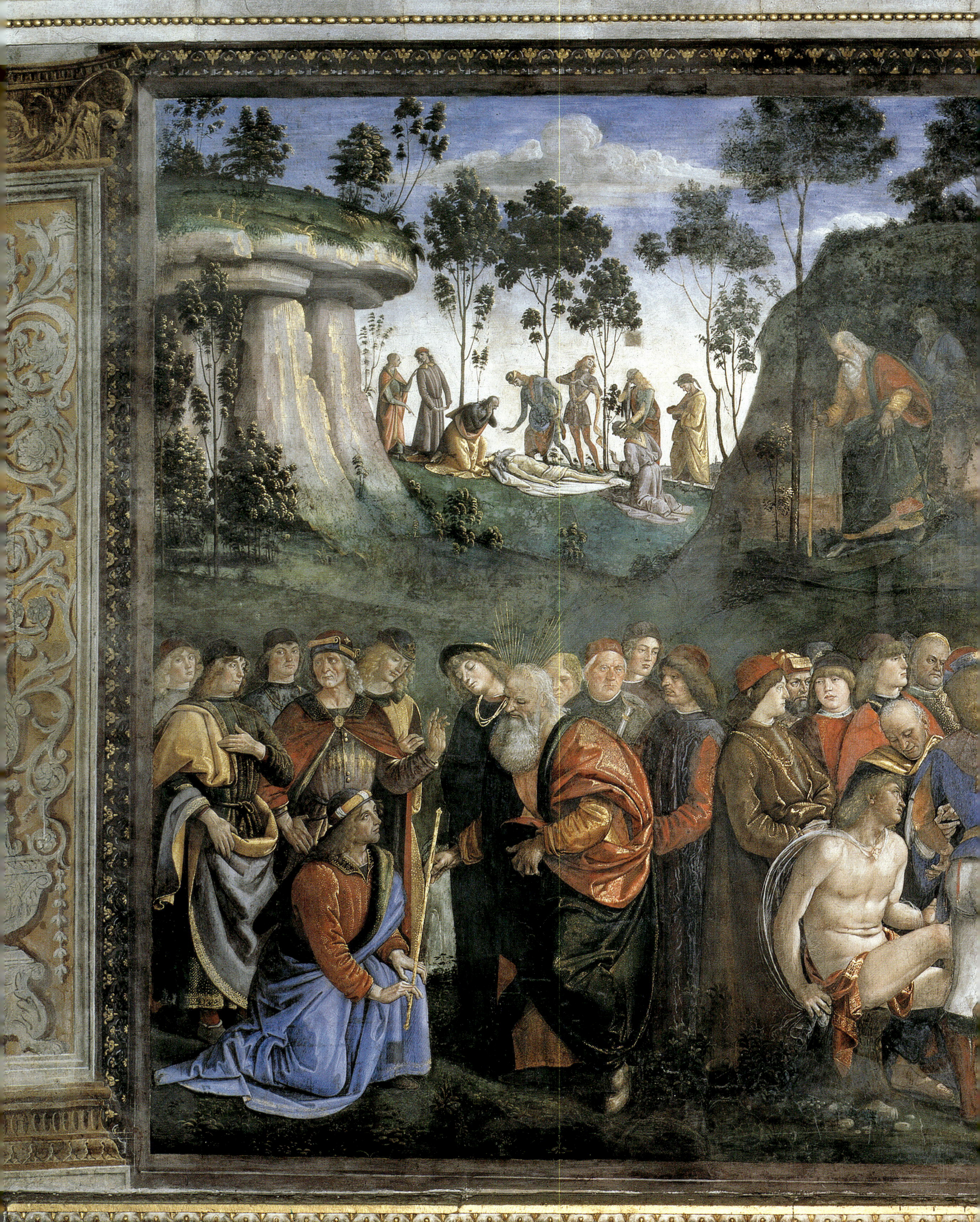
REPLICATIO

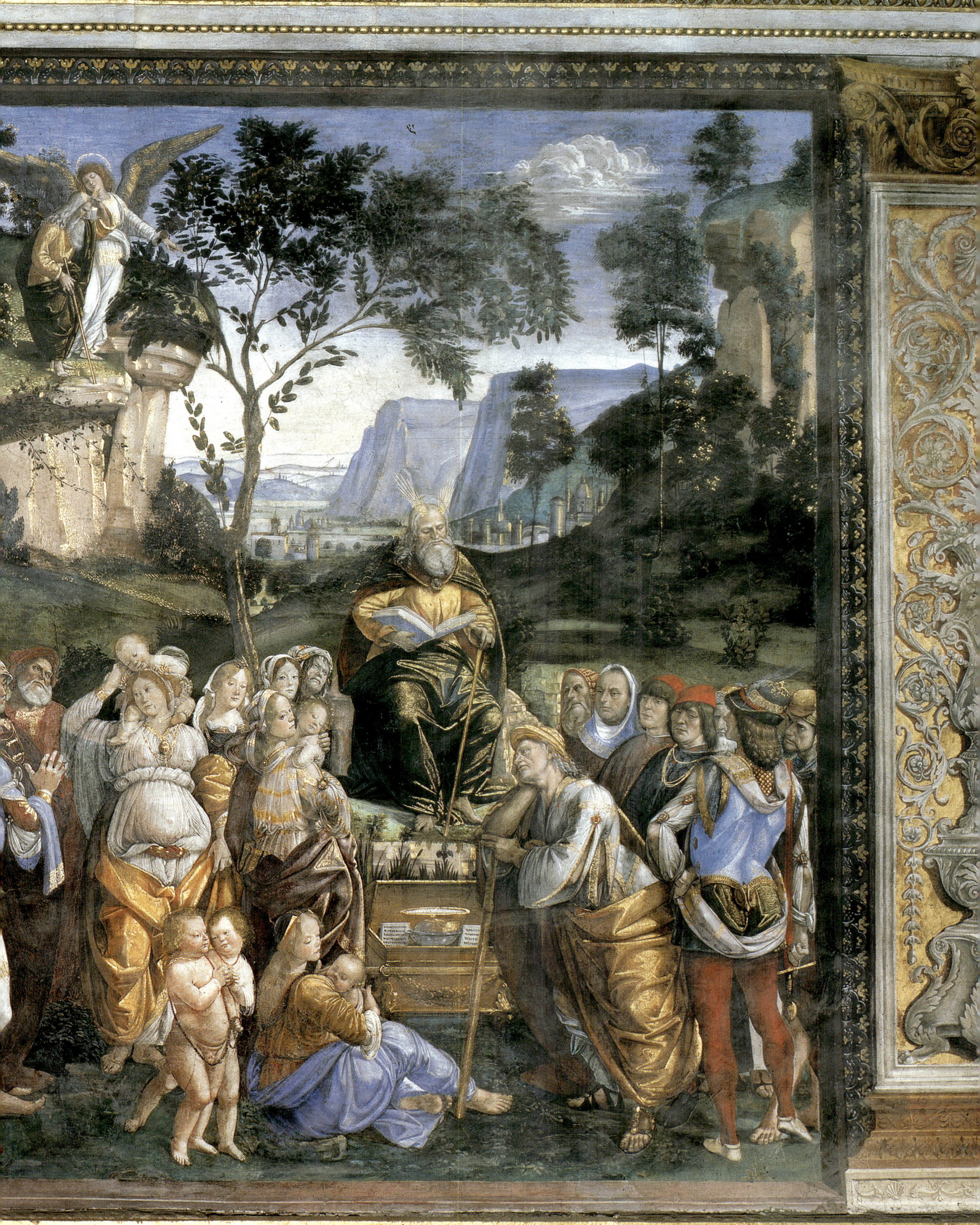
EGIS · SCRIPTAE · AMOISE

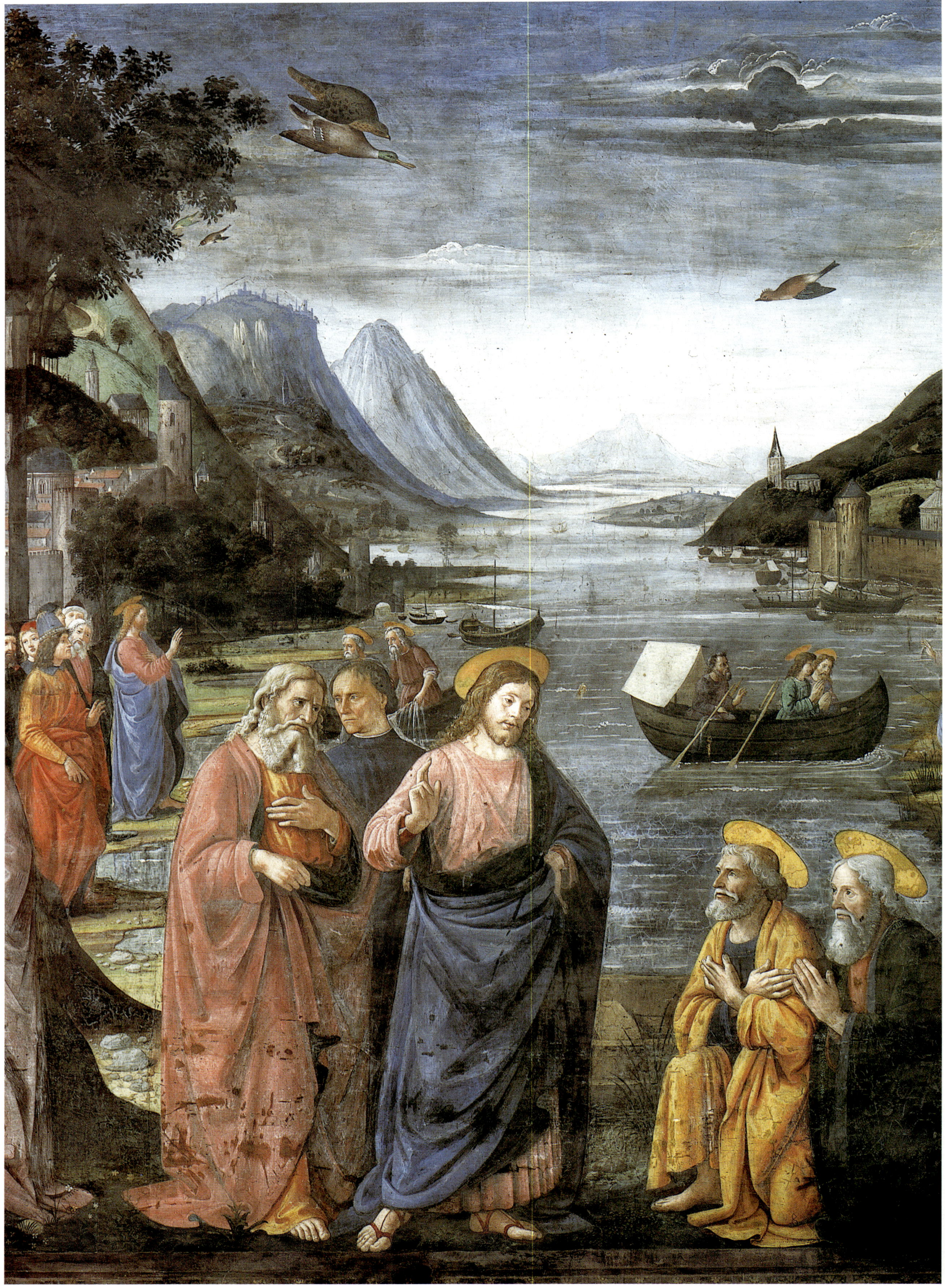

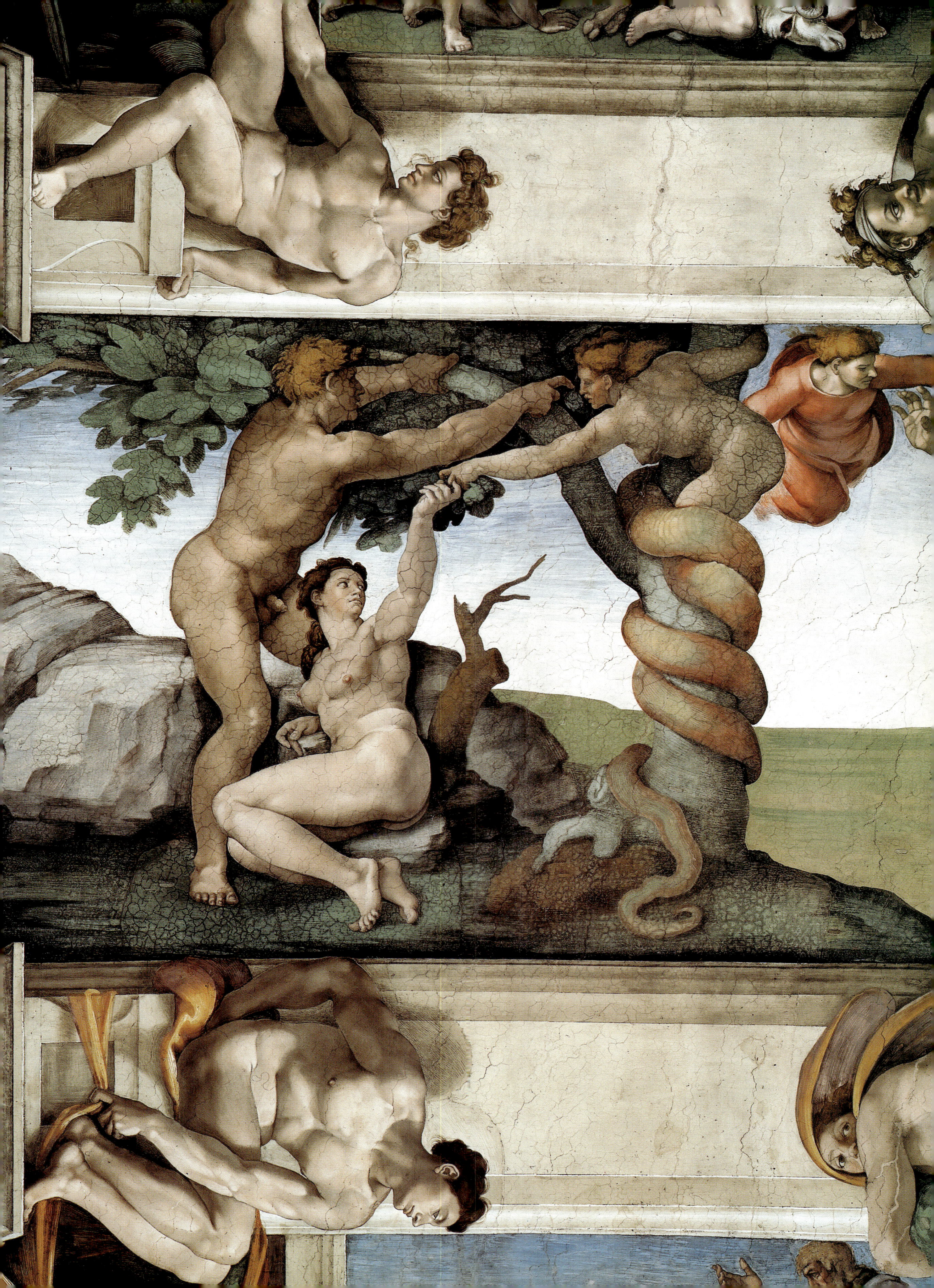

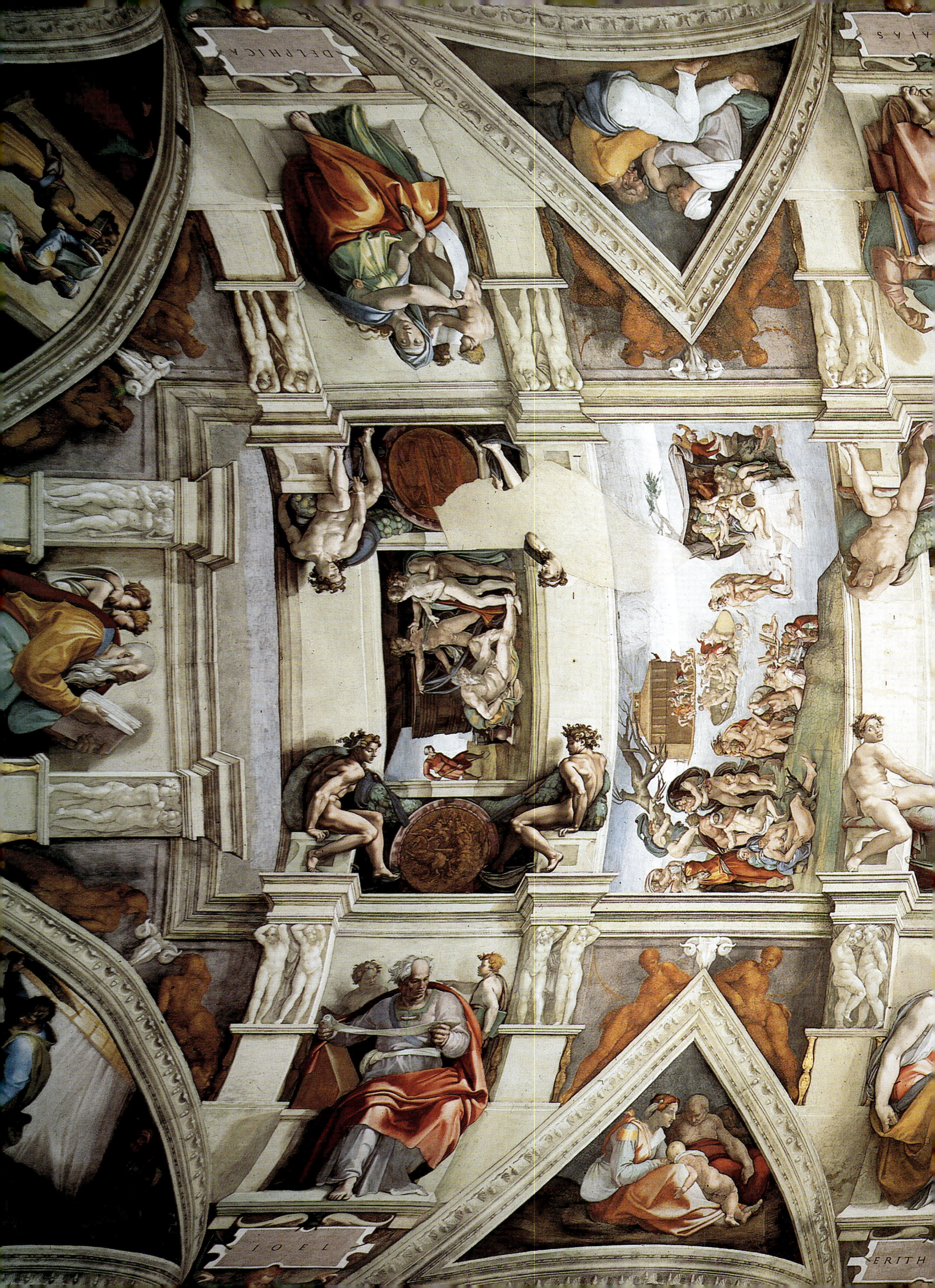
DELPHICA
IOEL

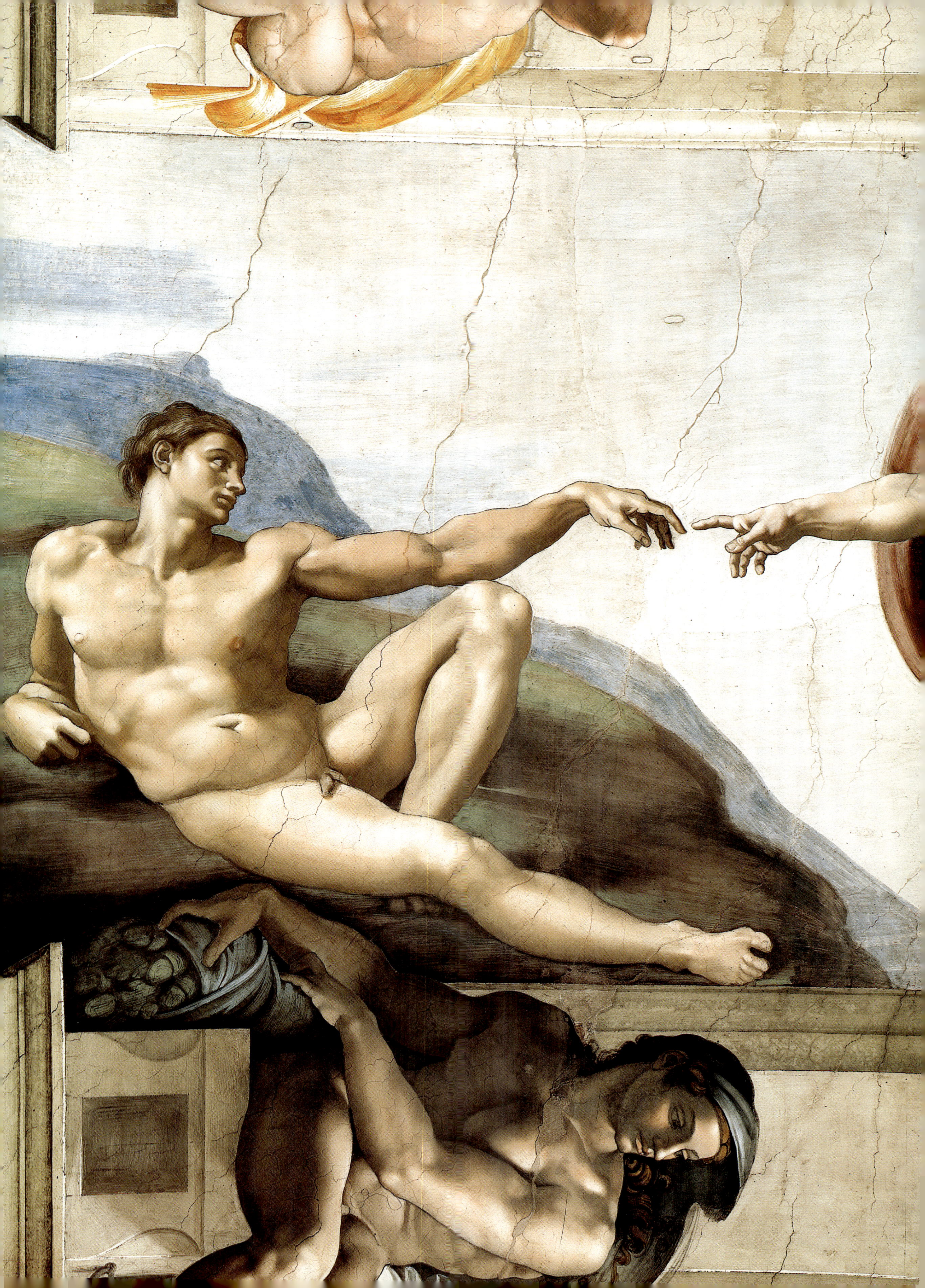

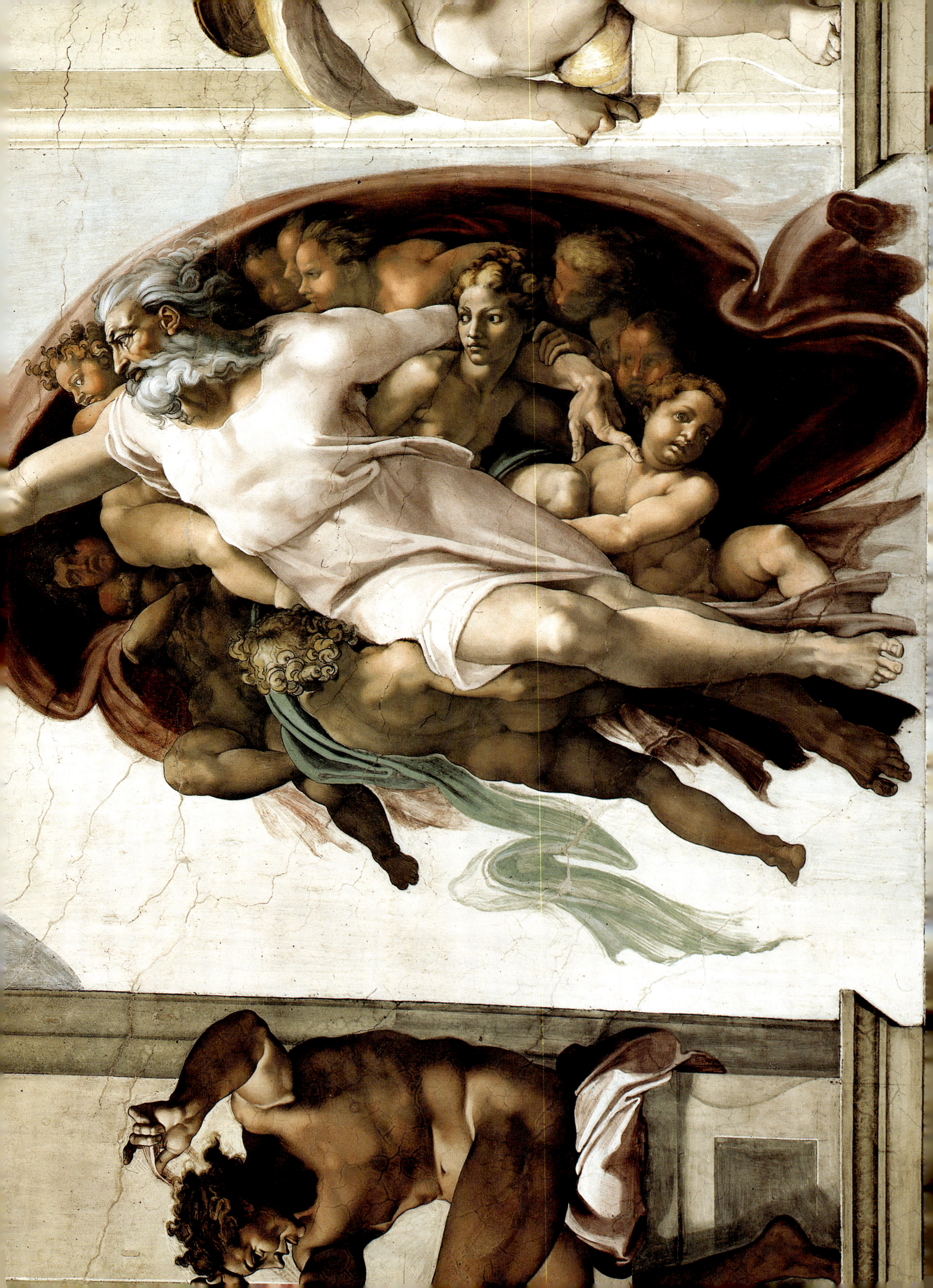

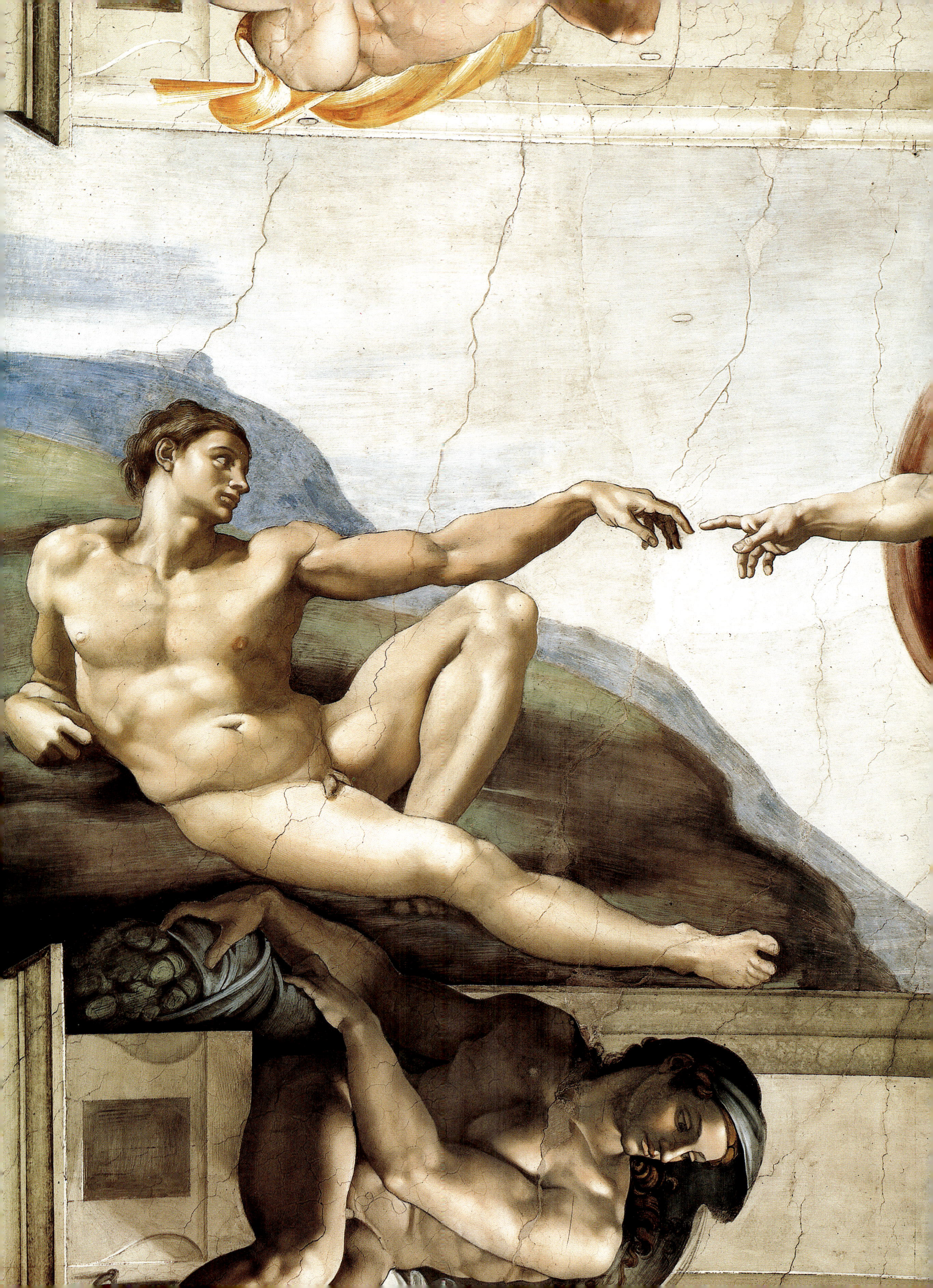

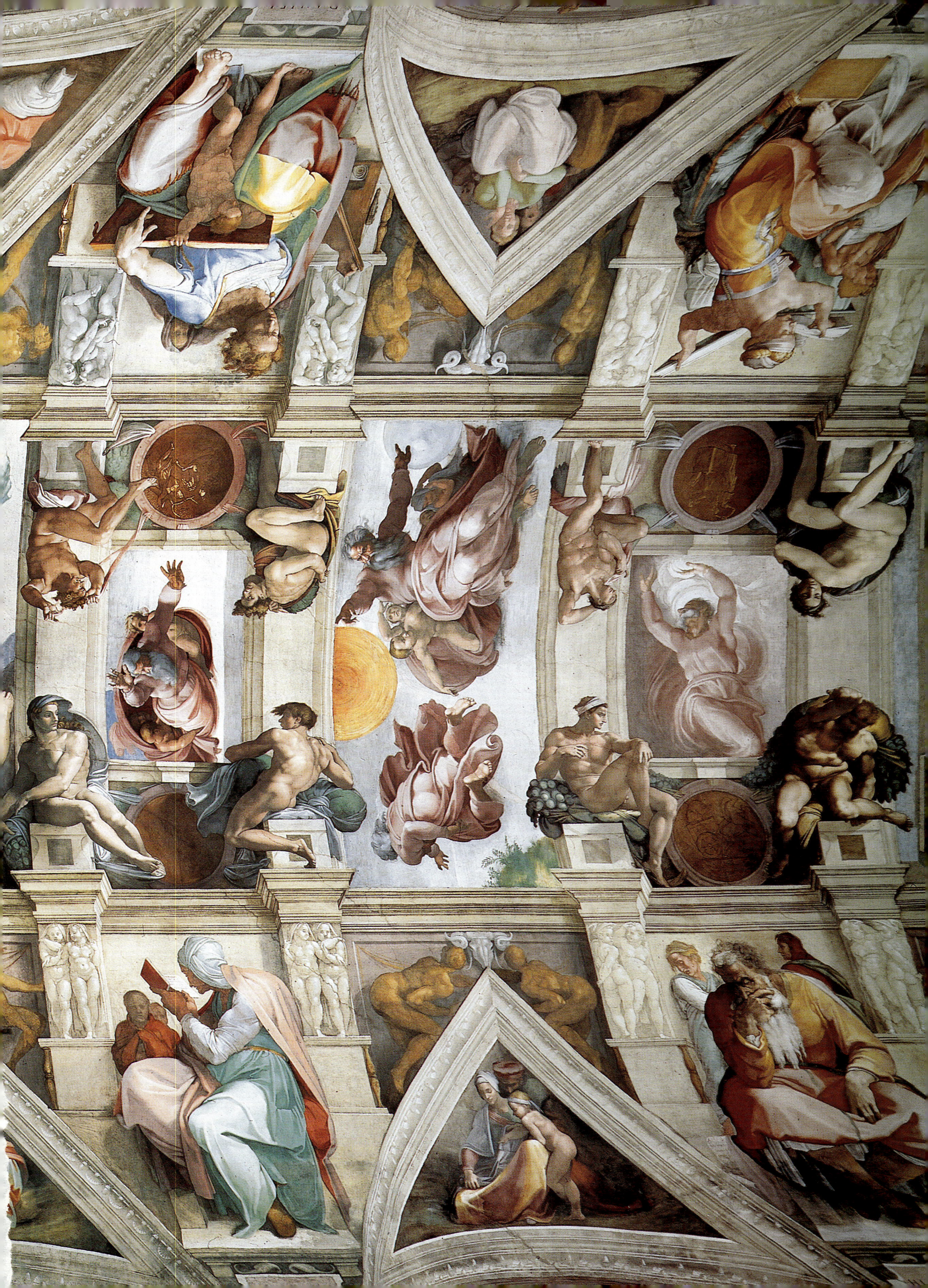

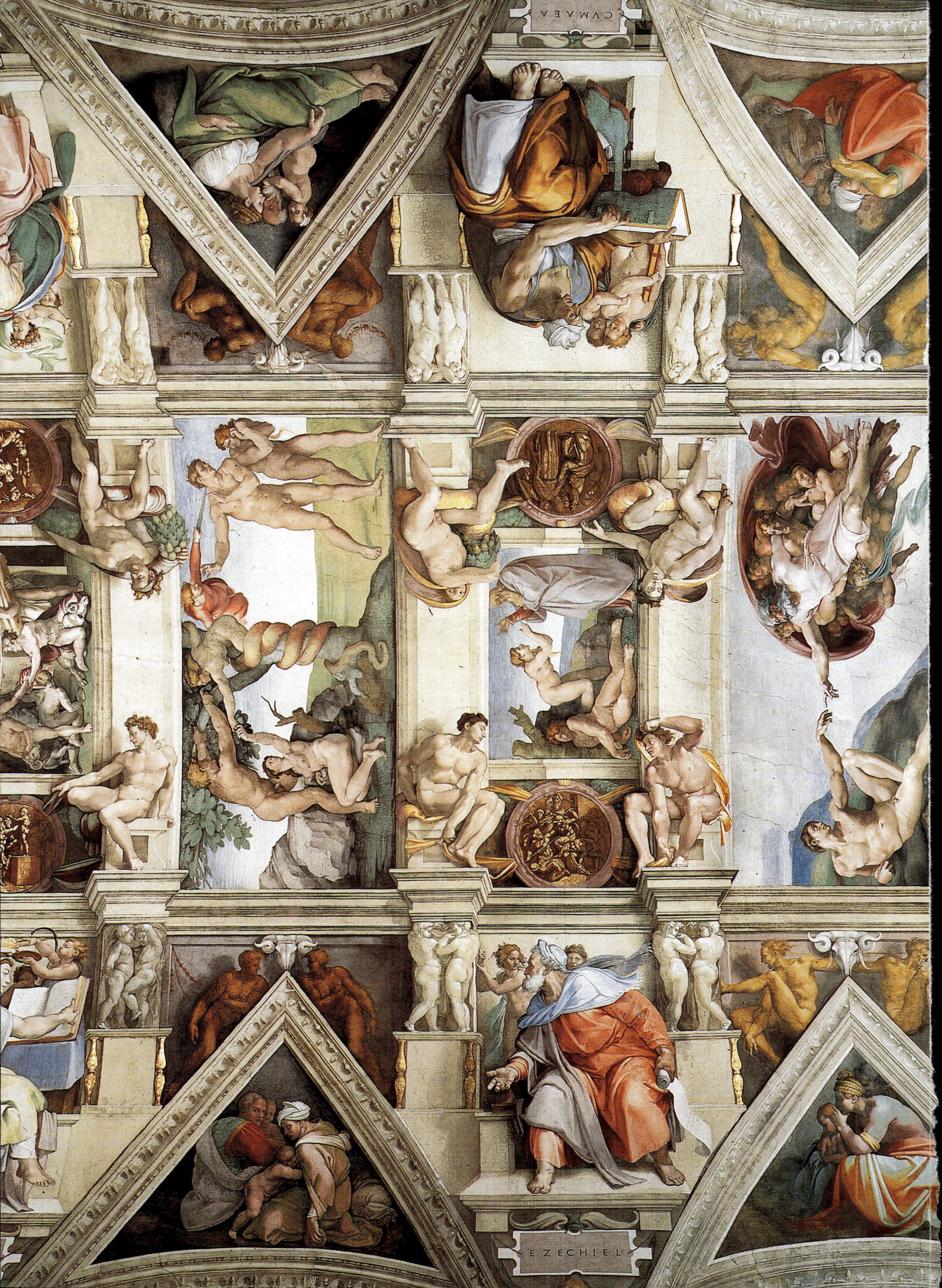
CVMAEA
EZECHIEL

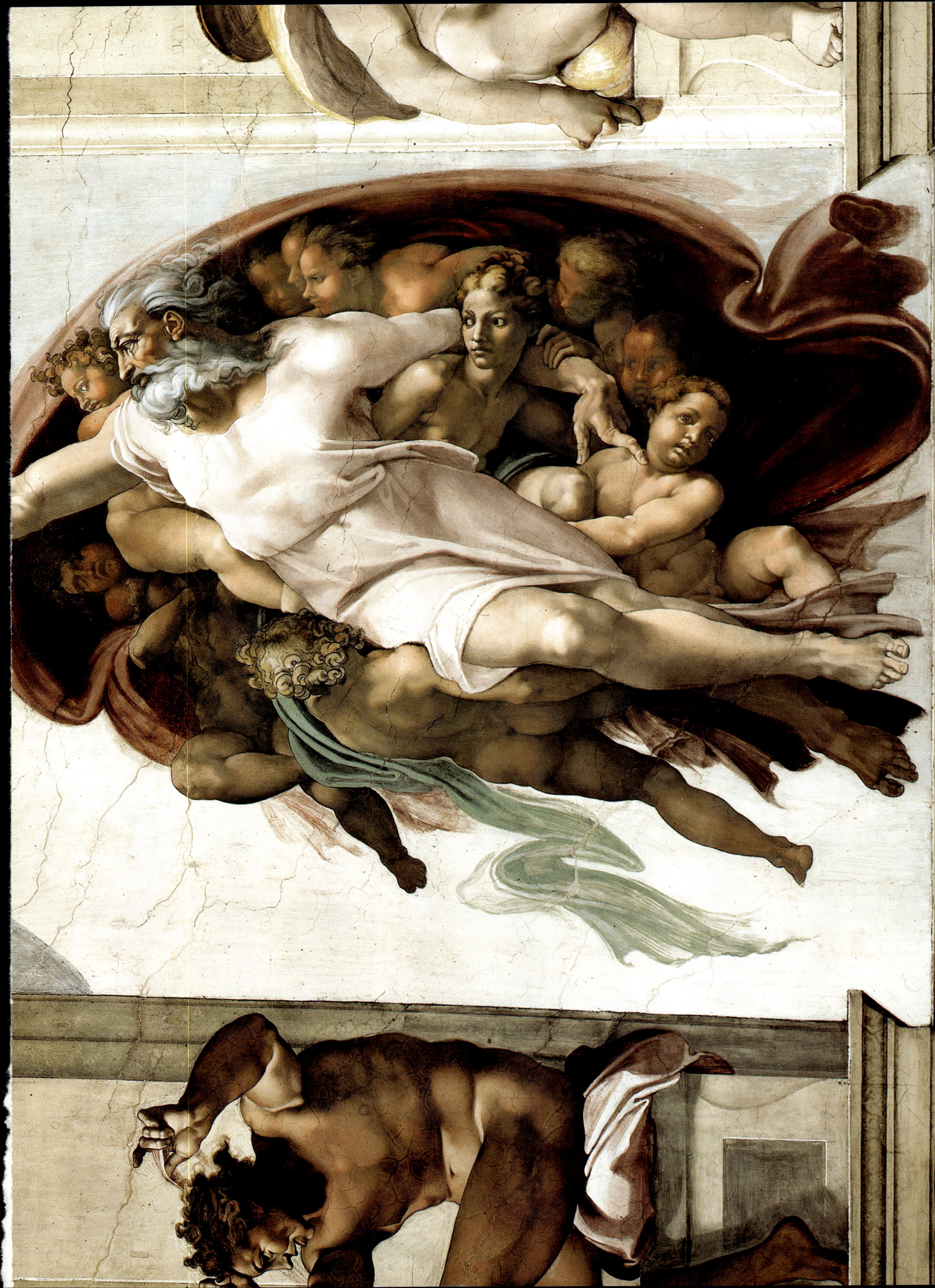

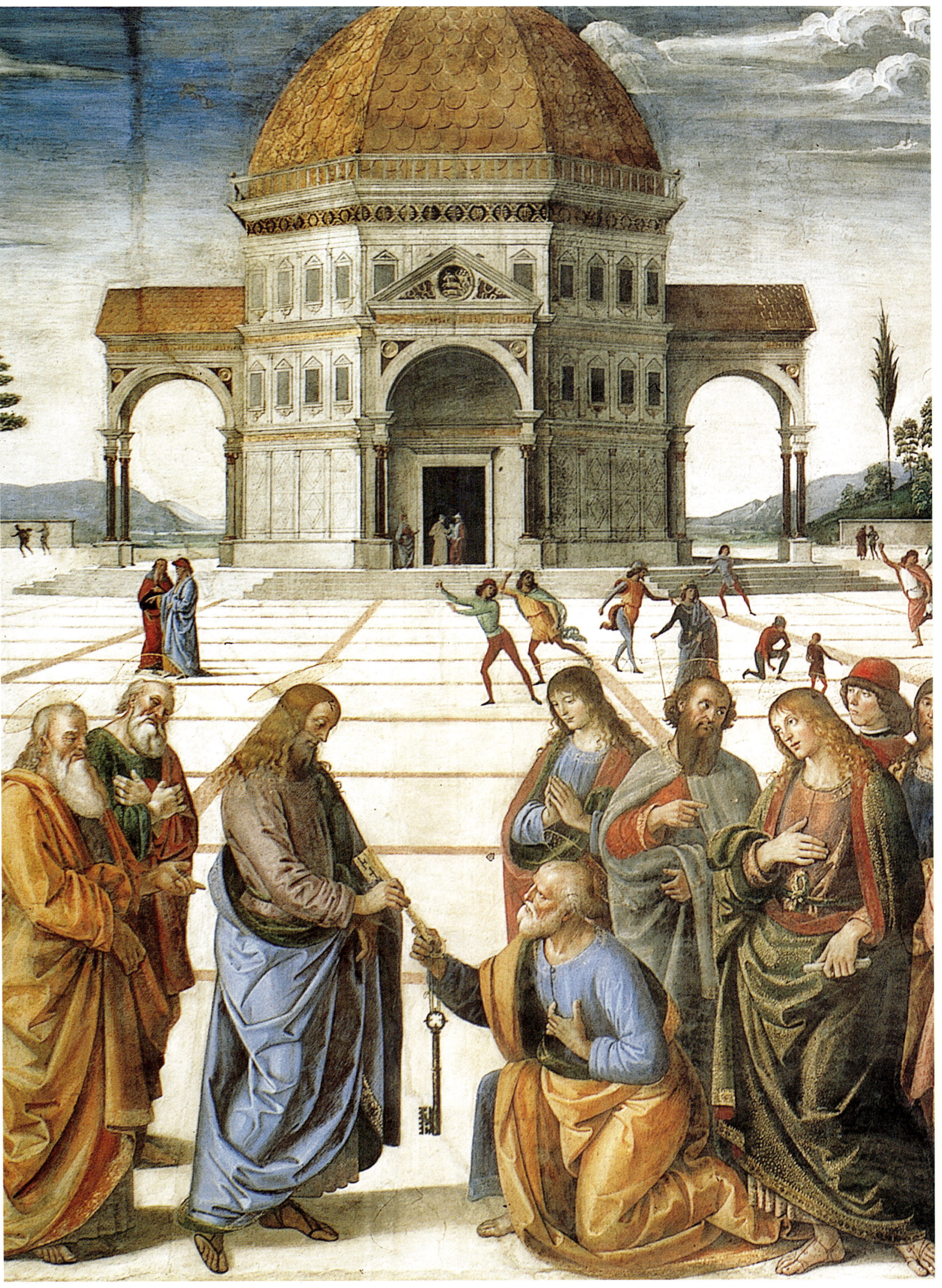

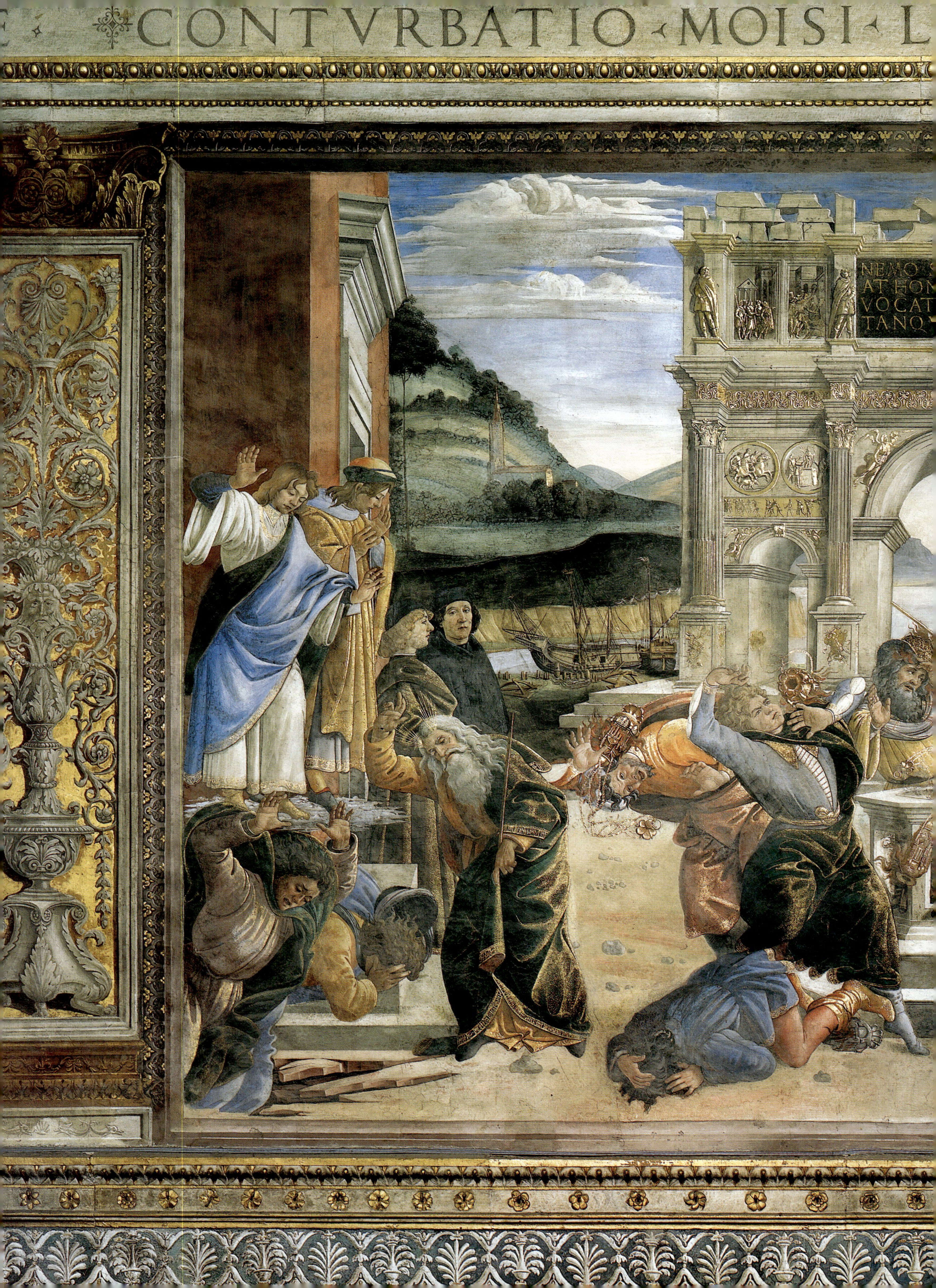

CONTVRBATIO MOISI L

NEMO
AT HON
VOCAT
TANQ

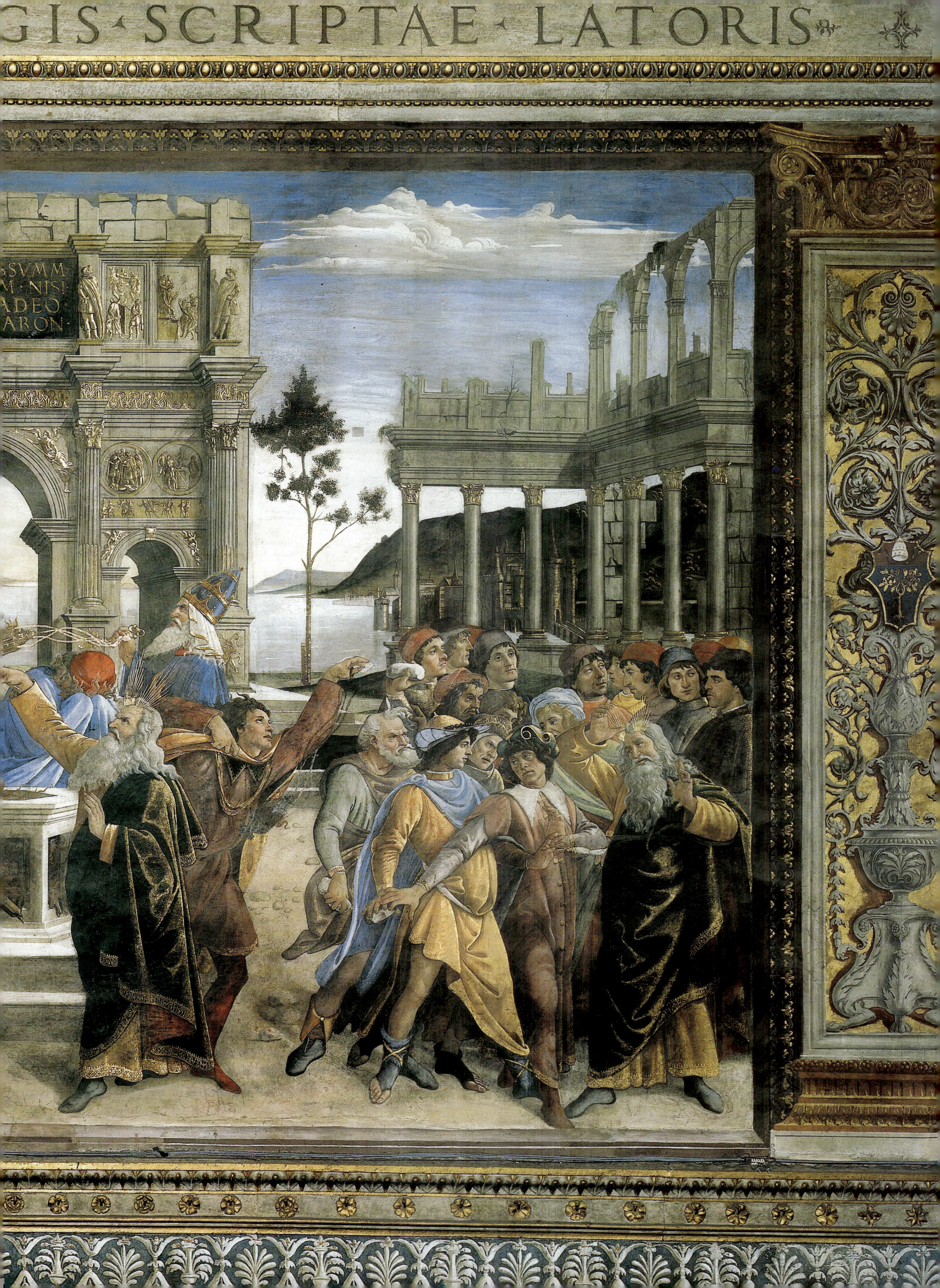

GIS SCRIPTAE LATORIS

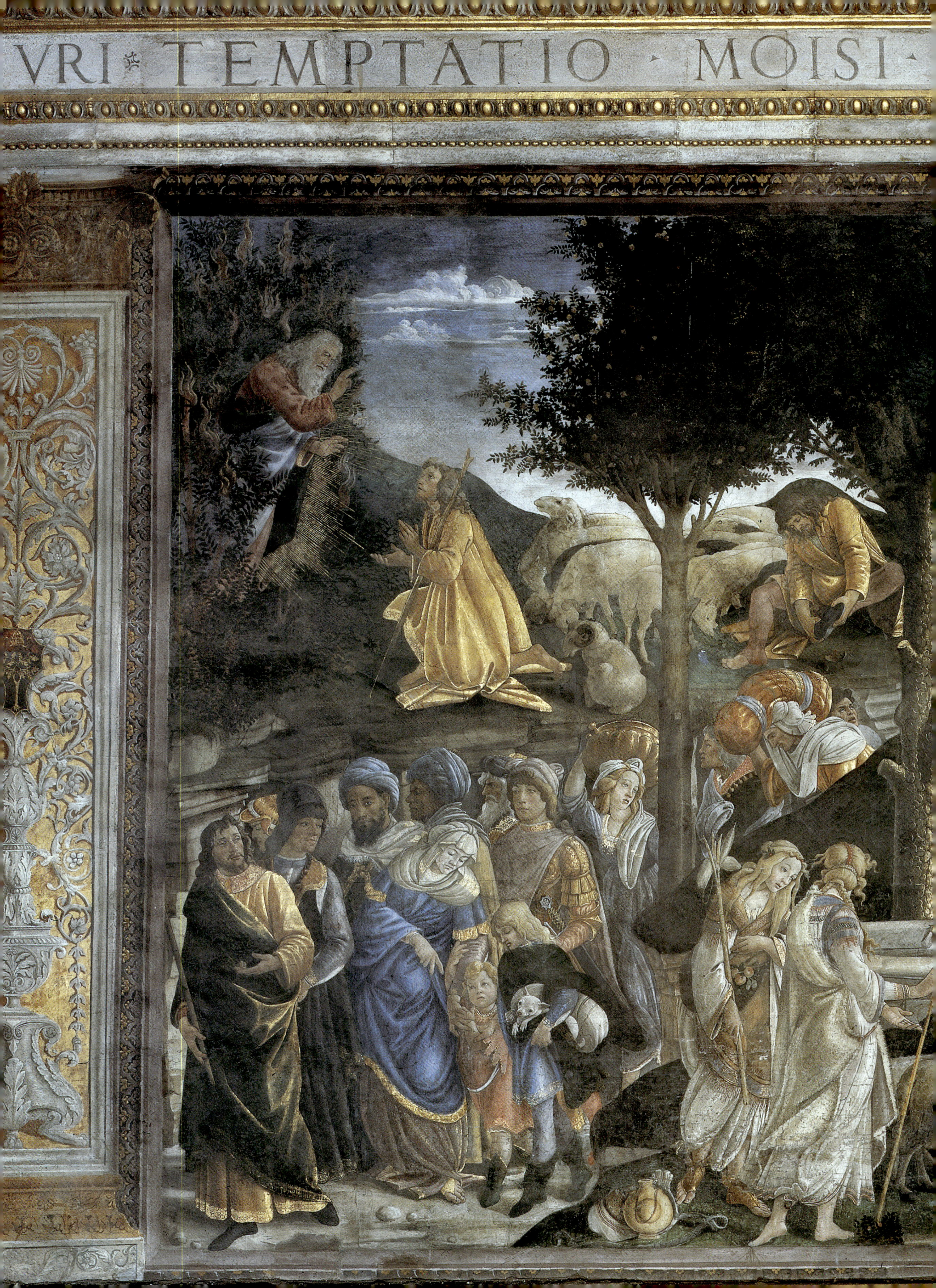

VRI · TEMPTATIO · MOISI ·

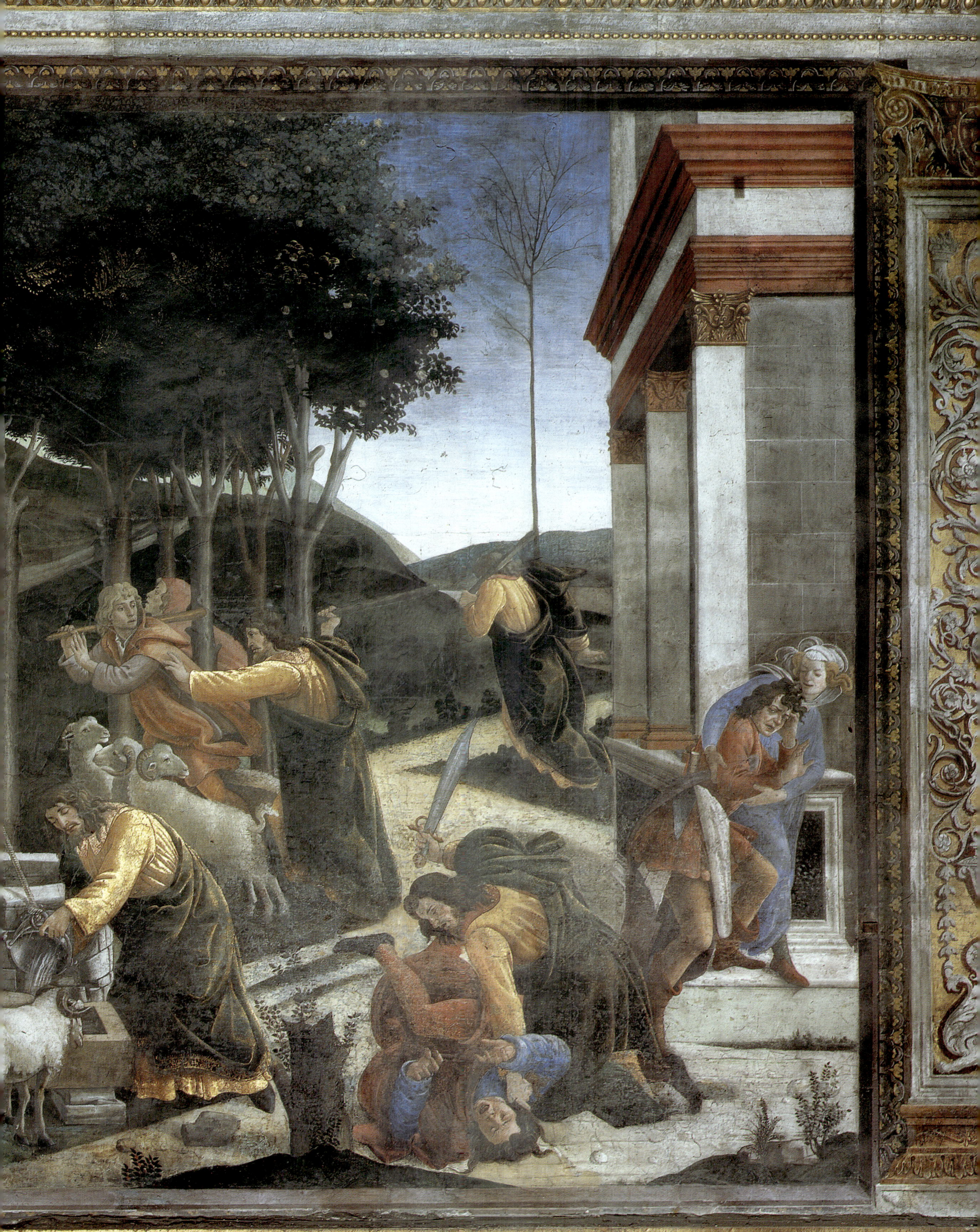
EGIS · SCRIPTAE · LATORIS

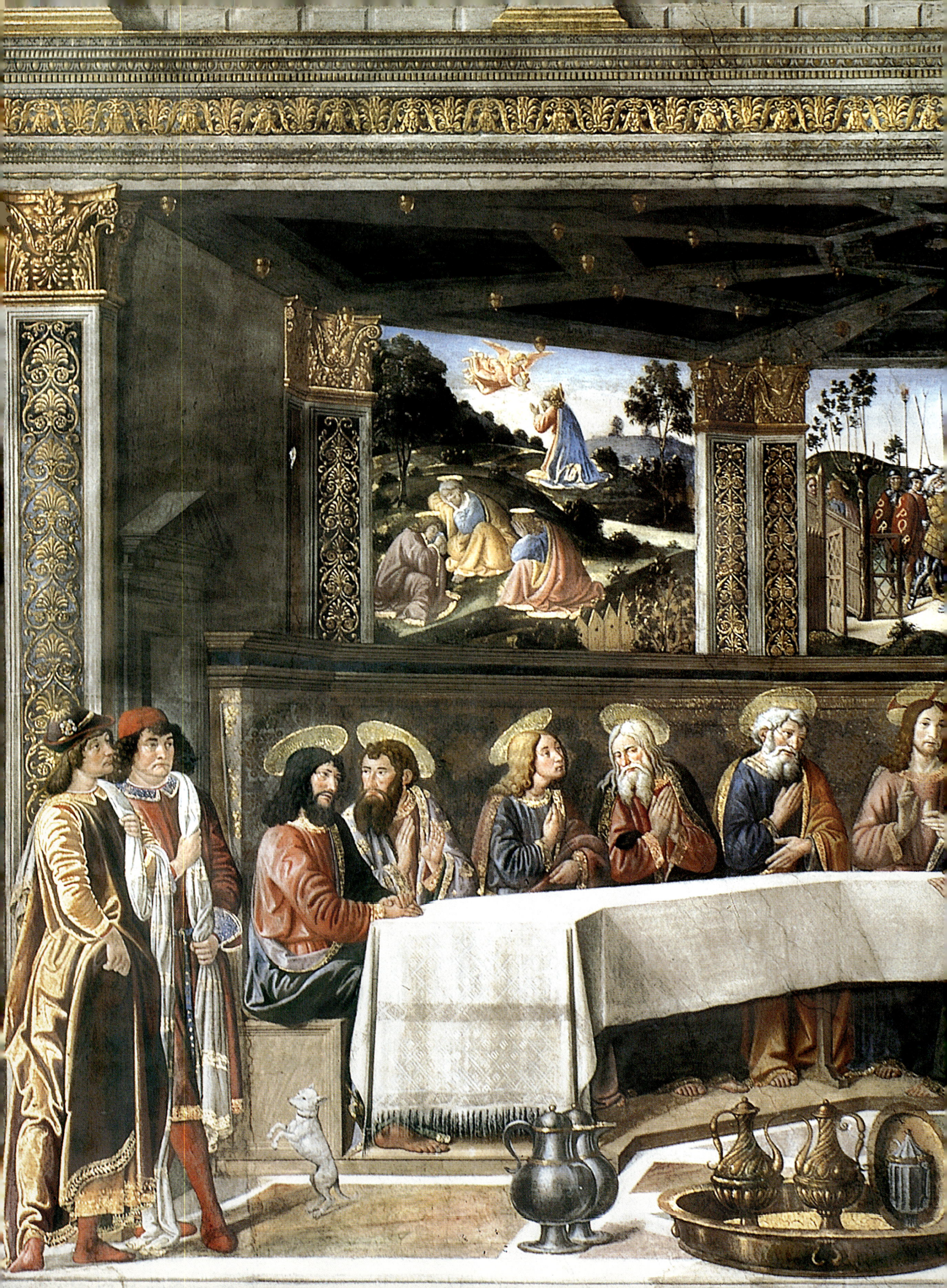

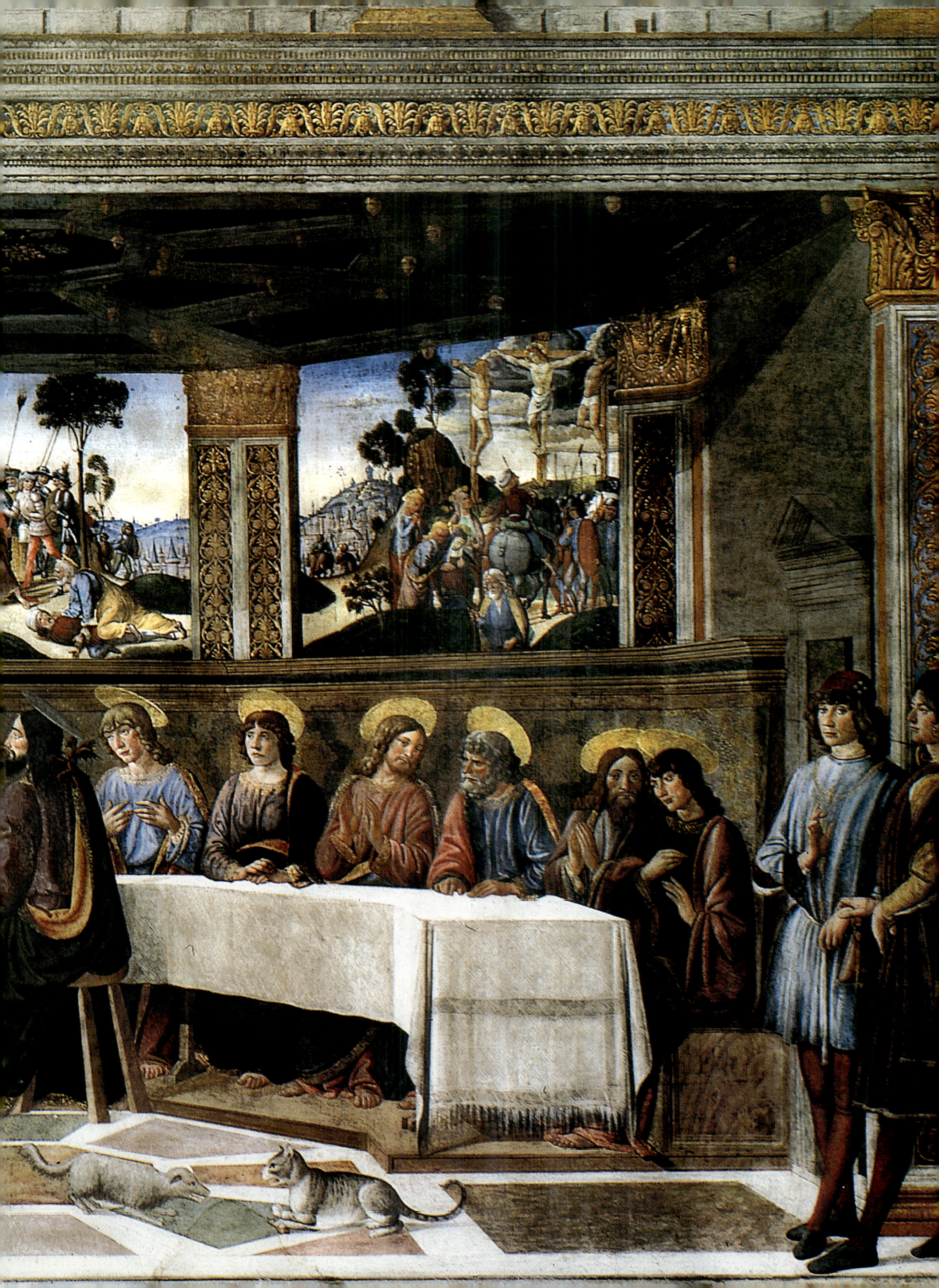

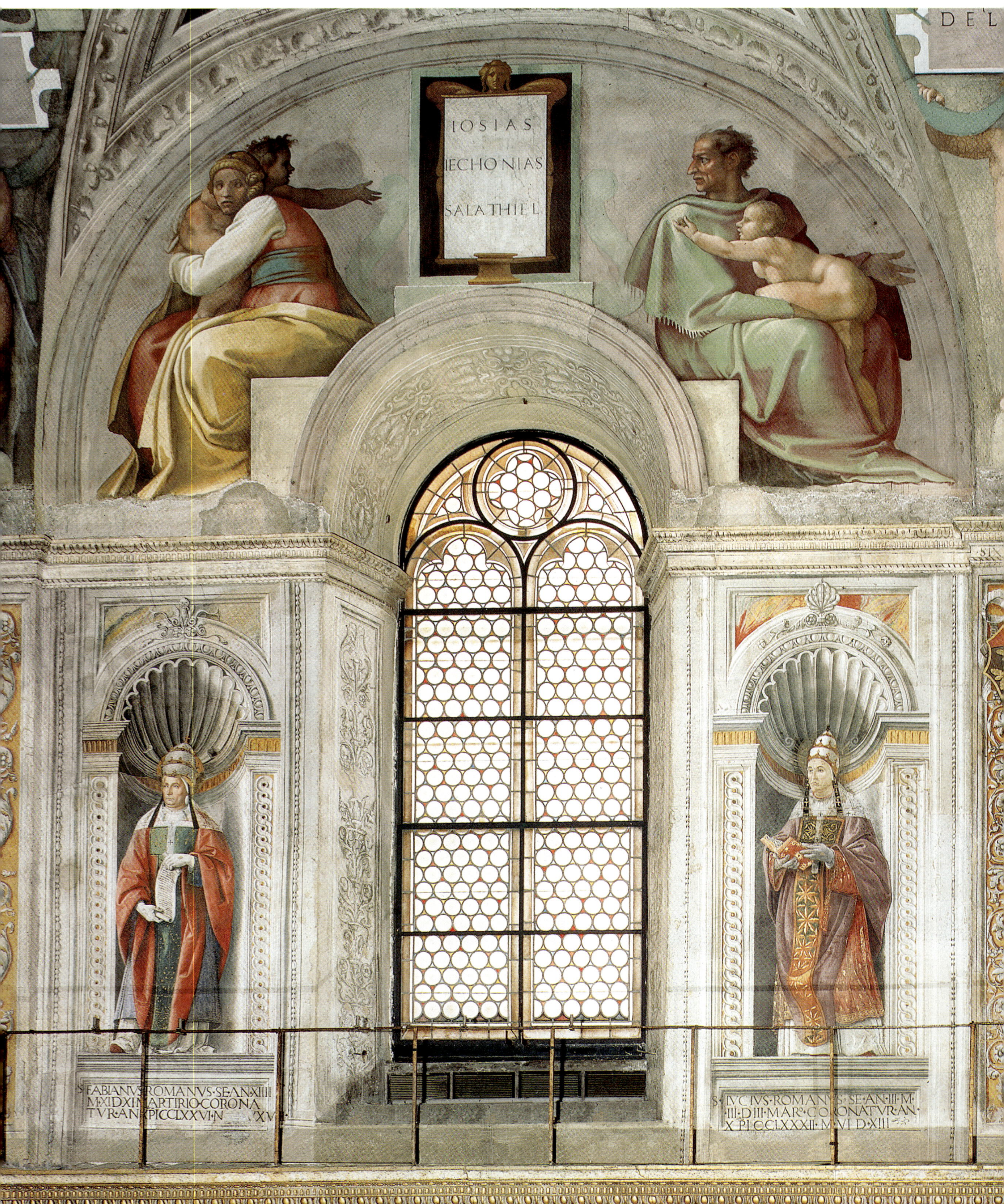
DEL
IOSIAS
IECHONIAS
SALATHIEL
S FABIANVS ROMANVS SE AN XIIII
M XI D XI MARTIRIO CORONA
TVR AN XPI CCLXXVI N XV
S LVCIVS ROMANVS SE AN III M
III D III MAR CORONATVR AN
XPI CCLXXXII M VI D XIII
CONTVRBATIO IESV CHRISTI LEGISLATORIS

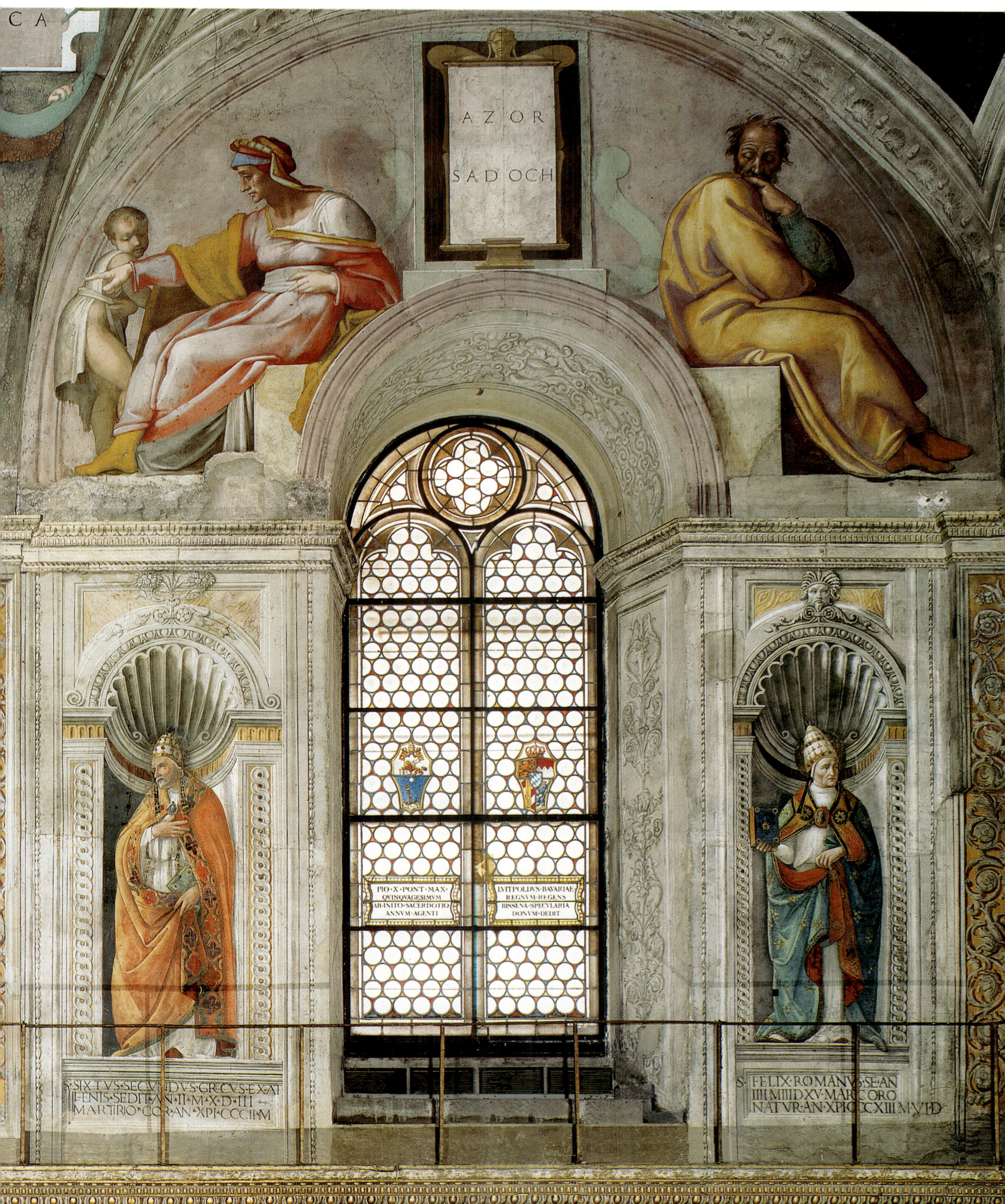
CA
AZOR
SADOCH
PIO·X·PONT·MAX·
QVINQVAGESIMVM
AB·INITO·SACERDOTIO
ANNVM·AGENTI
LVITPOLDVS·BAVARIAE·
REGNVM·REGENS
BISSENA·SPECVLARIA
DONVM·DEDIT
S·SIXTVS·SECVNDVS·GRECVS·EX·AT
HENIS·SEDIT·AN·II·M·X·D·III
MARTIRIO·COR·AN·XPI·CCCII·M
S·FELIX·ROMANVS·SE·AN
IIII·MIIII·D·XV·MAR·CORO
NATVR·AN·XPI·CCXIII·M·VI·D
REPLICATIO·LEGIS·EVANGELICAE·A·CHRISTO

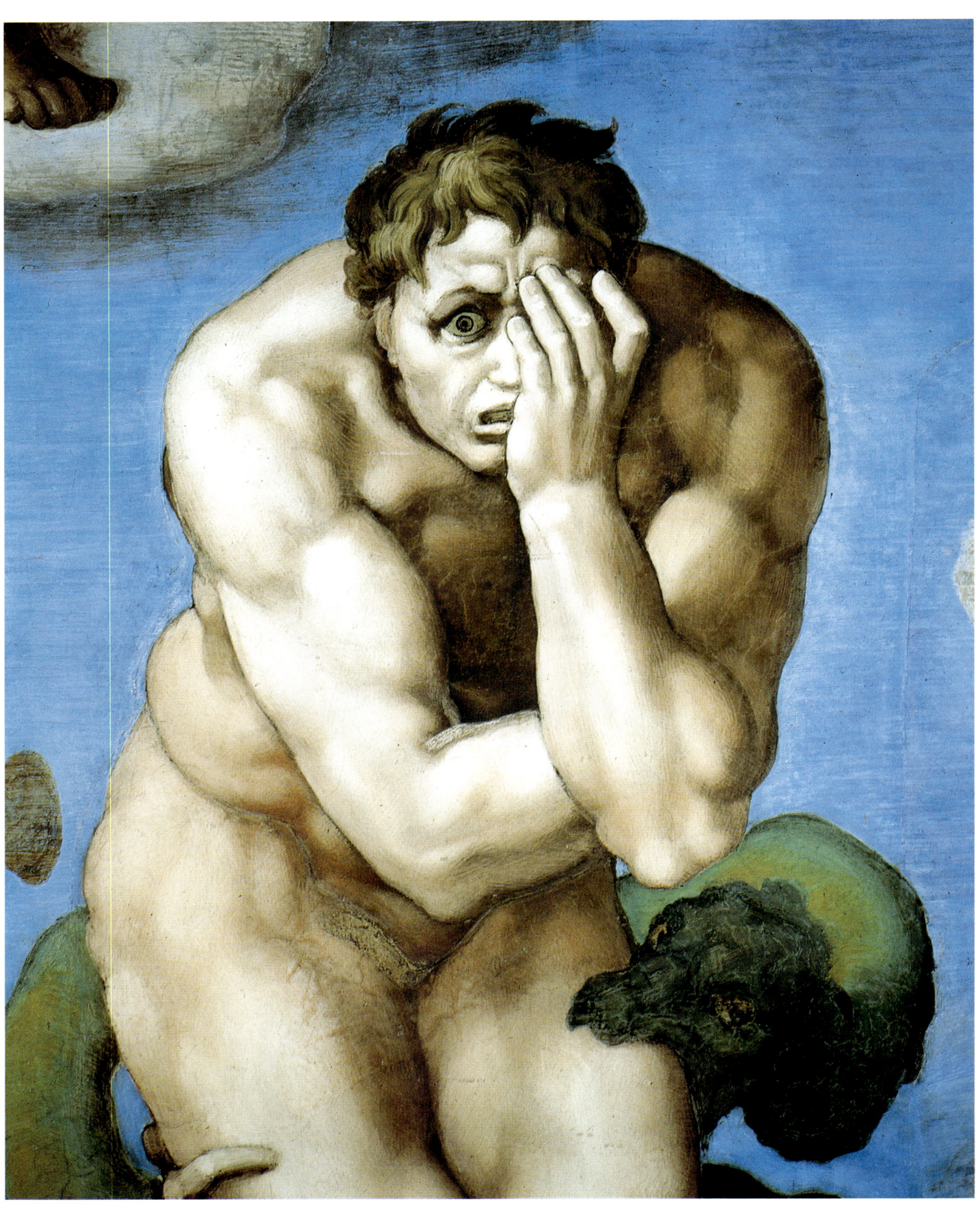

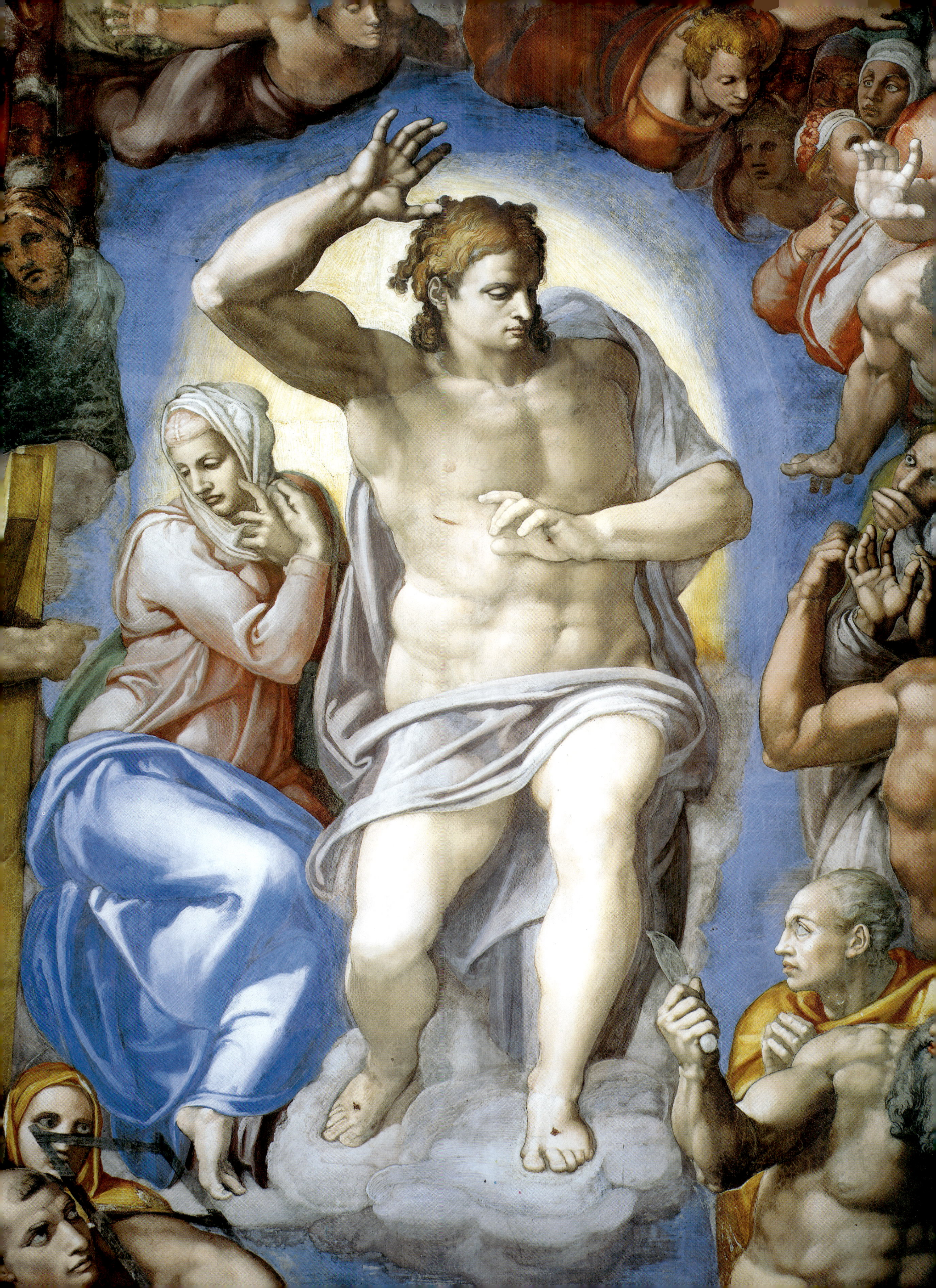

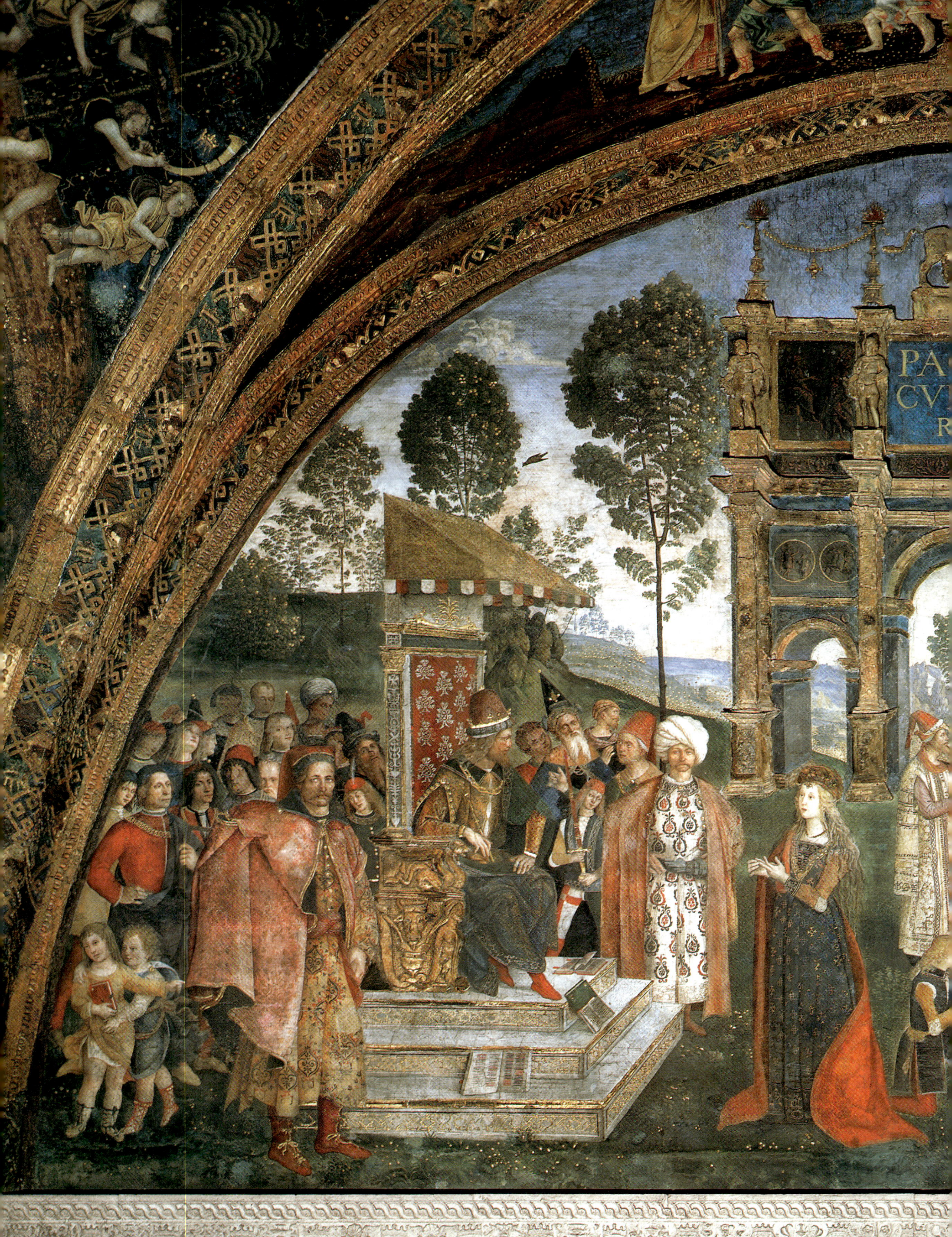

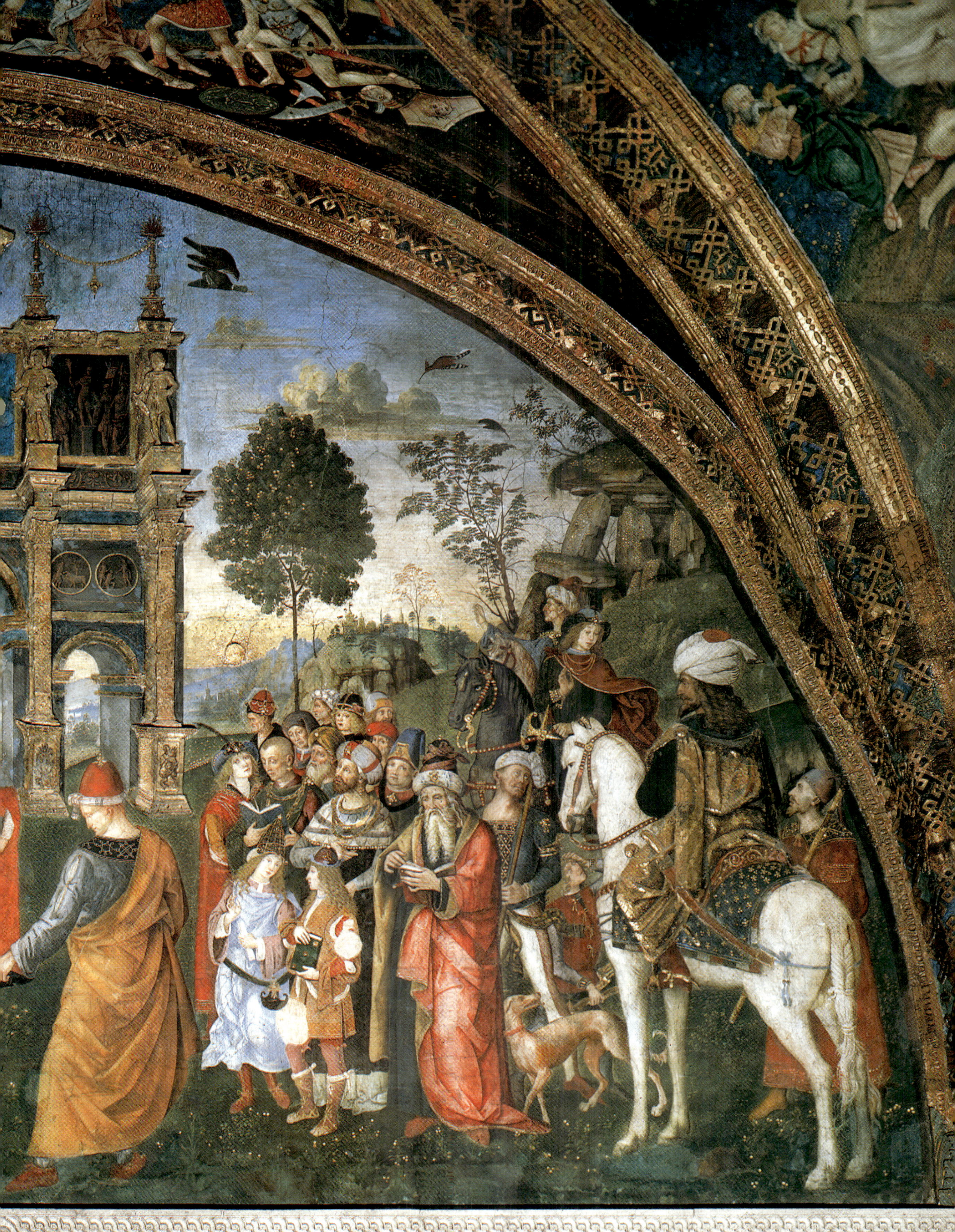

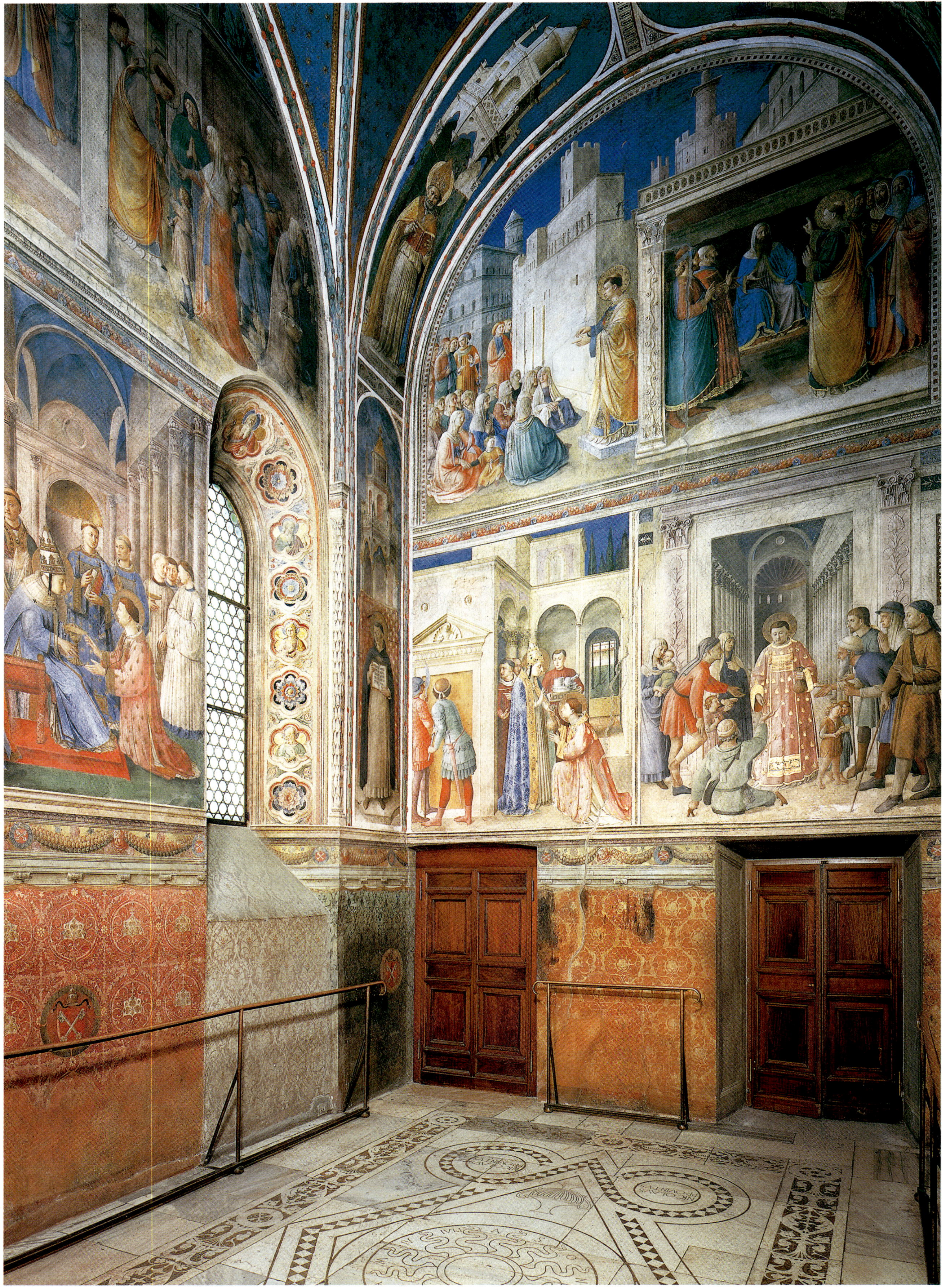

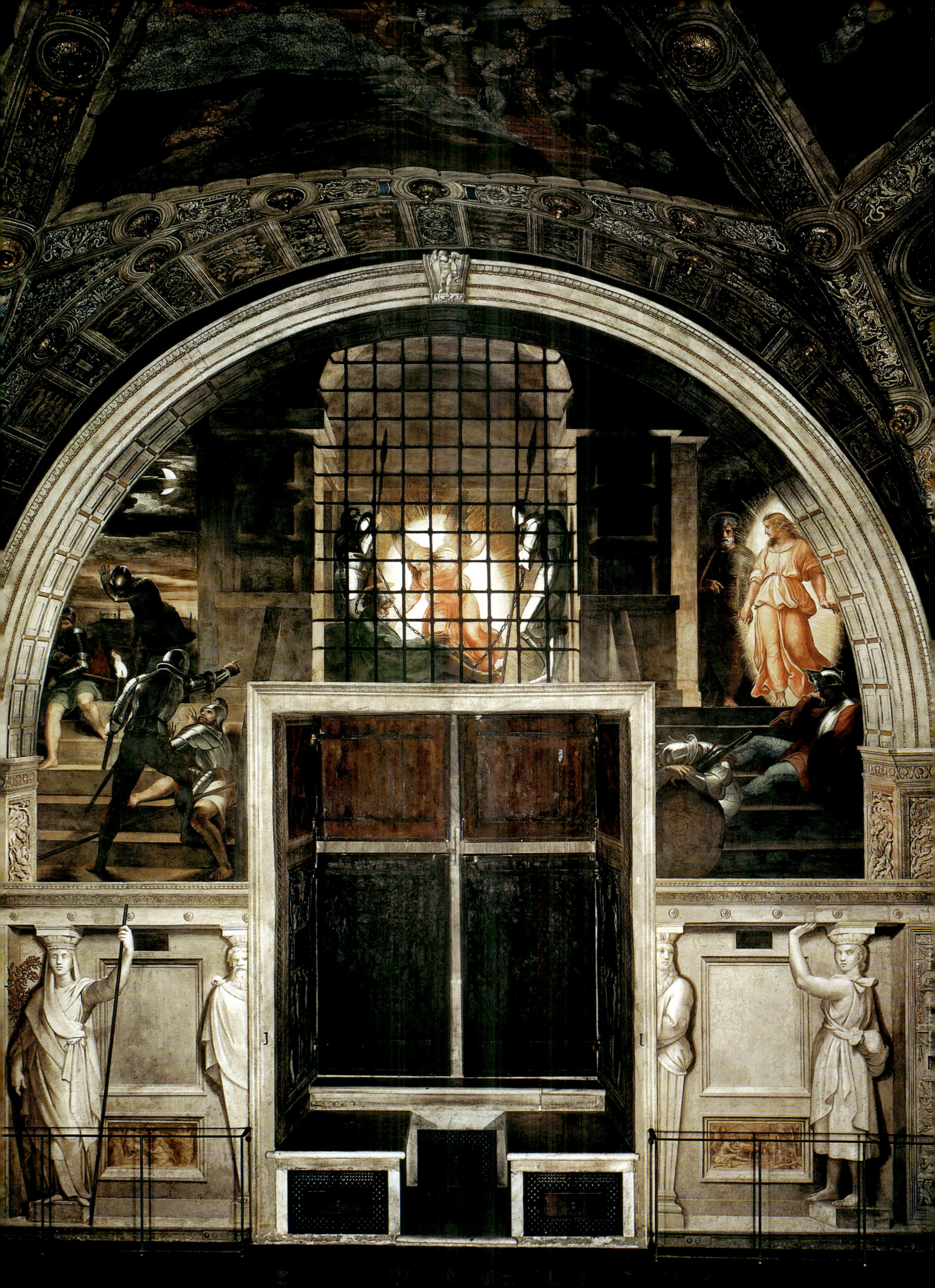

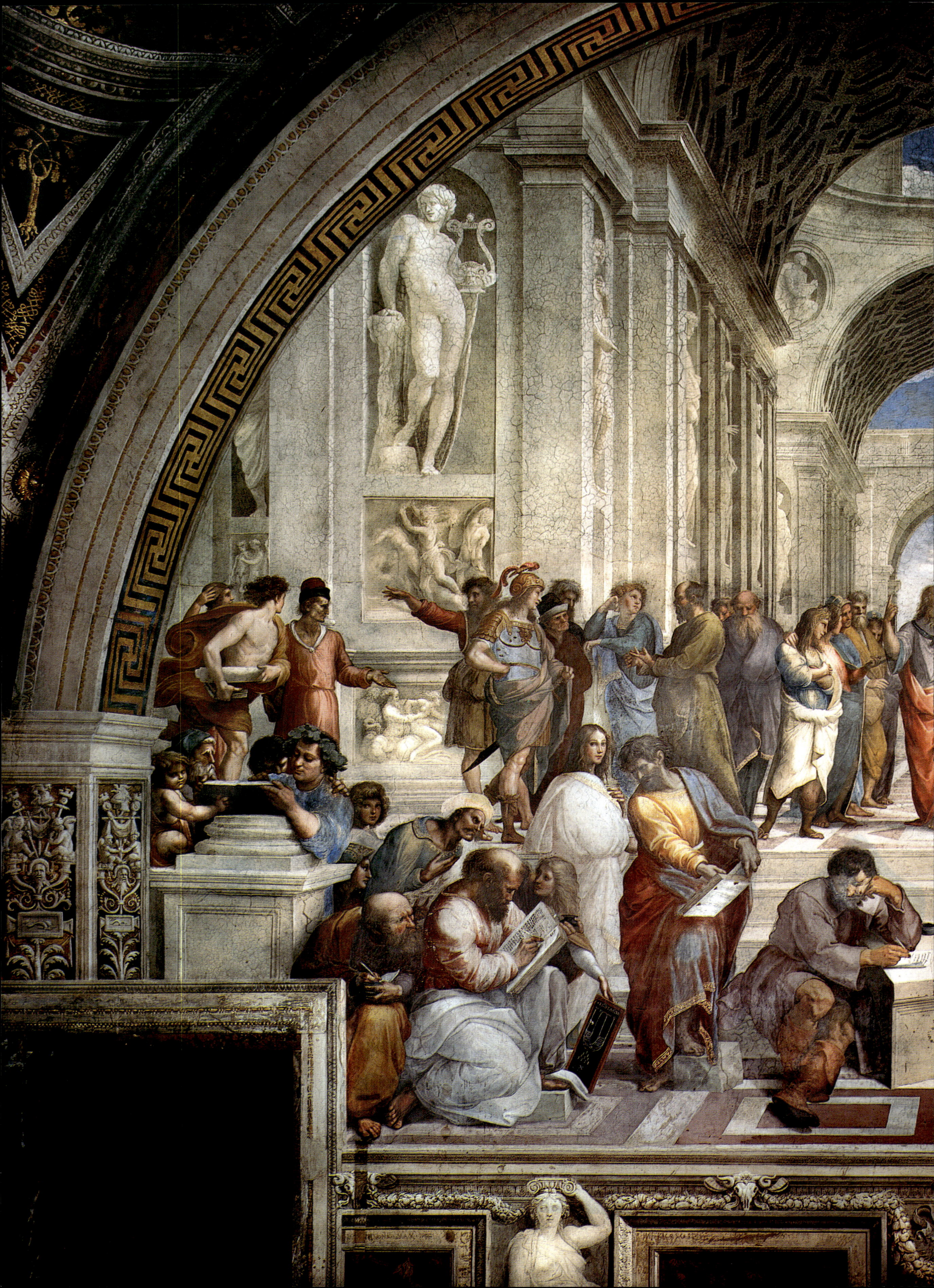

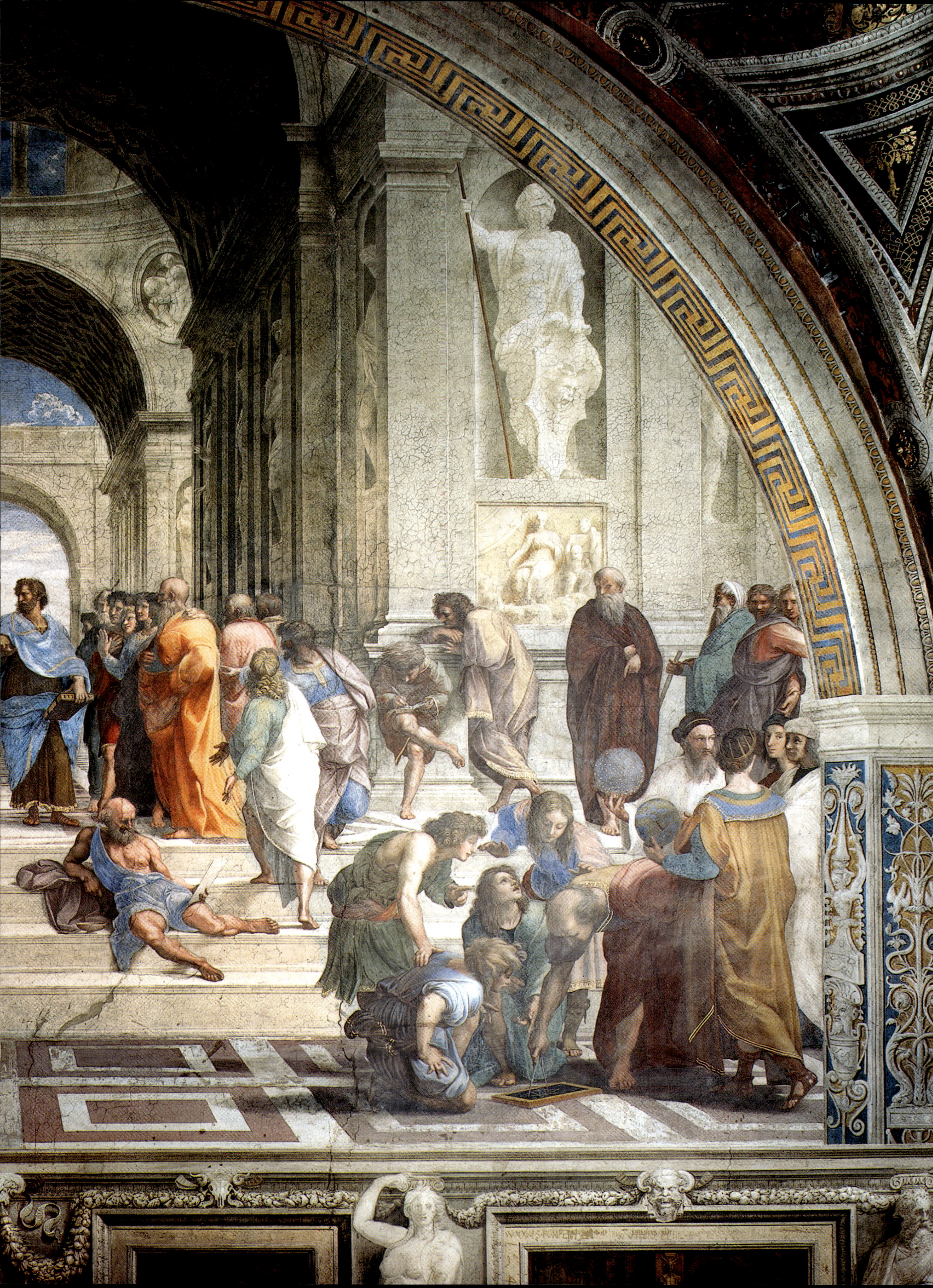

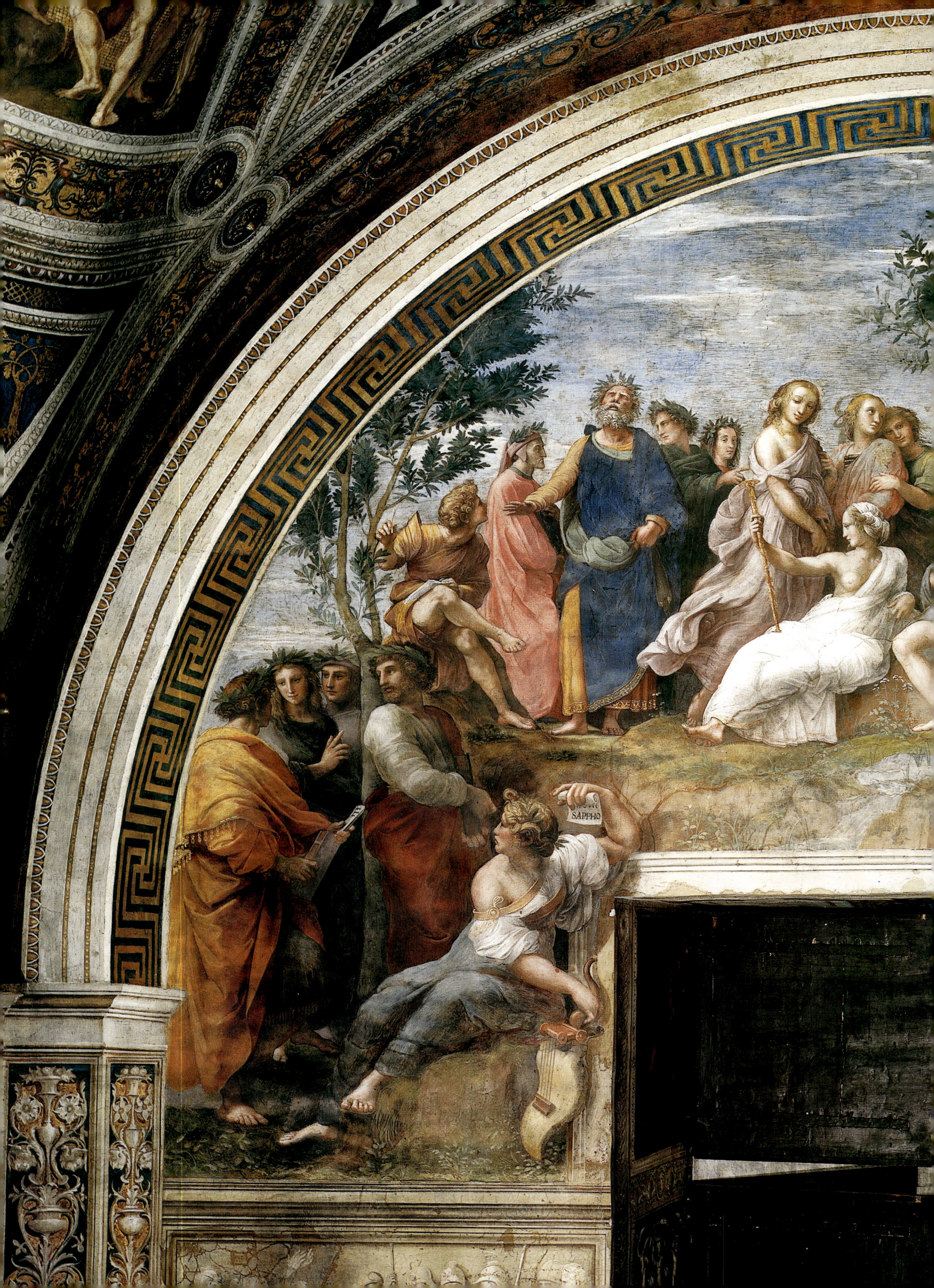
SAPPHO

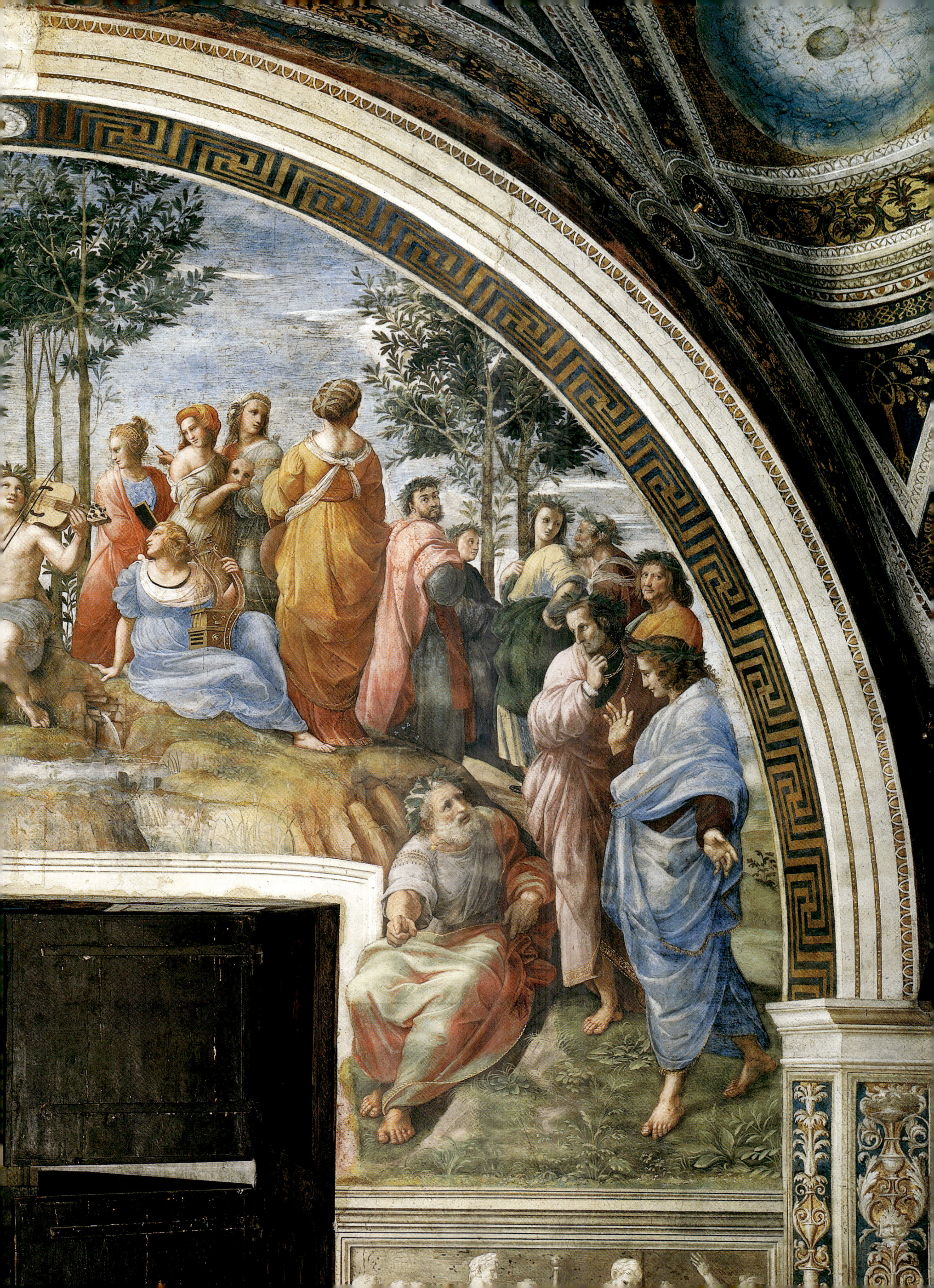

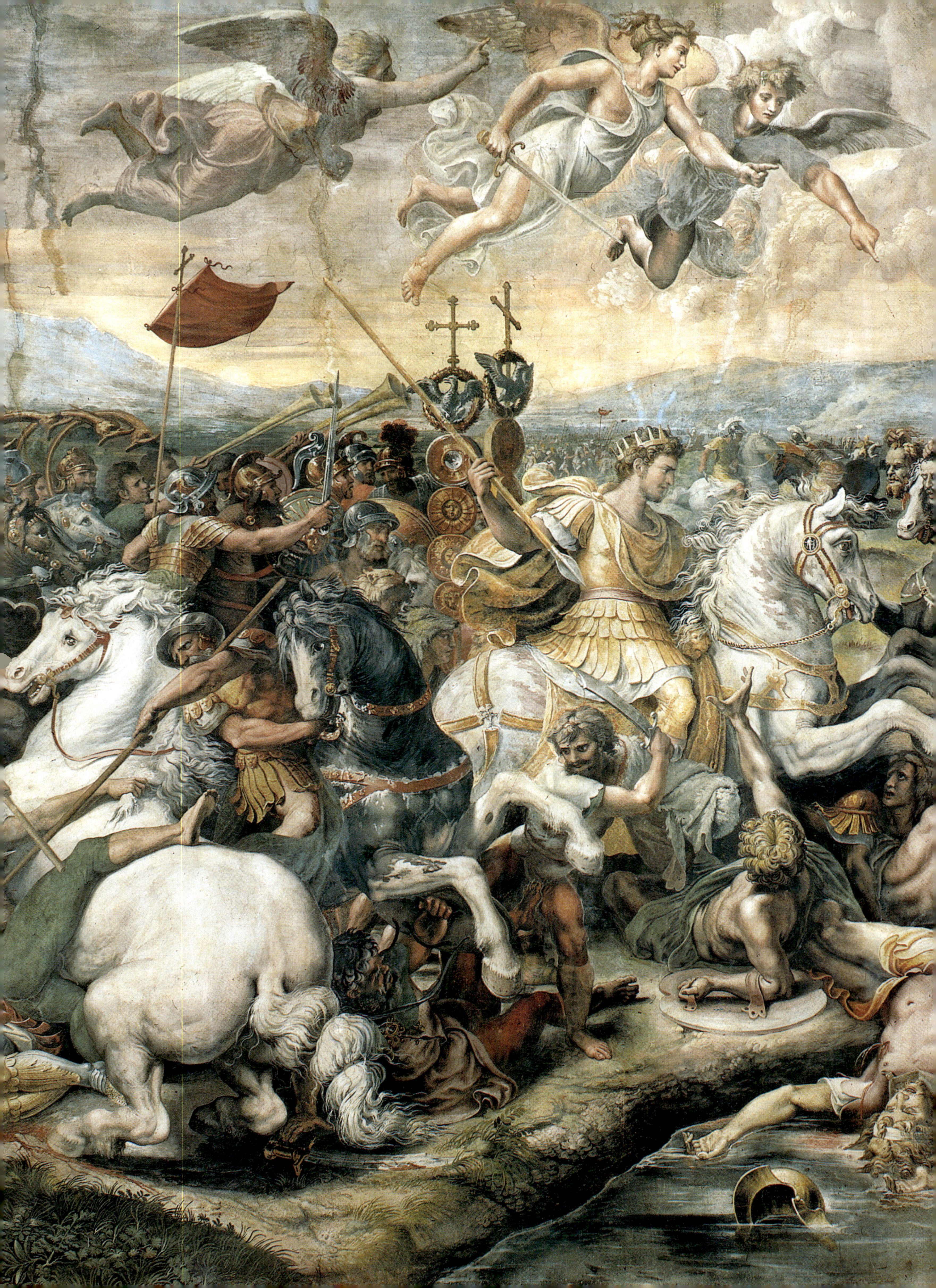

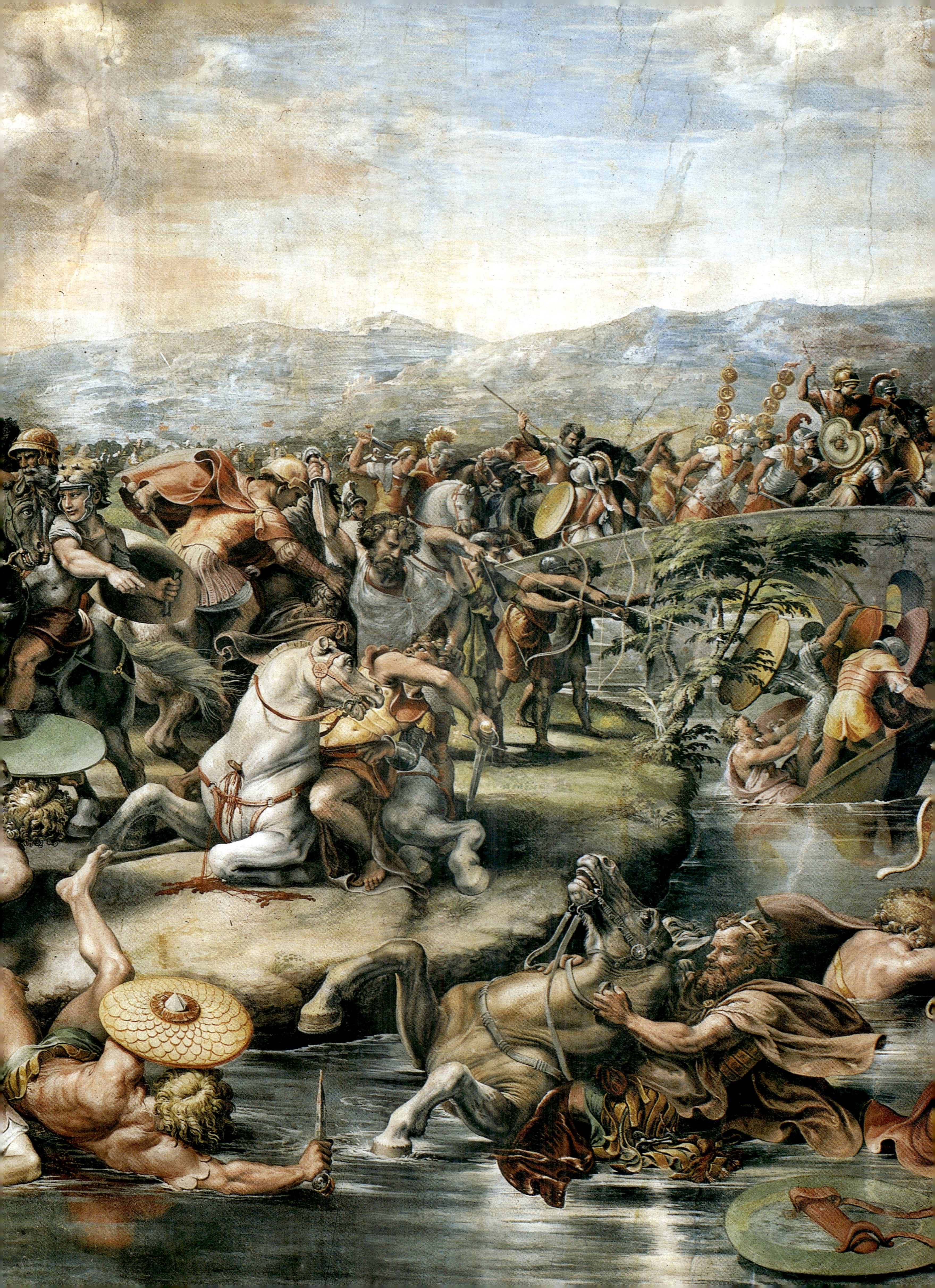

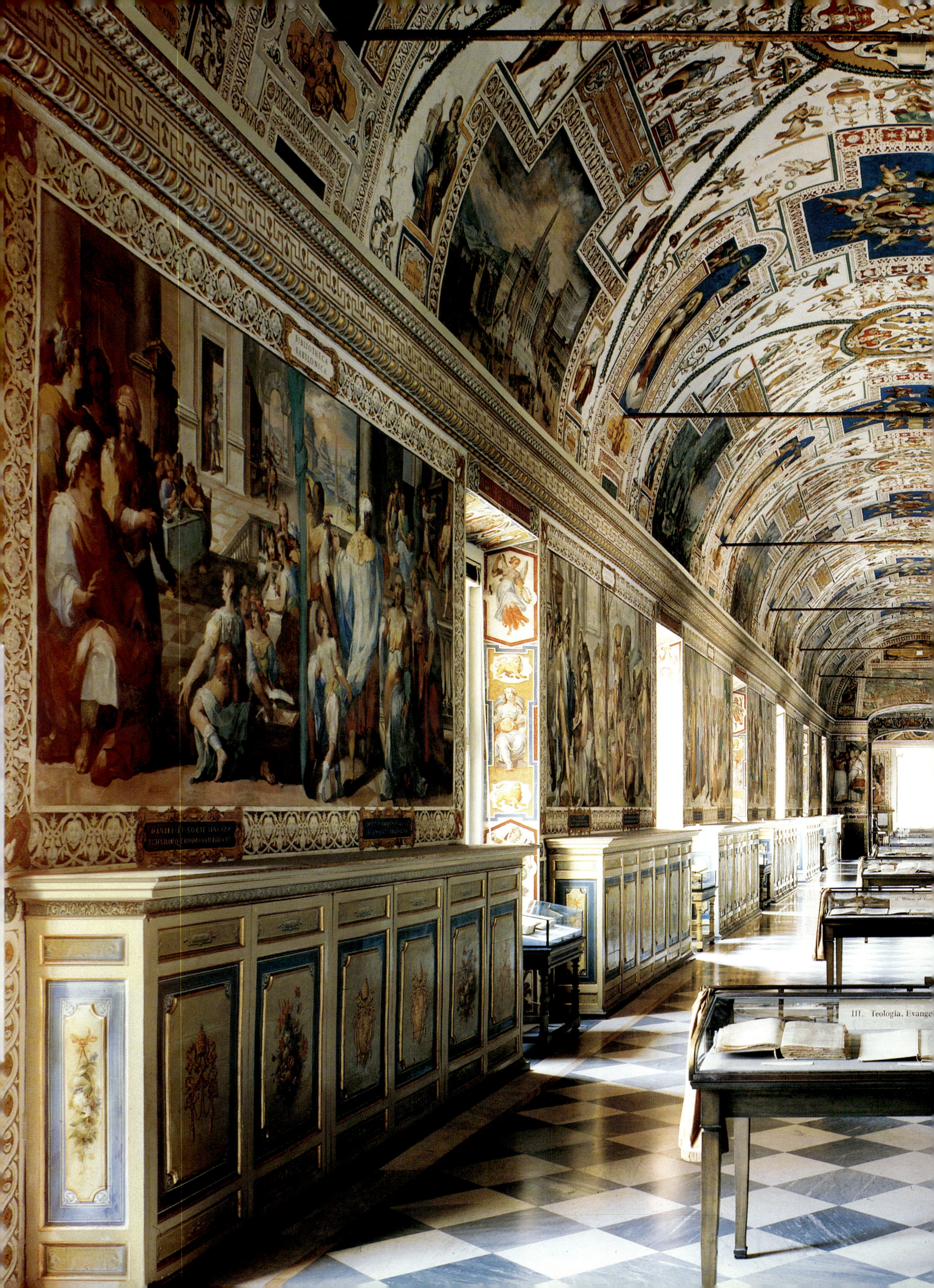
BIBLIOTHECA
BABYLONICA
III. Teologia. Evange

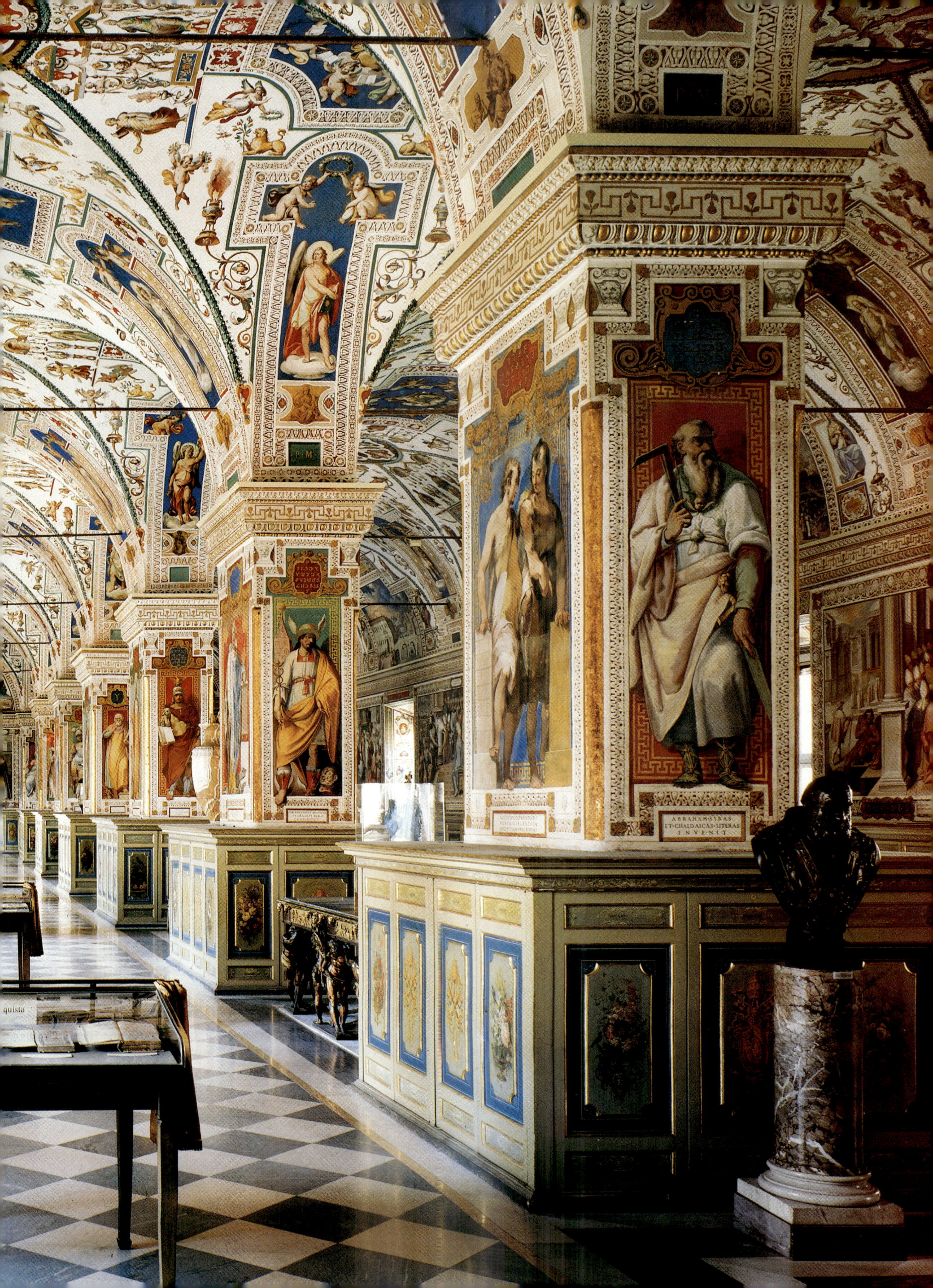
ABRAHAM·SYRAS
ET·CHALDAICAS·LITERAS
INVENIT
quista

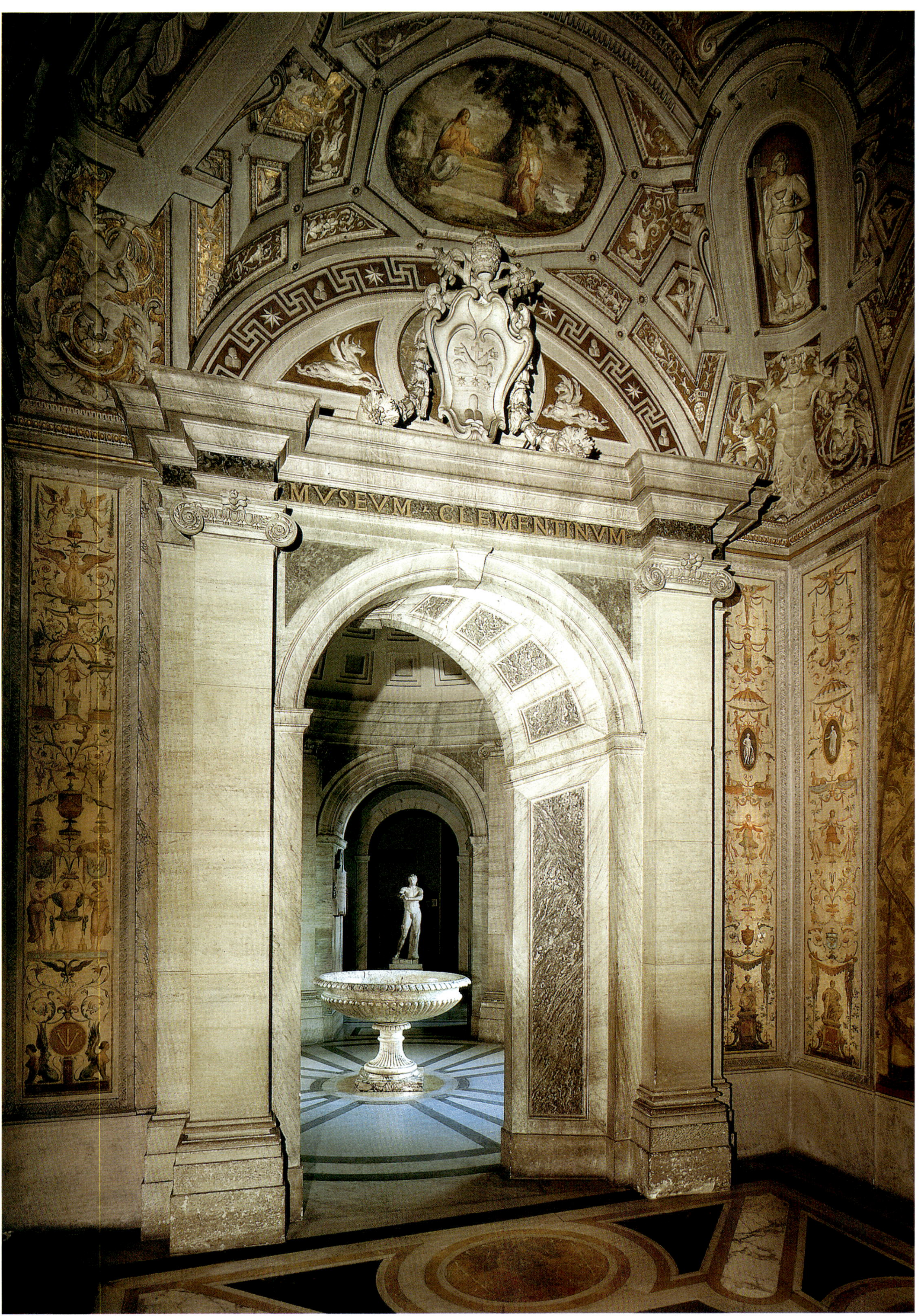
MVSEVM CLEMENTINVM

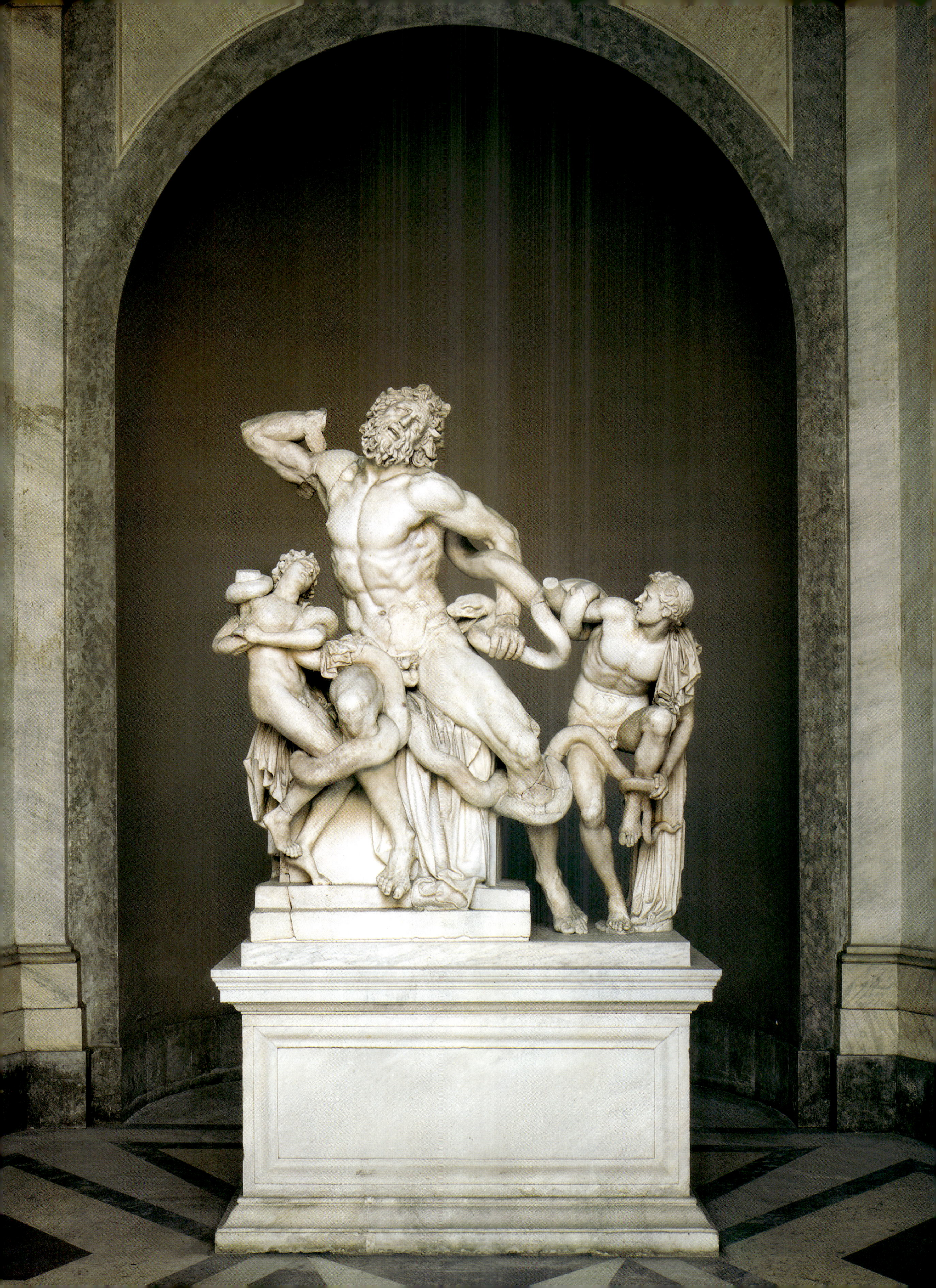

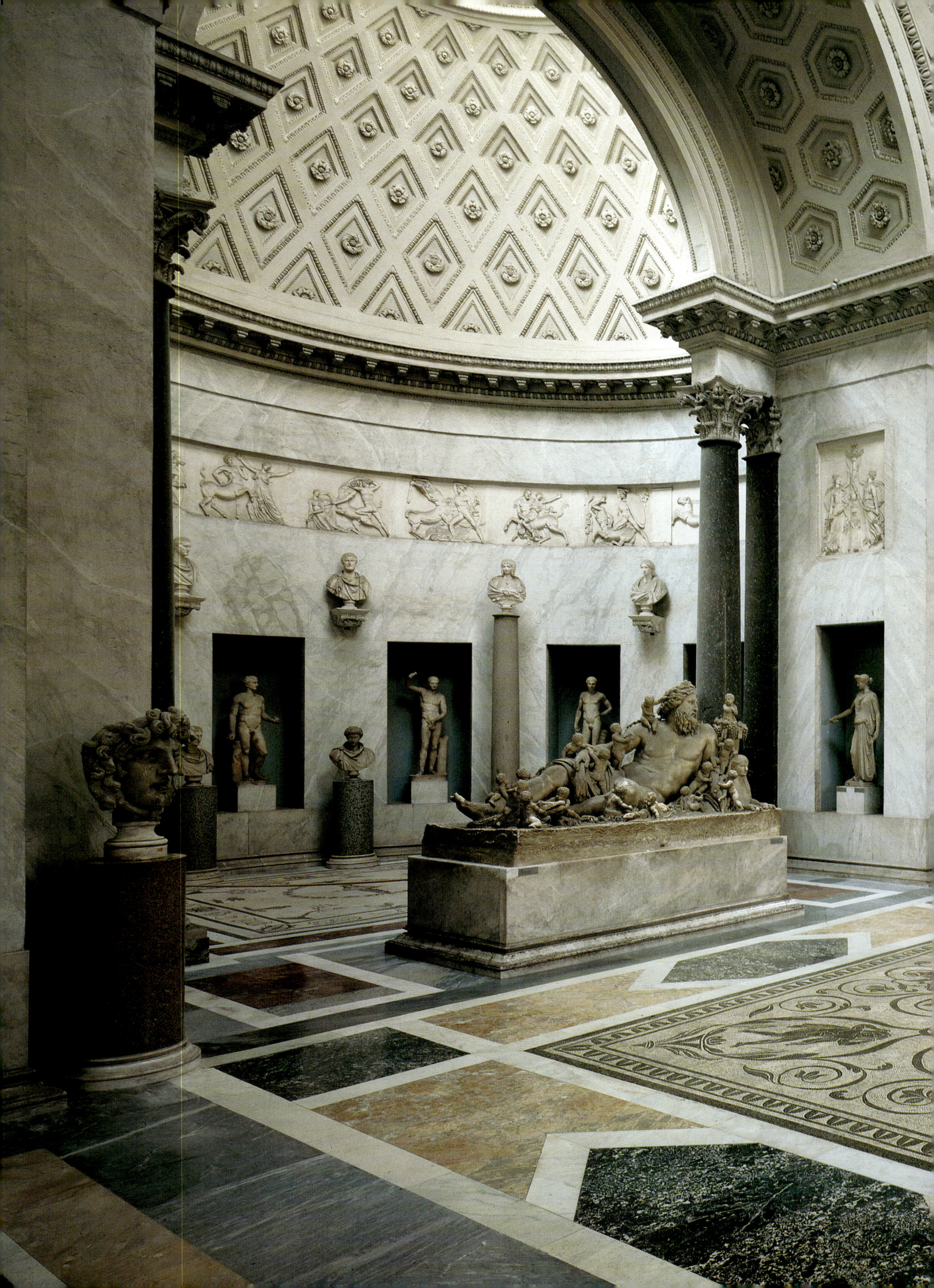

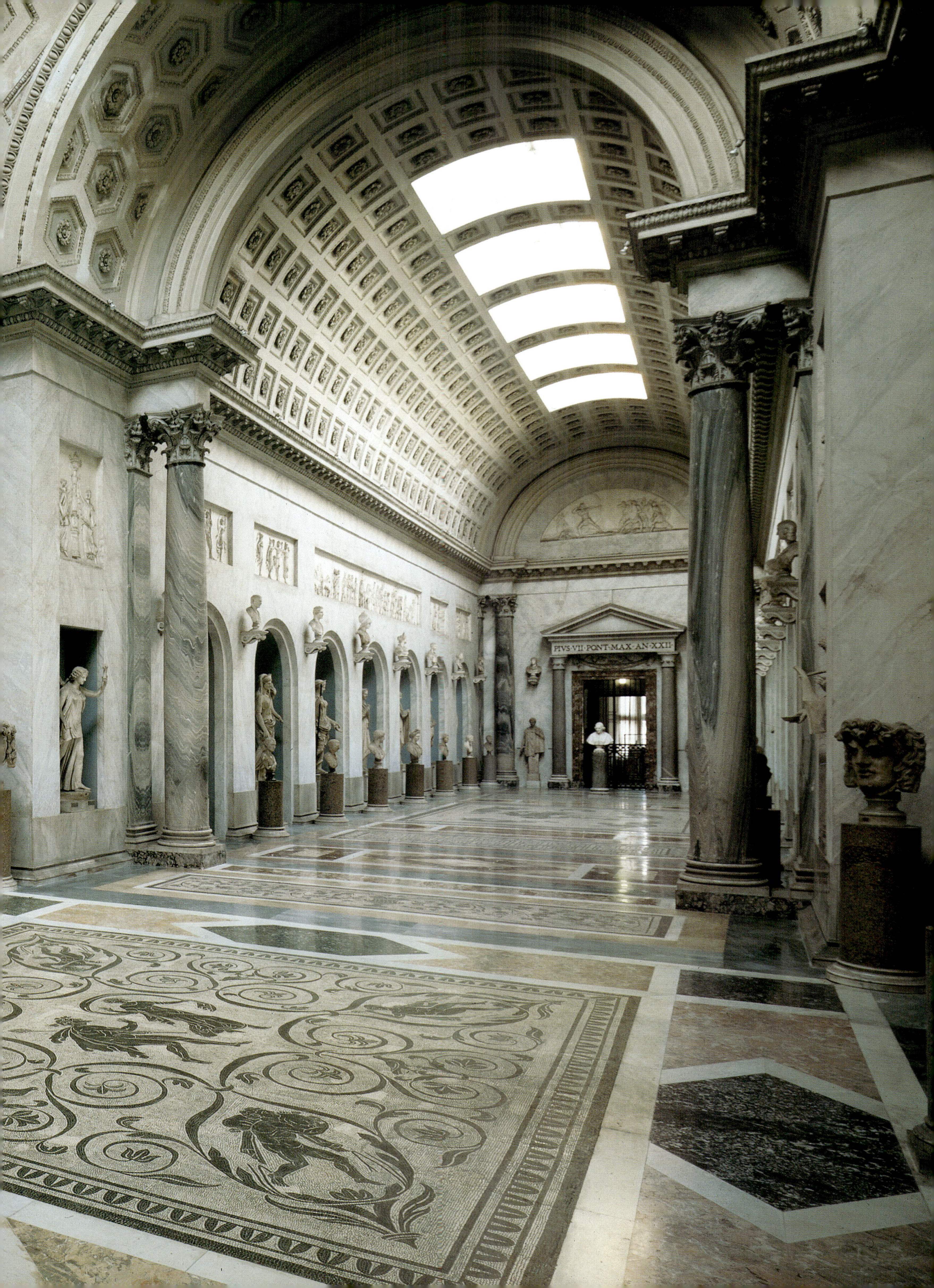
PIVS·VII·PONT·MAX·AN·XXII·

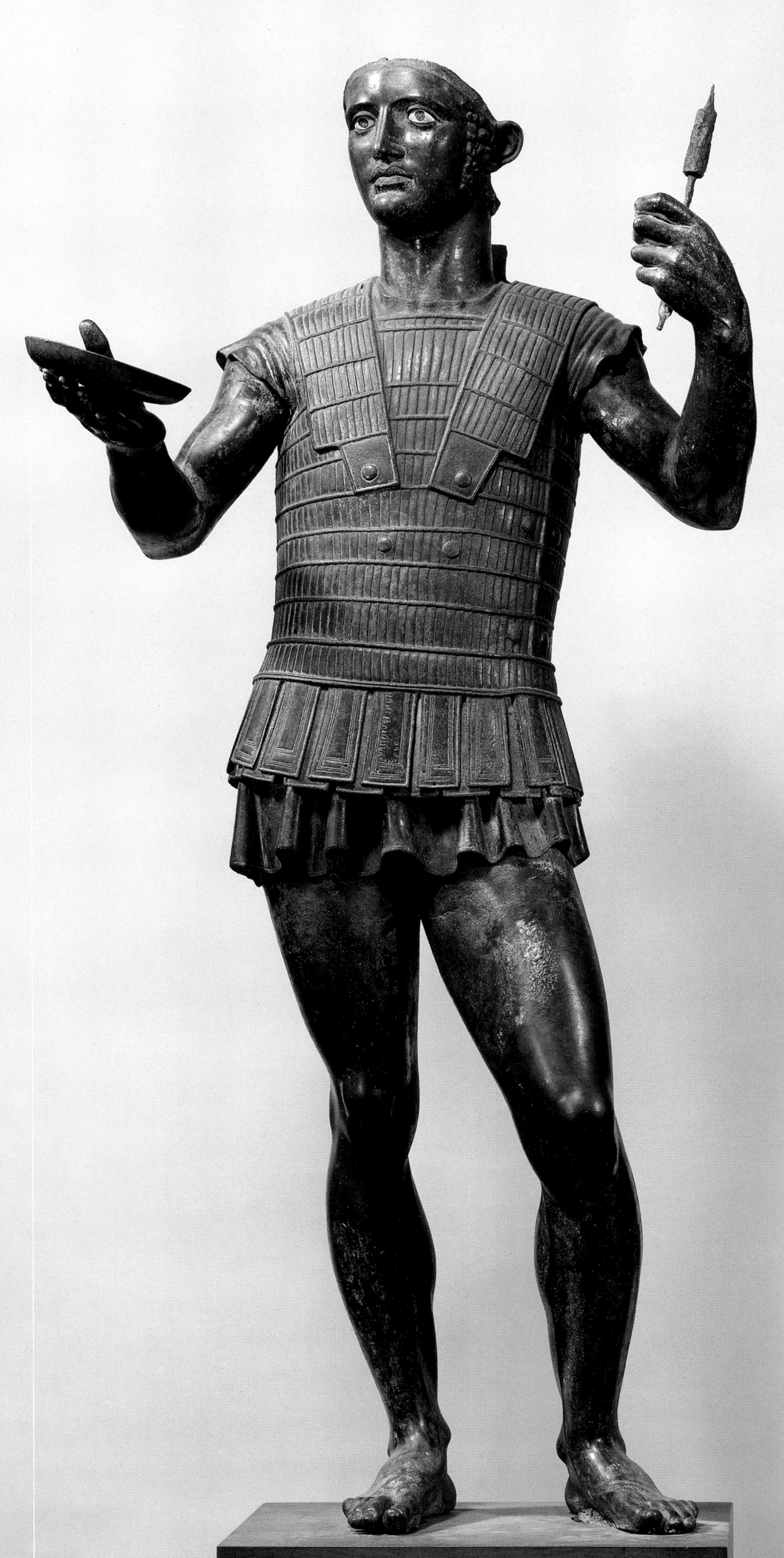

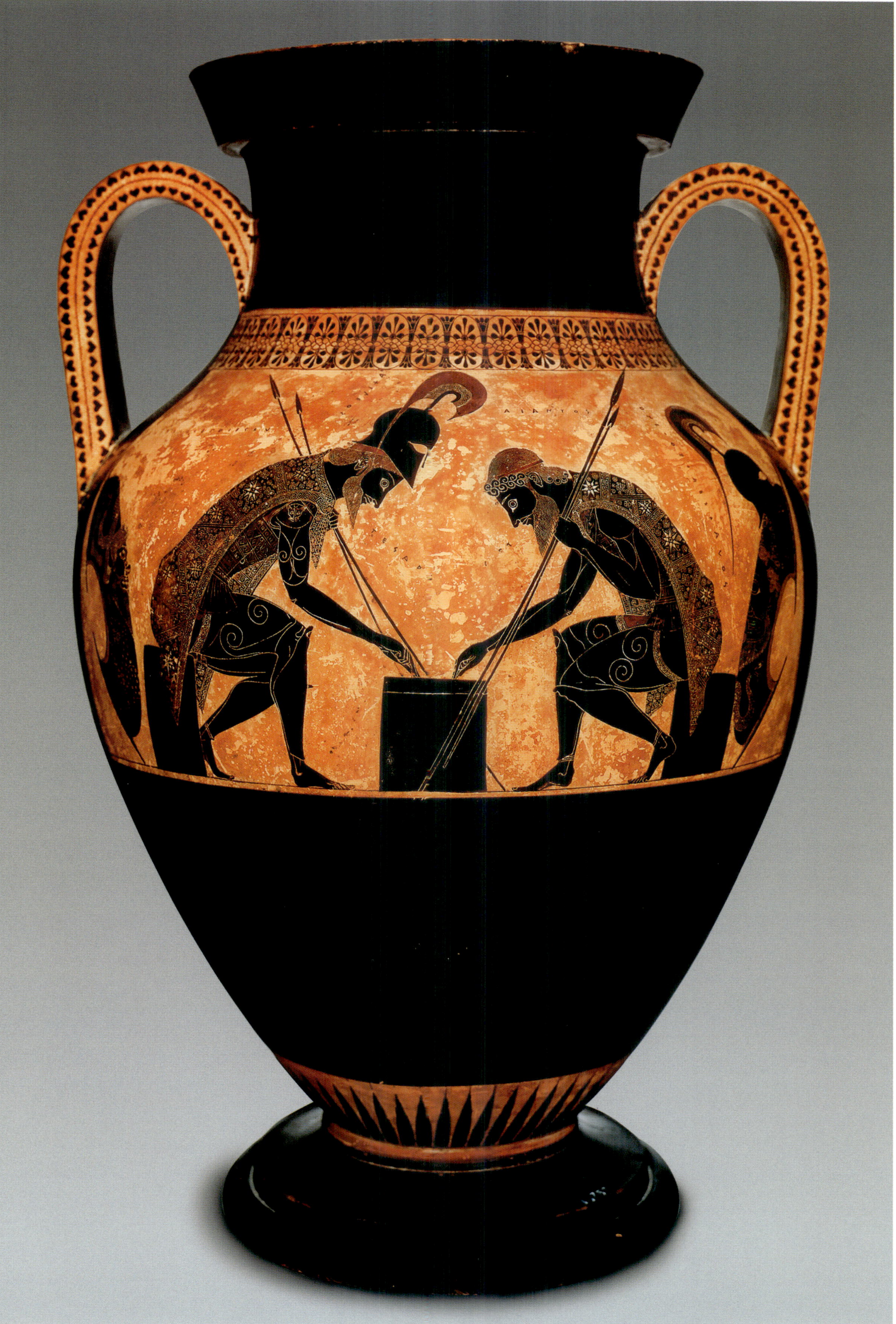

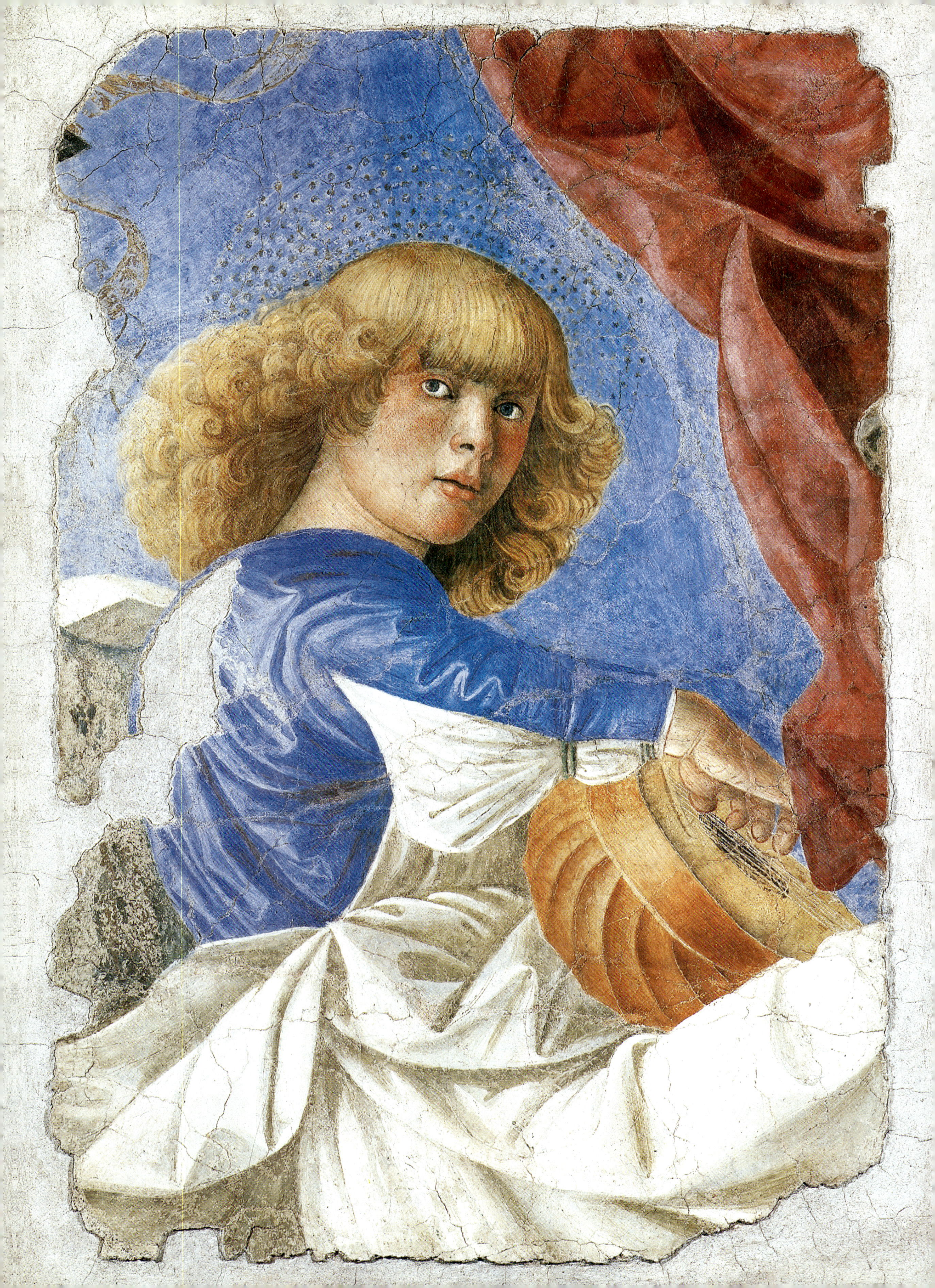

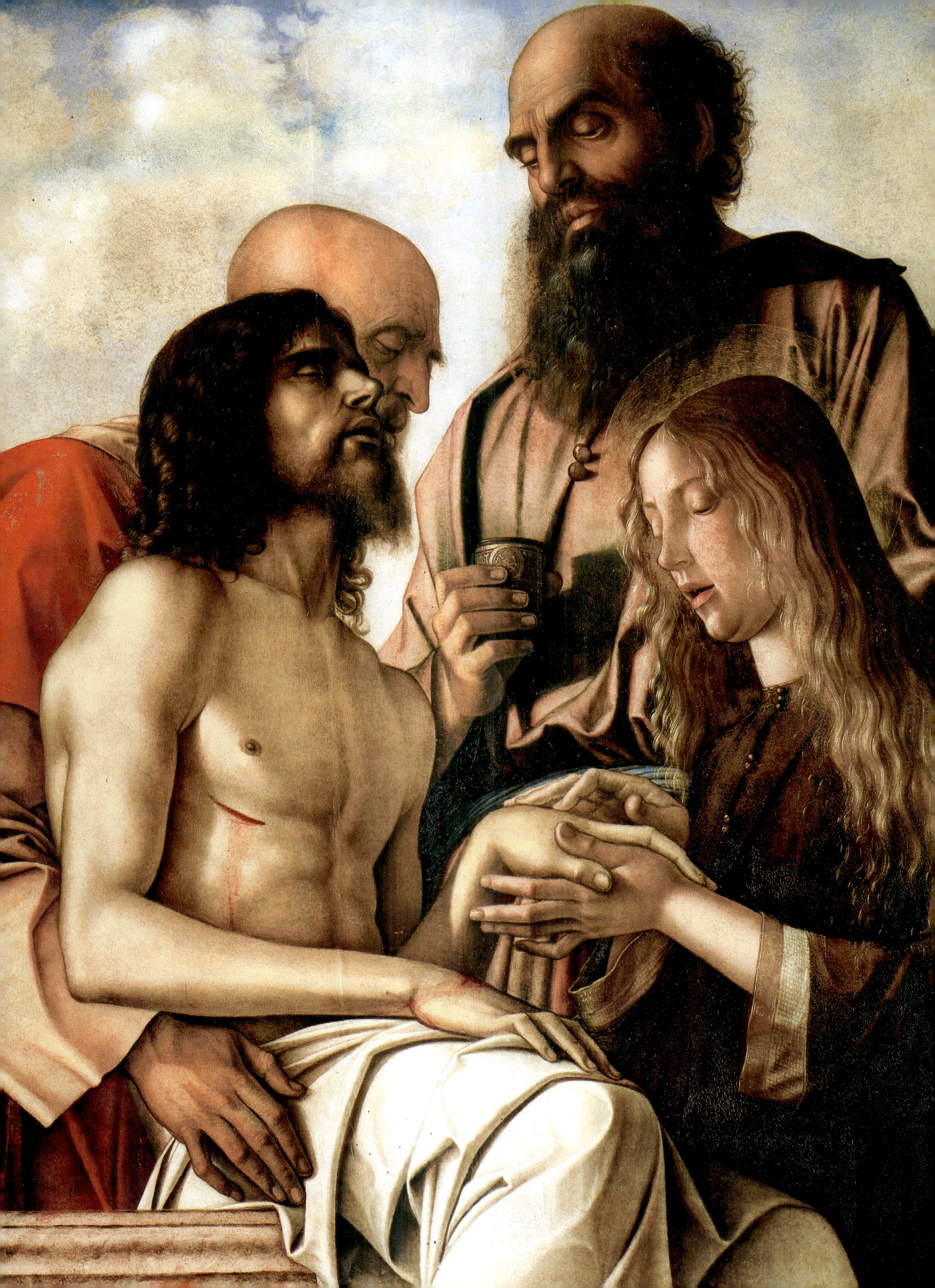

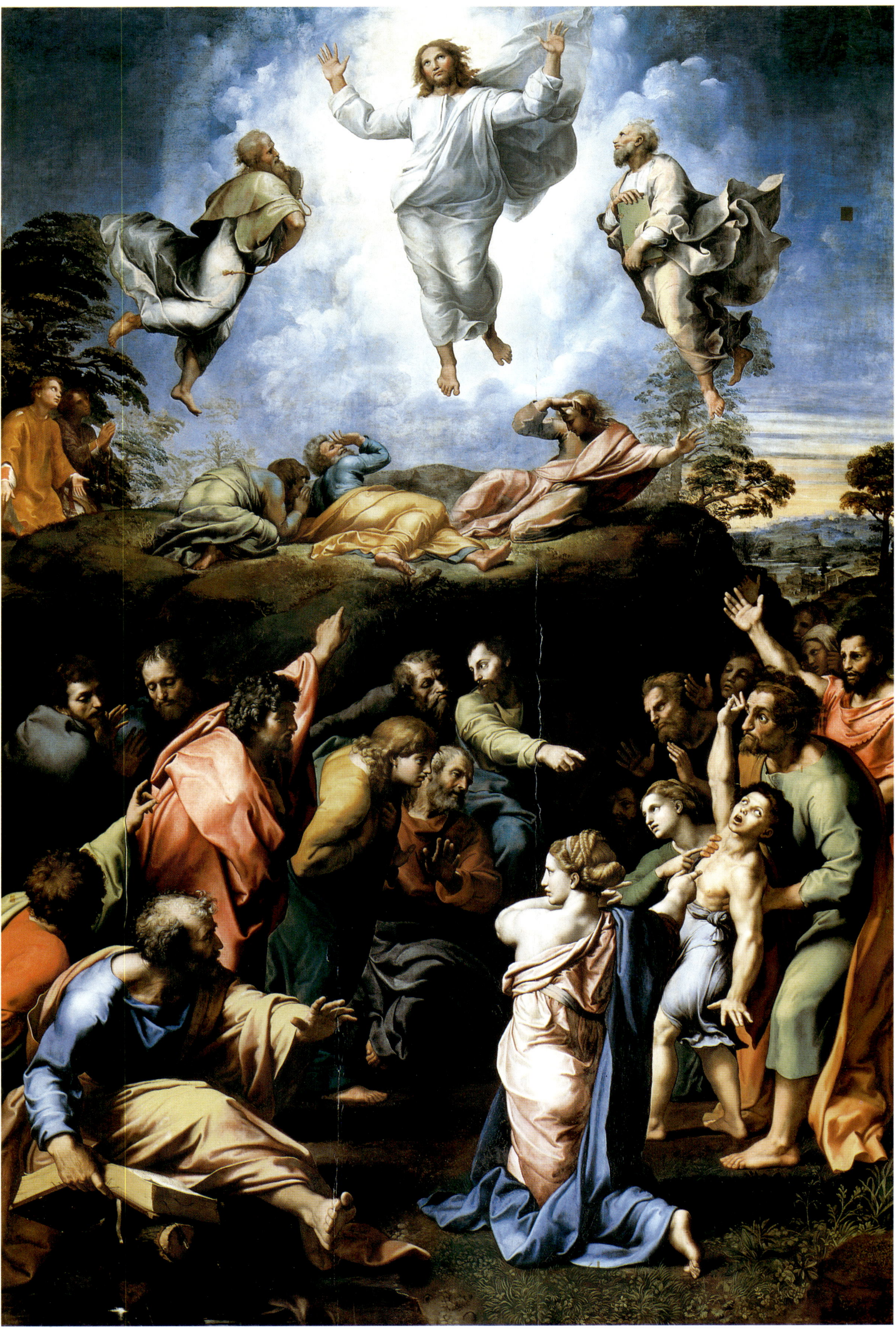

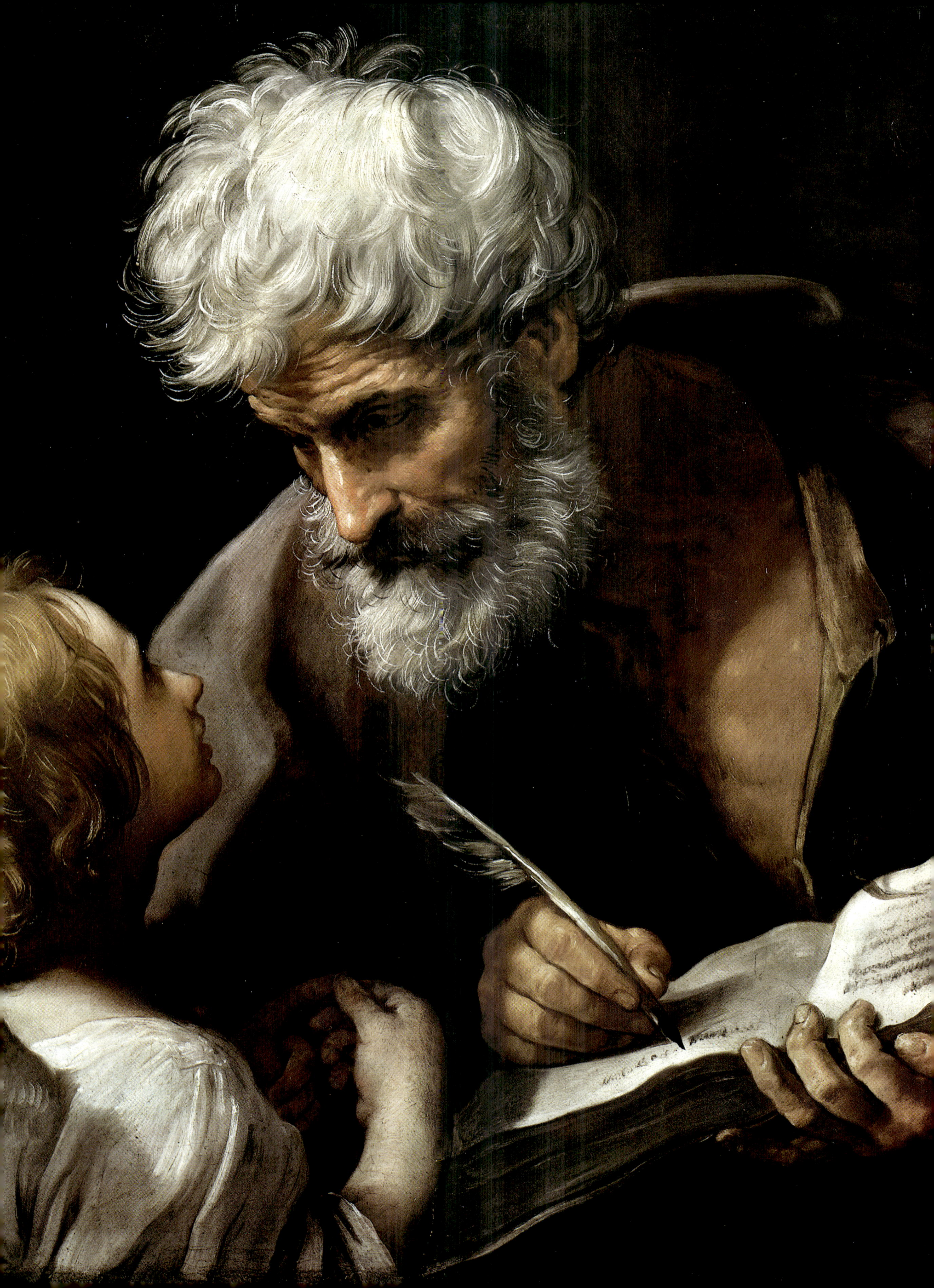

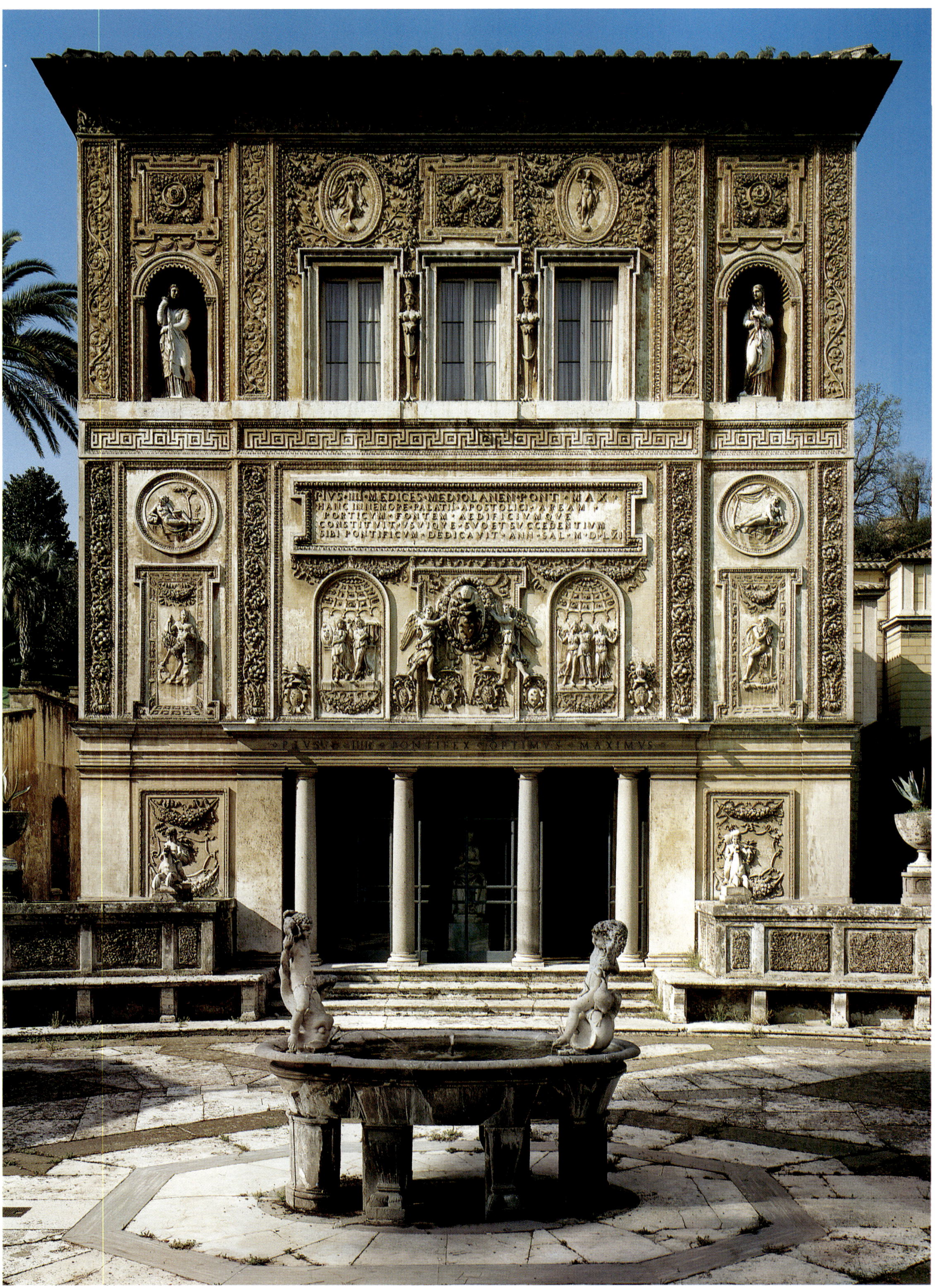
PIVS·IIII·MEDICES·MEDIOLANEN·PONT·MAX·
HANC·IN·NEMORE·PALATII·APOSTOLICI·AREAM·
PORTICVM·FONTEM·AEDIFICIVMQVE
CONSTITVIT·VSVIQVE·SVO·ET·SVCCEDENTIVM
SIBI·PONTIFICVM·DEDICAVIT·ANN·SAL·M·D·LXI
PIVS·IIII·PONTIFEX·OPTIMVS·MAXIMVS

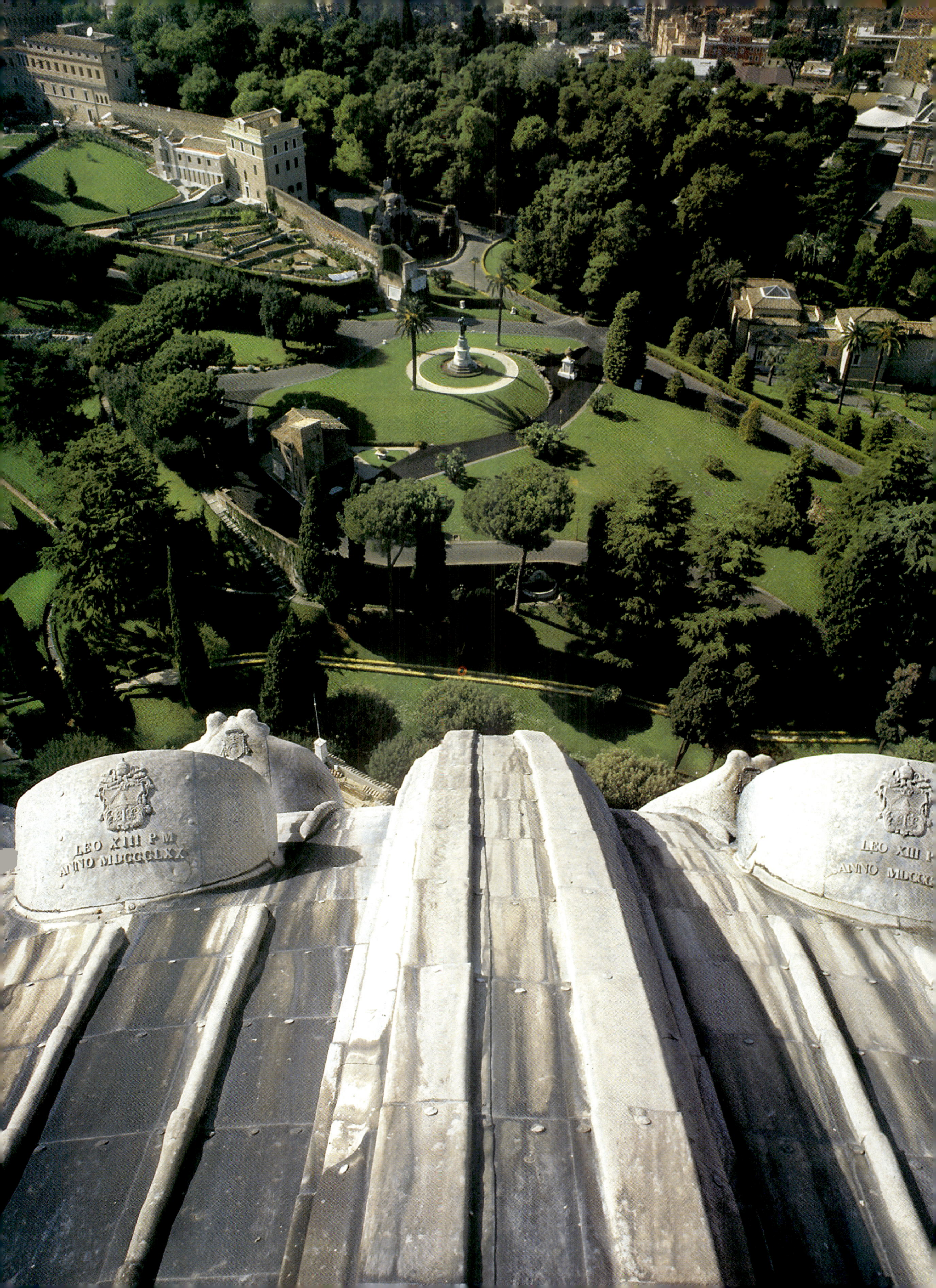
LEO XIII P M
ANNO MDCCCLXX
LEO XIII P
ANNO MDCCC

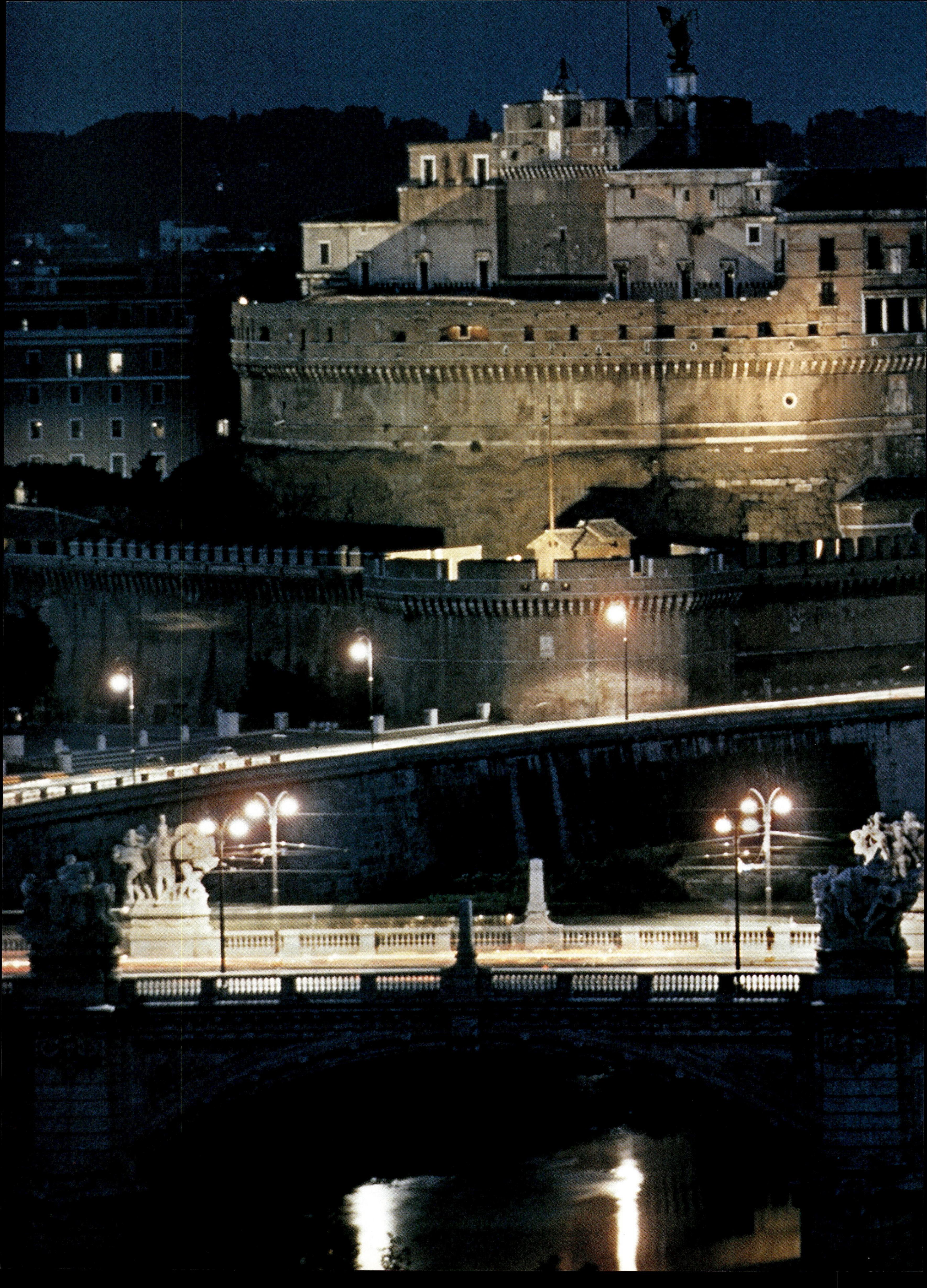

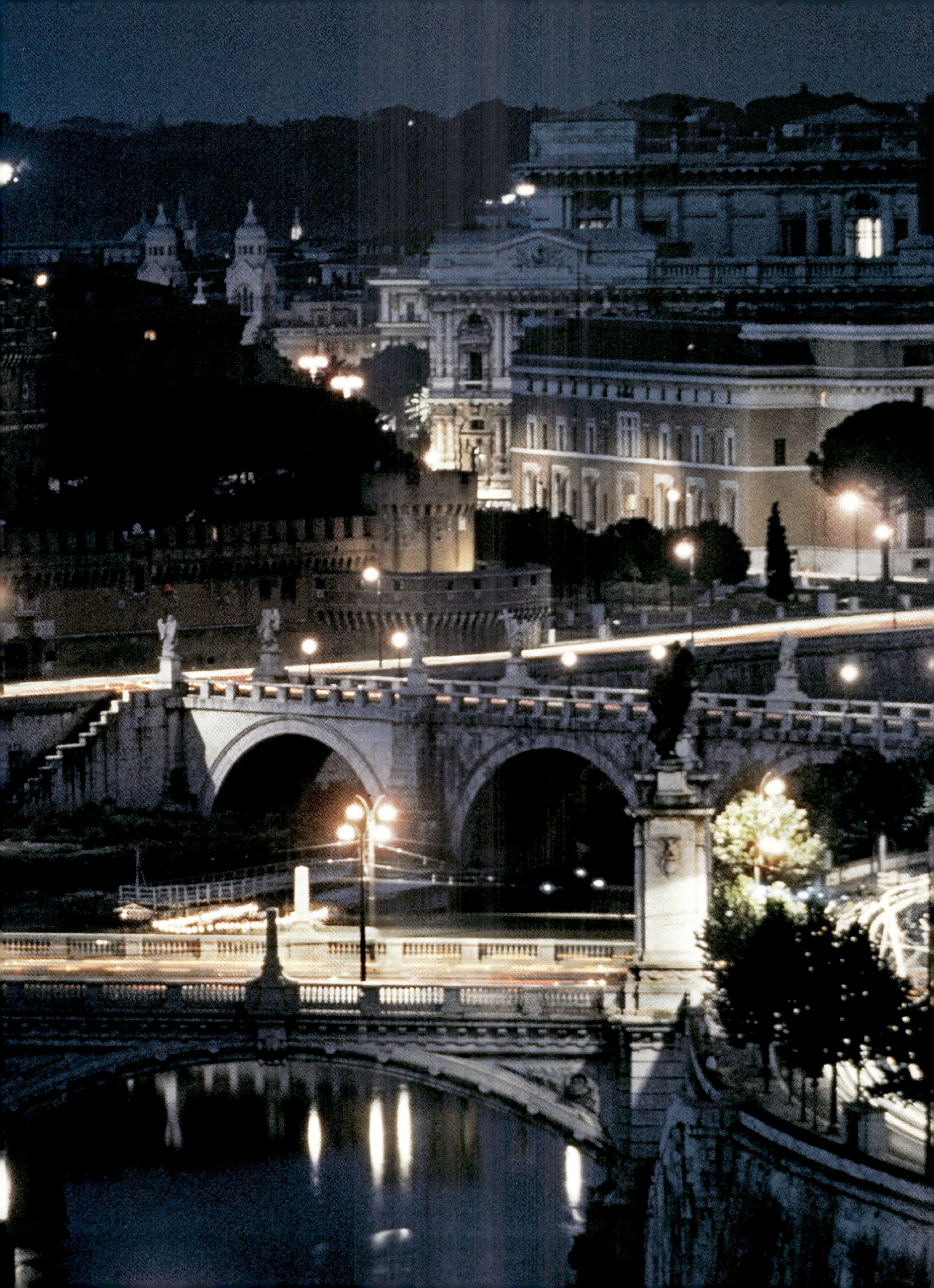

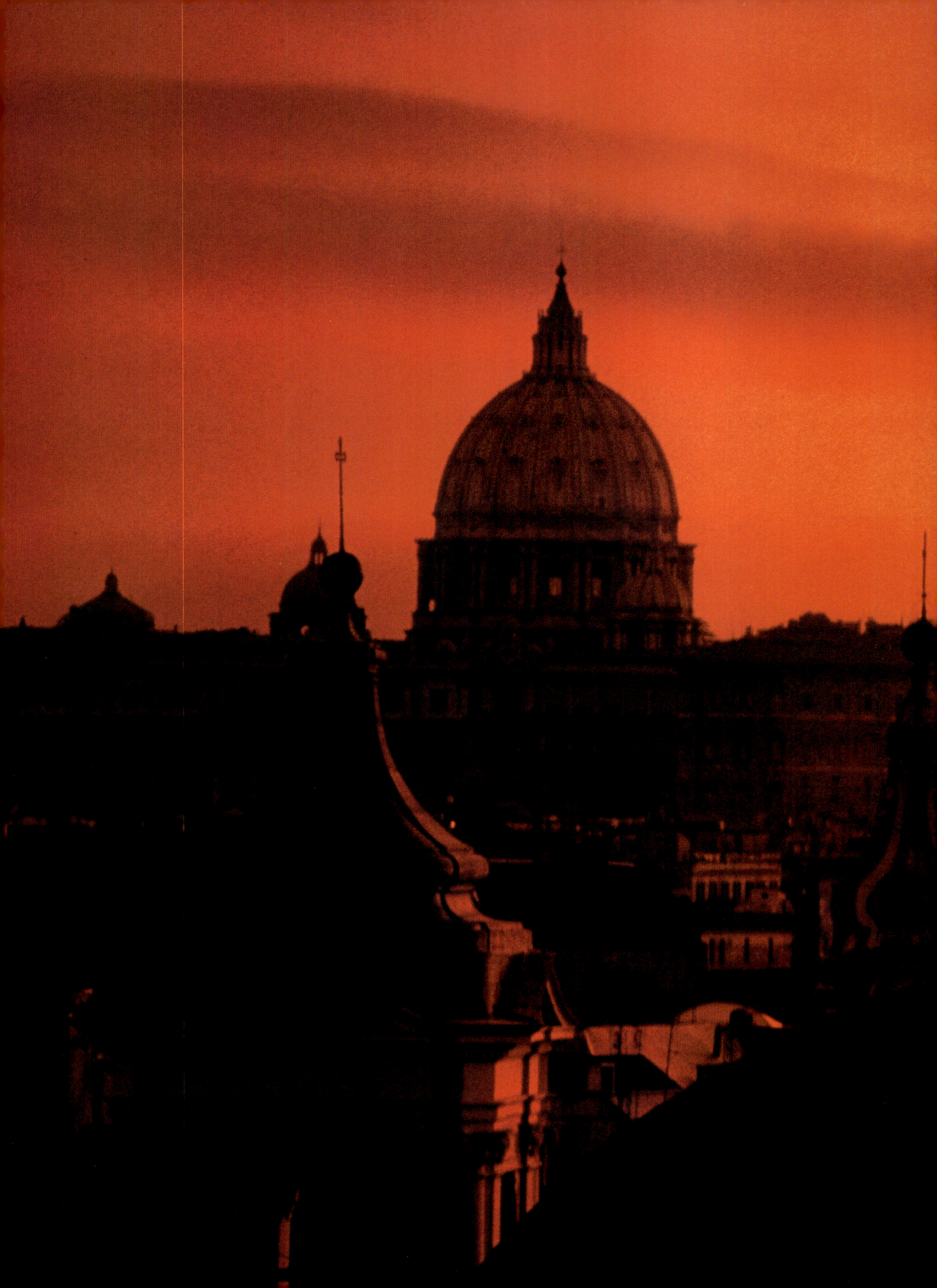

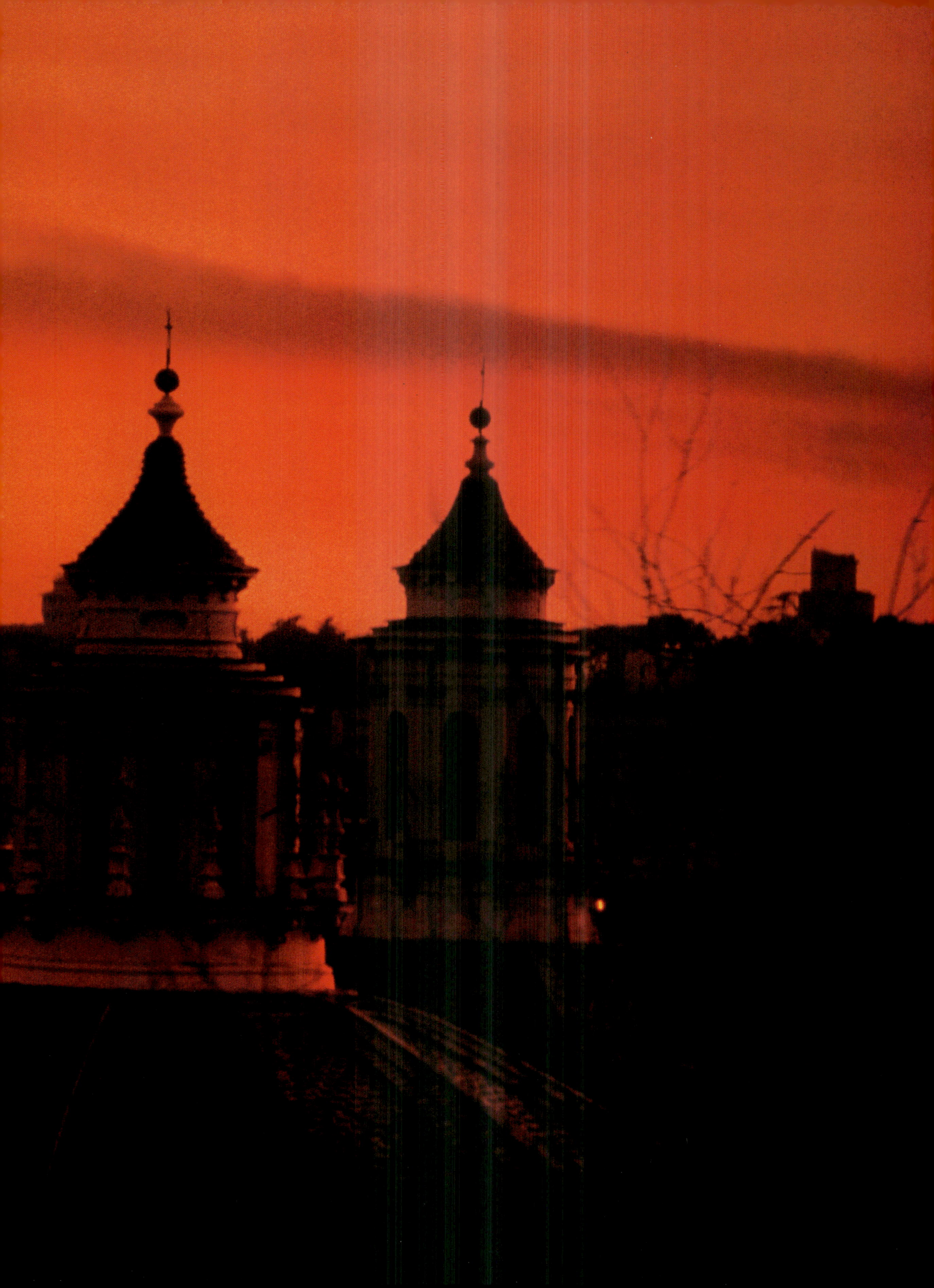

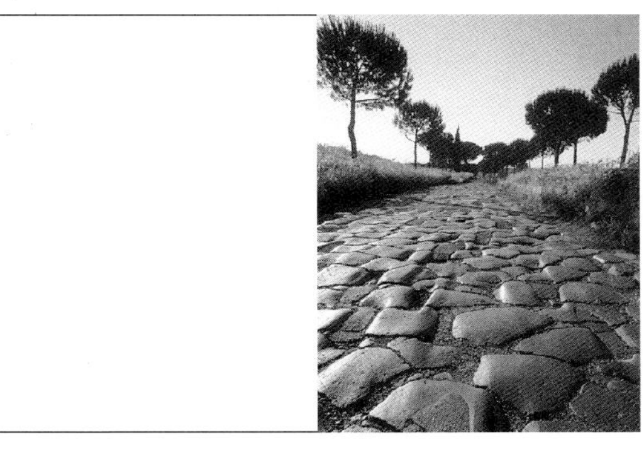

1. Many literary accounts say that Peter came to Rome from Palestine, travelling for the last part of the journey on the **Appian Way**, the *regina viarium*, with its paving still intact today. This road remains, therefore, the first testament to Jesus' apostolic message by means of the Galilean fisherman to whom the keys of the Church had been consigned. It is with the Appian Way, which has assumed a sacred nature because of the numerous catacombs along its last stretch, that the name of Rome's first Bishop, that is the first Pope, is associated. Here Jesus appeared to Peter who was fleeing the city to escape persecution by Nero. The church of *Domine quo vadis?* recalls that meeting which led the Apostle to turn back towards martyrdom. Peter's corpse, together with Paul's, was temporarily moved here in 258 during the umpteenth persecution of the Christians and hidden in the place known as *ad Catacumbas*, the same spot where an early church was erected and hence called *Apostolorum*, later to be dedicated to St Sebastian.

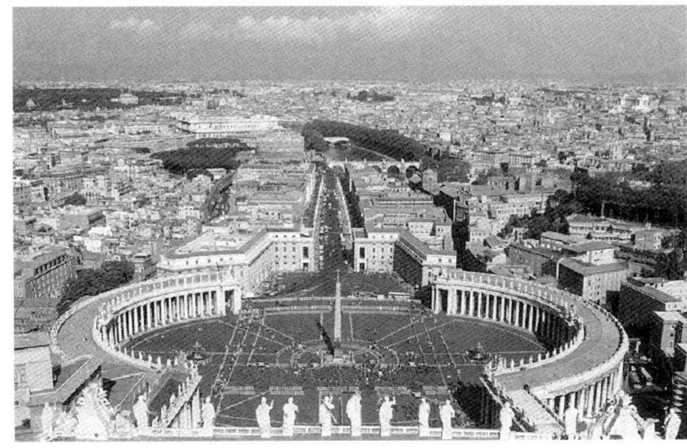

2. **St Peter's Square** seen from the Basilica's rooftop terrace, opening out towards Rome with Via della Conciliazione and the Tiber in the background. This sight is emblematical of the spectacular symbolic structure of the Vatican which, with its two hemicycles of Berninian colonnades, seems to be stretched out to embrace the world. In the foreground, 13 statues of the *Redeemer*, the *Baptist* and the *Apostles* except St Peter. In the centre of the Square, the obelisk. Aligned with it are the two fountains by Gian Lorenzo Bernini on the right and by Carlo Maderno on the left. The fountains are of equal distance from the colonnade which is made up of 284 columns and 88 pillars with the balustrade adorned by 140 statues of saints and large coats of arms of Alexander VII. The huge ellipse is 240 metres wide and measures 340 metres from the steps to the granite strip marking the Vatican City boundary.

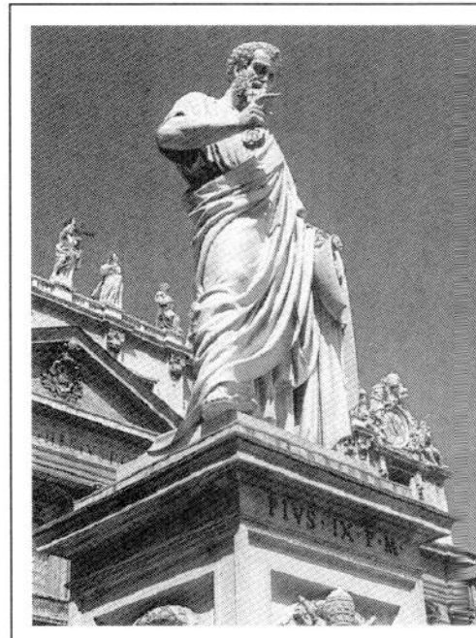

3. The colossal **Statue of St Peter** rising on the left of the parvis. By Giuseppe de Fabris, it was sculpted in 1838 for the basilica of St Paul's Outside the Walls (San Paolo Fuori le Mura), reconstructed after the disastrous fire in 1823. The statue of St Paul by Adamo Tadolini was to have the same destination. In March 1847 they were removed from storage in the wharehouses of the basilica under construction to be placed in the Square upon the request of Pius IX, substituting two statues of the same subjects but of smaller size executed in 1462 and now conserved in the old hall of the Synod.

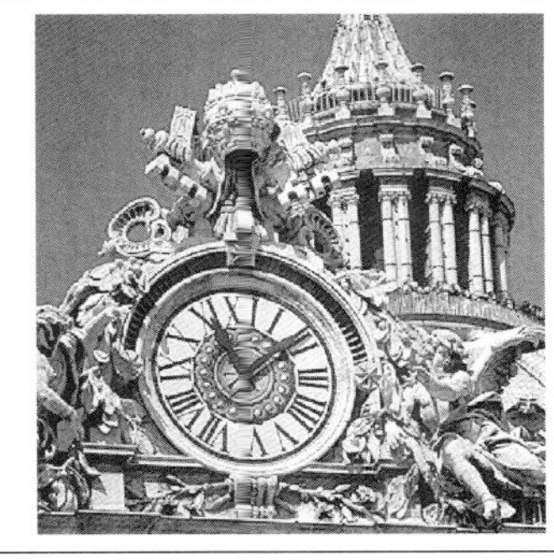

4. The **clock** with mosaic dial on the left of the attic on the Basilica's façade. Positioned above the bellfry, it couples a similar clock on the attic's right. Both were commissioned by Pius VI and constructed by Giuseppe Valadier. This one indicates the mean hour based on Europe's time zones, while the other indicates the real time. They are commonly known as *Oltremontano* (*Beyond the Mountains*) and *Italiano* (*Italian*). The dials were produced in 1727, using a precious enamel made up according to an ancient formula conserved by the Vatican City's "Mosaic Studio". This laboratory has recently carried out the restoration of the clocks which had been ruined by infiltrations over the centuries.

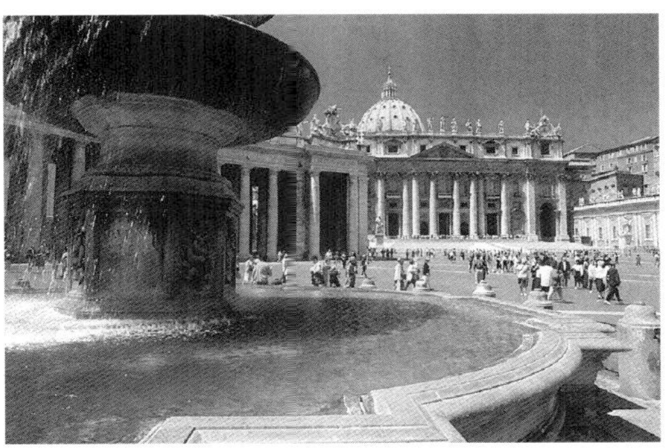

5. The **façade of St Peter's Basilica** (114 metres wide, 45 metres high) looks out on the three levels of steps with the gigantic statues of St Peter on the left and St Paul on the right. Constructed by Carlo Maderno from 1607 to 1614, it opens with a single order of Corinthian columns and pilasters with niches and loggias in between. The central portico is overlooked by the Benediction Loggia where the Pope appears on the most solemn occasions. The façade ends with a large attic topped by a crowning balustrade behind which the "dome" stands out. Some of the buildings making up the Apostolic Palaces can be seen on the right of the photo, while on the left in the foreground is the **fountain** erected by Bernini in 1677 during the pontificate of Innocent XI and symmetrical with Maderno's in the other hemicycle of the Square. Both are characterized by two basins with scale decoration supported by a stalk.

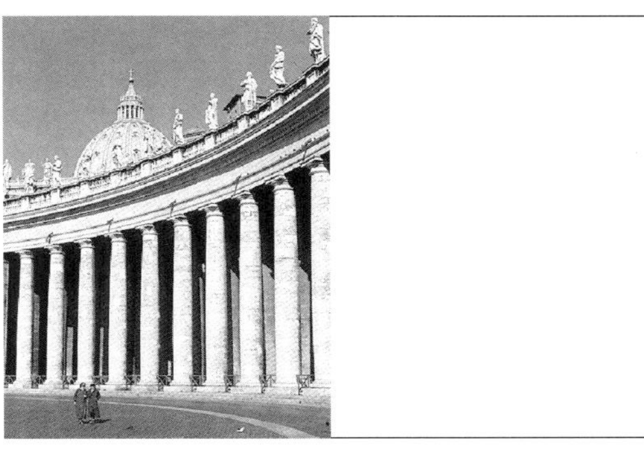

6. Detail of the **colonnade**. Conceived by Bernini and executed between 1656 and 1667 during the pontificate of Alexander VII, its decoration continued under the Popes Clement IX (1667-1669) and Clement X (1670-1676). It unfolds with two arcades of Tuscan columns (16 metres high and with a maximum diameter of 142 cms) in quadruple file delineating three aisles with a total width of 17 metres. Standing on one of the two marble disks in the pavement (which mark the focus points of of the Square's ellipse) the colonnade gives an incomparable optical effect: the columns of the outer three files disappear behind the columns of the innermost curve. This happens because of the gradual increase in the diameter of the columns from the internal to the external files, maintaining constant the distances between them.

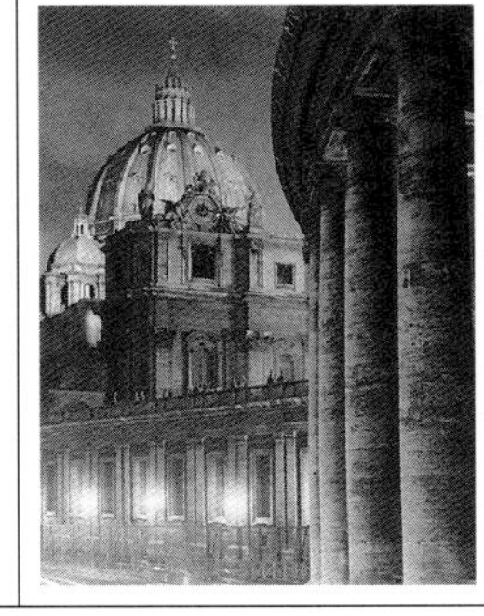

7. Nocturnal view from the Square of the Sant'Uffizio or Holy Office, situated on the Square's left side. Above is the **clock** with the bellfry containing six bells (one of the six is the famous bell weighing 100 quintals), the **dome** and the **cupola** over the Clementine Chapel erected by Giacomo Della Porta. This matches another cupola opposite (not visible in the photo) on the Gregorian Chapel. Both act as "counterweights" to Michelangelo's dome. In the right foreground is the outermost curve of the **colonnade** which ends in the straight, closed "wing" designed by Bernini as a connection between colonnade and façade. This "wing" is known as Charlemagne's "wing" because it

joins the left of the Basilica's portico where the equestrian statue of the Frankish king is positioned. It is often used for major exhibitions. This too is symmetrical with another closed "wing" to the right of the steps named after Constantine because it joins the right of the portico where the Emperor's equestrian statue stands.

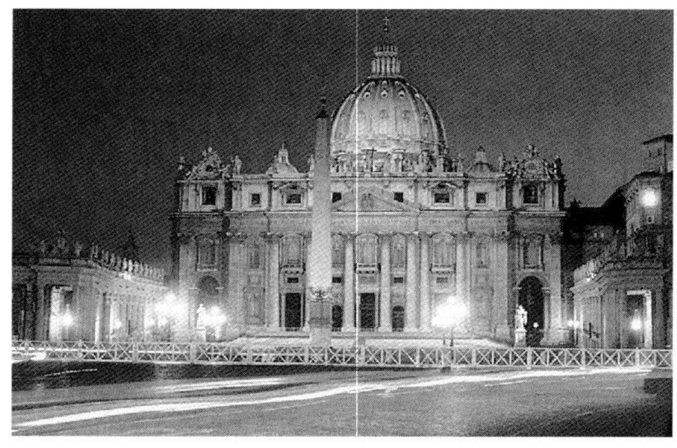

8. View of St Peter's Square with the **façade of the Basilica** in all its majesty, dominated by the dome. On the left behind Charlemagne's "wing" rises the cupola of Marchionni's Sacristy. On the right, above Constantine's "wing", soar the buildings of the Apostolic Palaces on the corner of the Court of St Damasus. In the centre stands the monolithic **obelisk** made of smooth bands of red granite and over 25 metres high with a base 8 metres high. Of Egyptian origin, it stood in Nero's circus and remained beside the Basilica until 1586 when Sixtus V had Domenico Fontana move it to its present position in the middle of the Square. It is crowned by the mounts and stars of the Chigi family's coat of arms, that of Alexander VII. Relics of the Holy Cross are preserved at the top. The base is decorated with four lions, heraldic symbol of Sixtus V, and bronze eagles added in 1713 by Innocent XIII in memory of the heraldic elements of his Conti family.

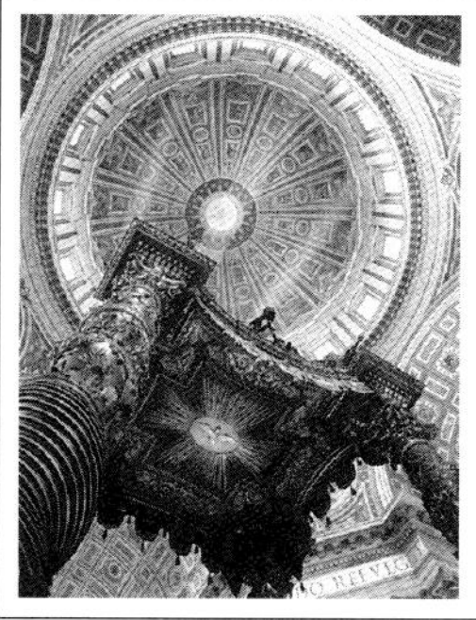

9. Bernini's bronze **baldachin** or **canopy** seen from the Papal altar below it, with the dove of the Holy Spirit in the centre of the splendid cornice enveloped in the magnificent panorama of the **dome**. The dome rests on four grand, vaulted arches on four pillars (each with a perimeter of 71 metres), is over 42 metres wide and more than 136 metres high from the pavement to the top. At its base, on a golden background, runs the Latin inscription regarding Christ's founding of the Church. From here the drum unfolds, punctuated by 16 windows between pairs of pilasters embedded in the wall supporting the cornice on which curves the cap. Between 1603 and 1612 this is divided into 16 large rib-like segments with stucco and mosaic decorations based on cartoons by Cavalier d'Arpino depicting the orders of Paradise with God at the summit. Sixtus V's dedication is in the eye of the lantern.

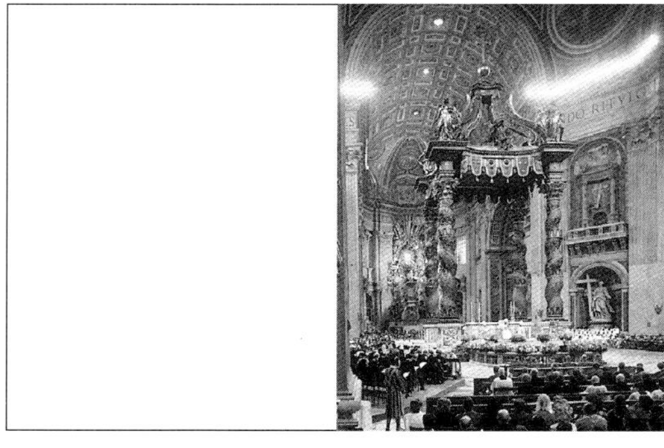

10. Religious function celebrated by the Pope at the altar beneath the bronze **canopy**. Executed by Bernini between 1624 and 1633, it was conceived as a spectacular Baroque "machine" for extolling the primacy of St Peter whose tomb is found below in the Confession. Leading to the place called the Confession is the balustrade with 99 perennially burning lamps. The canopy, born by four twisting columns each 20 metres high, is ringed by four angels emanating four volutes which join together at the centre as a support for a golden globe surmounted by the cross. At the base of the columns are splendid marble allegory decorations of *Mater Ecclesia* by the young Borromini, together with the coat of arms of Pope Urban VIII showing the bees of the Barberini family. In the apse in the background, keeping in scenic perspective with the canopy, stands the so-called **Throne of St Peter (Cattedra di San Pietro)**, another of Bernini's ingenious Baroque fantasies completed between 1658 and 1666. The wooden chair is enclosed in a large bronze "case" supported by colossal statues of the Doctors of the Church: St Augustine, St Ambrose, St Athanasius and St John Chrysostom. Encircling the Throne is a triumph of angels with a sheaf of golden rays exalting the *Glory* illuminated by an oval window of white and yellow stained glass where the dove of the Holy Spirit stands out.

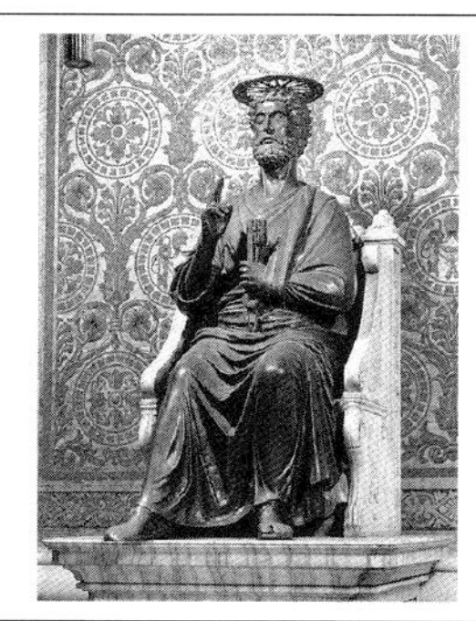

11. The **bronze statue of St Peter**, which stands against the last column in the Basilica's nave. Retained in the past to be an anonymous work of the 5th century, it has been correctly dated as 13th century, probably by Arnolfo di Cambio (1245-1310) who used an ancient statue of Jove, according to a strange legend. The Saint is depicted in a blessing pose and is seated on a marble chair dating from the 1800s, while the jasper pedestal dates from 1757 and is the work of Carlo Marchionni. In the *Ad Augendum* papal brief of 1857 Pius IX conceded a 50 day indulgence to whoever had kissed the foot of the statue, which appears so worn due to a thousand year old devotion which in any case preceded the brief. On the feast-day of Saints Peter and Paul on 29 June the statue is dressed in rich pontifical vestments and is the object of special religious functions aimed at exalting the preeminence of the Prince of the Apostles.

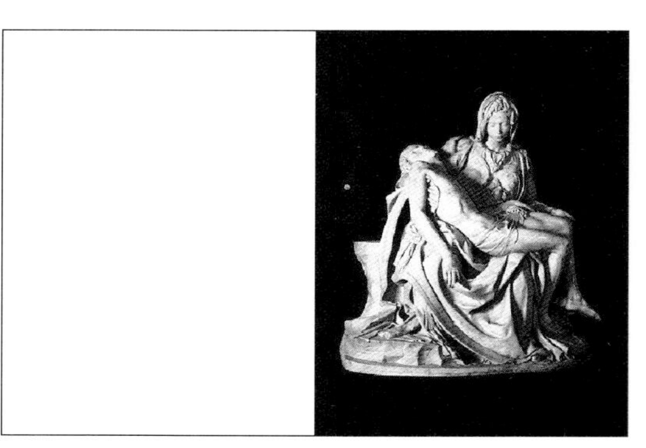

12. **Michelangelo's Pietà**, located in the chapel of the same name which is the first in the Basilica's right aisle. A work by the young artist commissioned by Cardinal Jean Villier de la Grolaie, Charles VIII's legate to Alexander VI in Rome, it was executed between 1498 and 1499 using a single block of marble from Carrara. It is the only work bearing the sculptor's signature, on the band falling from the Madonna's left shoulder. Damaged by the hammer blows of a madman in 1972, it was restored to perfect condition that same year by the "Vatican Marble Laboratory" reconsigning to us the complete, marvellous composition which depicts the Virgin who is holding the dead Christ on her knees. In addition, the restoration work brought to light Michelangelo's monogram on the Madonna's right hand - an "M" traced between the lines of the palm - which had been illegible for almost five centuries.

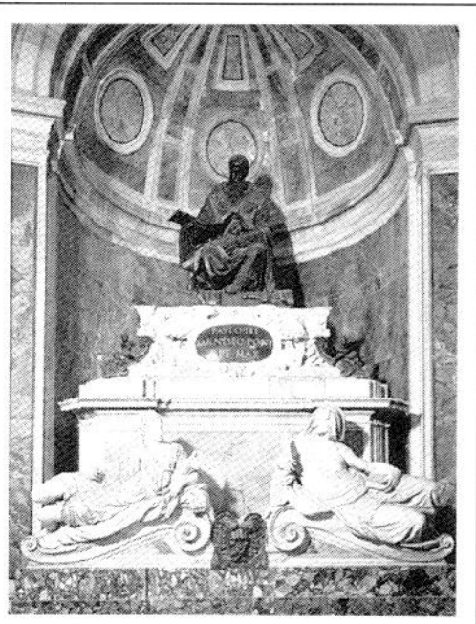

13. **Pope Paul III Farnese's funerary monument** by Guglielmo Della Porta is situated in the left niche of the apse in St Peter's Basilica. Beneath the bronze statue of the Pope are the marble representations of *Justice* and *Prudence* which are held to be Giulia Farnese, the Pope's sister, and Giovannella Caetani, his mother. Originally conceived as an isolated pyramidal tomb, it was to have been placed triumphantly in the centre of the apse. However the unfavourable views of many of the artists working on the Basilica's decoration, that of Michelangelo above all, resulted in the reduction of the monument's size to its present form. Two planned statues of *Abundance* and *Peace* were also eliminated. Having been moved, therefore, to the niche on the right-hand side of the apse, it was later

moved to the niche on the left so as to make room for the monument to Urban VIII. The long and tormented labour took more than 20 years, from 1551 to 1575.

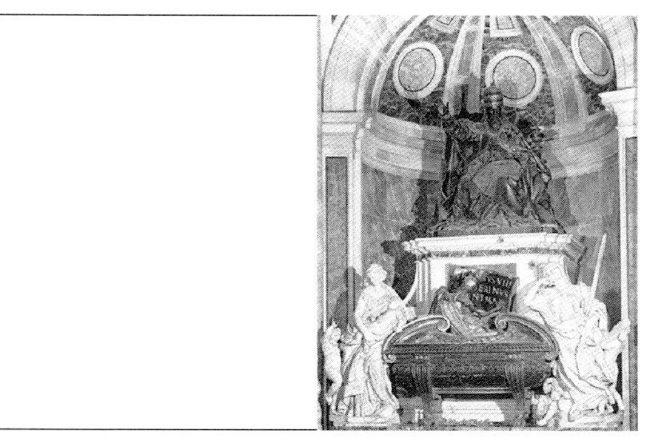

14. **Urban VIII Barberini's funerary monument.** Gian Lorenzo Bernini worked on his masterpiece from 1627 to 1647. The difference in its conception from that of the monument to Paul III is obvious: here the Pope is represented in all his power and majesty with the Triple Crown, symbol of the Pope's power as Father of Princes and Kings, Rector of the Orbe and Vicar of Christ. Bernini places the two figures *Charity* and *Justice* almost outside the niche in a free interpretation of space, characteristic of the artist. Above the sarcophagus, Death carves the Pope's name on a scroll, while bees symbolizing the Barberini family alight here and there almost irreverently in keeping with the artist's capricious personality and the Pope's impetuousity. The grandeur of the figures along with the composition's arrangement make it one of the outstanding masterpieces of the 17th century.

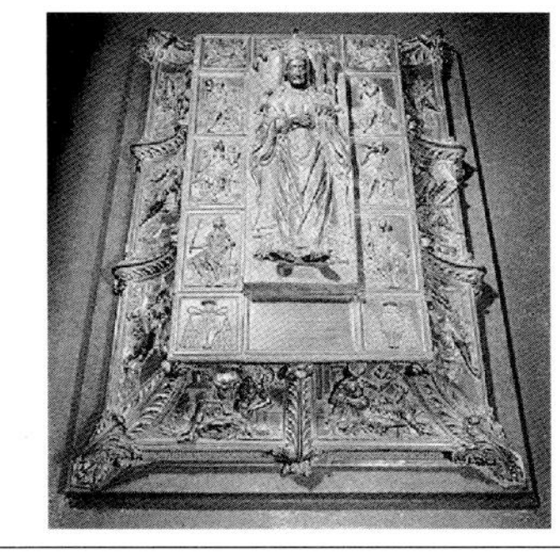

15. The marvellous **funerary monument to Sixtus IV**, part of the Museum of the Treasury of St Peter's. Antonio Pollaiolo's masterpiece is signed and dated 1493. It is a great bronze catafalque on which lies the Pope wearing the Triple Crown, his head resting on two richly embroidered cushions and his body laid out on a raised base surrounded by panels depicting the cardinal and theoloical virtues, four coats of arms of the Della Rovere family and an epigraph. On the concave edges of the bier in trapezoidal shaped segments divided by volutes of acanthus leaves the female allegorical figures of Rhetoric, Grammar, Perspective, Music, Geometry, Theology, Philosopy, Arithmetic, Astrology and Dialectics stand out. All these figures refer to the humanistic spirit which enlightened Sixtus IV (1471-1484). He founded the Vatican Apostolic Library and had the Papal Chapel, later to be called the Sistine in his memory, constructed. The monument is a true expression of the Christian Renaissance, capable of exalting the regality of the sovereign Pope and his patronage even in the tragedy of his death.

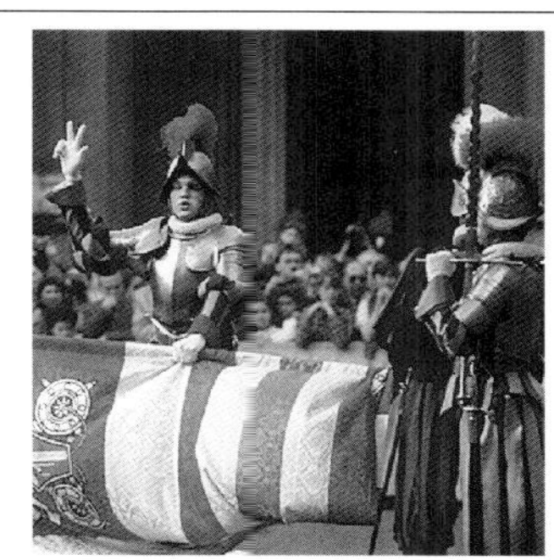

16. The **swearing-in of the Swiss Guard.** The ceremony takes place in the Apostolic Palace's Court of St Damasus on the morning of 6 May: each recruit holds high his right hand pointing upwards with three fingers in a sign of the Trinity and with his left hand grasps the yellow, red and blue flag divided by the white cross on which stands the coat of arms of the current commander of the corps, accompanied by the bearings of the reigning Pope and of Julius II, founder of the Guard. The swearing-in recalls the terrible date of 6 May 1527 when 147 halberdiers were massacred by the Lansquenet horde in defence of Pope Clement VII's retreat to Castel Sant'Angelo during the sacking of Rome.

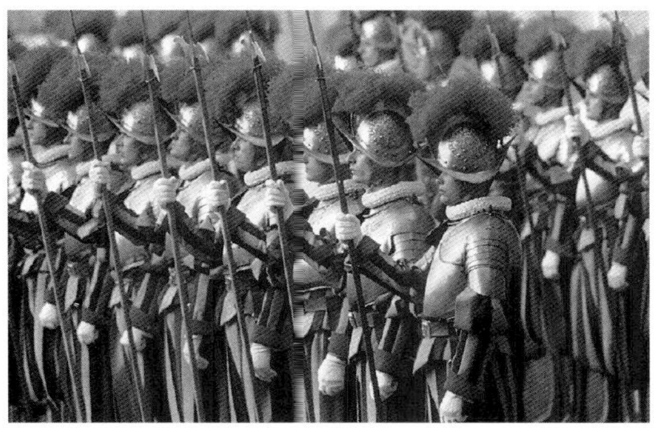

17. The soldiers of the **Swiss Guard** in file wearing full uniform. The Papal bodyguard was established on 21 January 1506 in accordance with the wishes of Pope Julius II and is recruited in the Catholic cantons of German-speaking Switzerland. The grand uniform, according to tradition, was designed by Michelangelo and is characterized by the billowing yellow and blue sleeves with red cuffs, the showy Spanish-style headpiece topped by red Ostrich feathers, the ruff, the armour and the two metre long halberd weighing six kilogrammes. The Guard is commanded by a colonel whose motto is "Fortiter et fideliter". The soldiers stand guard at the Bronze Gate, at the Arch of the Bells and at St Anne's Gate. Always stern in their surveillance, they are impeccable in their salute such as the special *Schultern* reserved for the Cardinals, tossing the heavy halberd and catching it in flight.

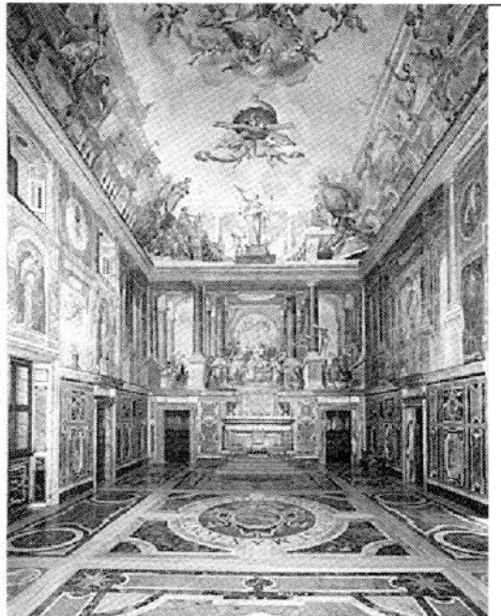

18. The **Clementine Room** (**Sala Clementina**), the grand vestibule of the Pope's formal apartment on the second floor of the Sistine Palace. It is named after Clement VIII who commissioned Giovanni Fontana and Giacomo Delle Porta to complete the work in 1595. The Pope's name appears, in fact, on the doorposts, in the epigraph above the throne and in the pavement at the centre of the room with the majestic Aldobrandini bearings. The sumptuous fresco decoration is by the Alberti brothers, Giovanni and Cherubino, and exalts the figure of Pope Clement I, from the *Baptism* on the wall in the background to the *Martyrdom* on the opposite wall, not visible in the photo. Also in the series is his *Triumph* on the ceiling, completed in the context of the glory of the Papacy and the Roman Church, with the symbolic keys of St Peter and the female allegorical figures of Art, Science and the Catholic Apostolate and was completed for the Jubilee of 1600. In times gone by the Pope celebrated the rite of the washing of the feet in this room each Holy Thursday in the presence of pilgrims.

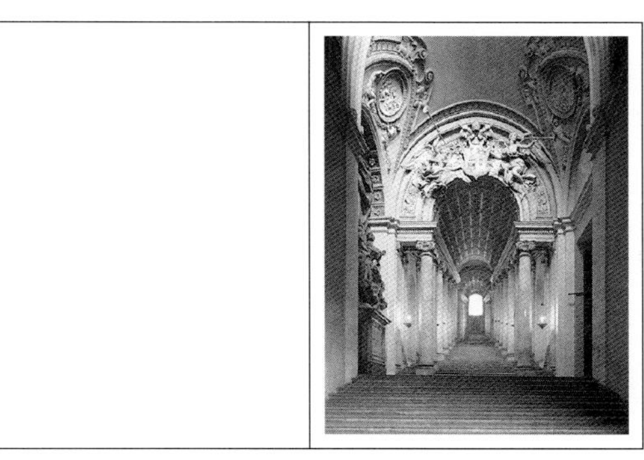

19. The striking **Royal Staircase** (**Scala Regia**) at the end of the so-called Constantine's "wing" which one enters from the Bronze Gate. The stupendous staircase was built in 1665 by Bernini as a triumphal entrance to the Royal Hall (Sala Regia), adjacent to the Sistine Chapel, substituting an old stairway. The artist himself defined it "the most daring operation he had ever done". It unfolds over two flights, punctuated by a landing. The first flight has six pairs of Ionic columns on each wall supporting a barrel vault with stucco decoration. The second flight opens with a marvellous arch (decorated with two angels holding the coat of arms of Pope Alexander VII Chigi, commissioner of the work) from which rises an internal colonnade, its architrave bearing the barrel vault with stucco decoration. The flight gradually becomes more narrow and low, creating an extraordinary perspective effect. In fact, the progressive lowering of the vault and of the height and width of the columns towards the bottom makes the stairway seem longer than it really is.

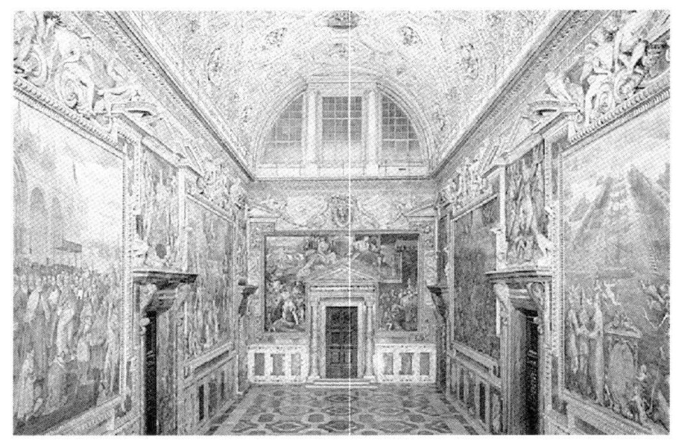

20. The **Royal Hall** (**Sala Regia**) which one enters from the stairway of the same name, the Royal Staircase. Begun in 1538 by Antonio da Sangallo on the commission of Paul III (recalled in the inscription on the architrave of the door opening onto the Pauline Chapel), it was not completed until 1573 during the pontificate of Gregory XIII. It was intended as a reception room for private audiences with sovereigns. As such it was frescoed with themes exalting the Pope's power with the aim of stirring reverent respect in the guests. On the left, Francesco Salviati's *The Subjection of Barbarossa to Alexander III* and on the far wall, to the right of the door, Federico Zuccari's *Henry IV Before Gregory VII*. On the right-hand wall is Lorenzo Sabatini's *The Alliance between Holy See, Spain and Venice* with the personification of the three states in the three large figures in the foreground. The largescale "naval review" symbolizes the power of a Crusade blessed by the Pope. The barrel vault has rich stucco lacunars by Perin del Vaga, while the stucco work on the walls is by Daniele da Volterra.

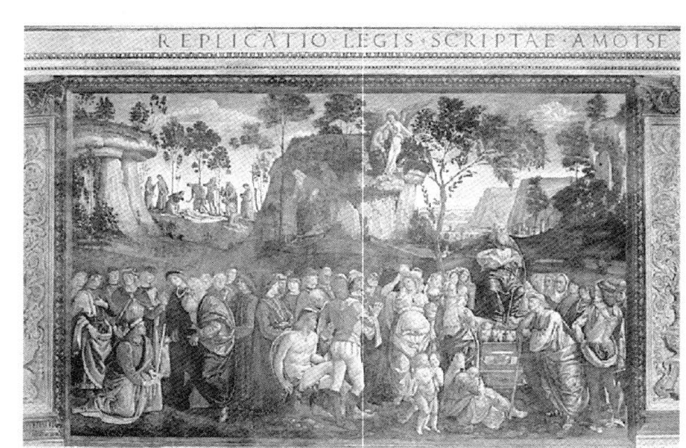

21. Fresco with **Episodes from the Life of Moses** on the right-hand wall of the Sistine Chapel. This is part of Sixtus IV's iconographic programme concentrated on the exaltation of the universal supremacy of the Roman Pontiff and unfolding over a series of six panels recalling the life of Moses and an equal number inspired by the life of Christ. Executed in 1483 by Luca Signorelli and Bartolomeo Della Gatta, this is the last in the sequence dedicated to Moses. Depicted in the panel are: in the foreground, *The Handing over of the Rod to Aaron* and on the right, *The Reading of the Testament*; further back to the right, *The Promised Land* in the form of a city, *The Angel Shows Moses the Promised Land* and *Moses Moving Towards Death* in the centre, while on the left is the *Lamentation over the Death of Moses*. It may be held that the young nude in the centre foreground, representing the tribe of Levi, inspired Michelangelo's "Atlases" on the vault of this same Chapel.

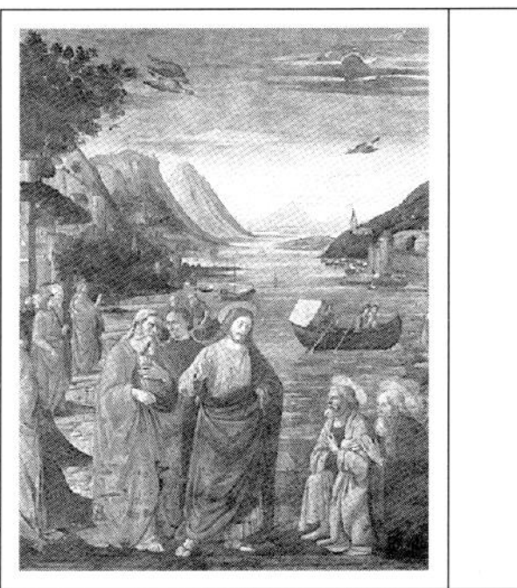

22. **The Calling of the First Apostles** is the fresco on the left-hand wall of the Sistine Chapel. Part of the series of panels inspired by the life of Christ and carried out by various artists commissioned by Sixtus IV, it was painted by Ghirlandaio in 1482. Reproduced here is a detail representing in the foreground, *Peter and Andrew Kneeling Before Jesus*; further back on the right, *The Two Apostles Going to Cast the Nets* and to the left *The Two Apostles Hauling in the Nets with the Benediction of Jesus*. In the background is a beautiful landscape of the lake at Tiberiad, also known as the Sea of Galilee, with fancifully medieval buildings, but in line with the geographic features of Jesus' time: the dark and desolate hills to the East, fertile and woody land to the West and a glimpse of Mount Tabor to the North - the mountain of the Transfiguration. This episode, narrated in detail in Luke's Gospel, is fundamental to the symbolic sense of the figure of Peter, "fisher of men", and of his "little boat" signifying the reason for the Church's existence.

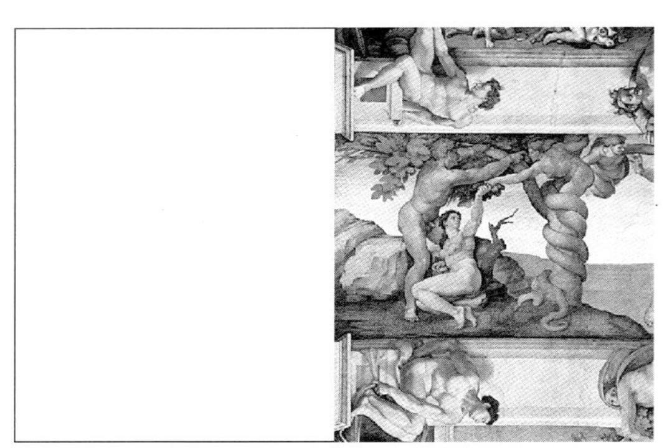

23. **The Original Sin** is one of the frescoes on the vault of the Sistine Chapel, recently restored to bring back the splendour of its original colours. Painted by Michelangelo between 1508 and 1512 for Julius II, it depicts episodes from *Genesis* from the creation of the universe to the continuation of life on earth through Noah's family. The *Expulsion from Paradise* is to the right of this scene and we can make out the angel executioner in the photo shown. That very same angel seems to grow out of the tree in the centre to which the tempter is clinging. In fact, the fresco is conceived as a triptych centred on the tree. The ancestors of humanity are beautiful, captured in all their virginal purity. In the two panels above and below, two of the four naked youths seem, with their gestures, to comment on the event taking place.

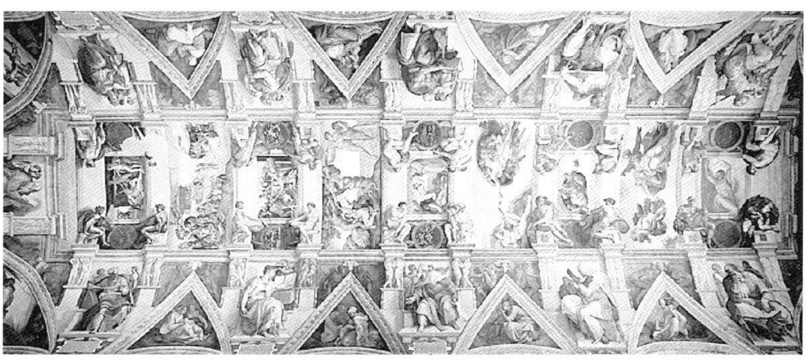

24. The **vault of the Sistine Chapel**. In the centre are nine episodes from *Genesis* spanning over four large panels and five smaller, framed panels, each born by four naked youths ("ignudi") acting as "Atlases", holding festoons and false bronze medallions adorned with figures. The episodes are, from the right, *God Separates Light from Darkness* (with an almost immaterial figure of the Creator), *God Creates the Moon, Sun and Plants* (with the Creator depicted twice), *God Separates the Land from the Water, The Creation of Man, The Creation of Woman* (rising in prayer from Adam's side, drawn to God's right), *The Original Sin and Expulsion from Paradise, Noah's Sacrifice, The Flood* (the first fresco executed by Michelangelo in 1508) and *The Drunkenness of Noah*, signal of the recommencement of life on earth, linking up with the cycle that unfolds on the walls covering the lives of Jesus and Moses. Depicted alternately along the curved part of the ceiling are seven prophets (*Joel, Ezechiel, Jeremiah, Jonah, Daniel, Isaiah* and *Zechariah*) and five sybils (*Erythraen, Persian, Libyan, Cumaean* and *Delphic*), each assisted by an angel. Four biblical scenes are depicted in the corner-spandrels: the *Punishment of Haman*, the *Bronze Serpent, Judith and Holofernes*, and *David and Goliath*. All allude to the Redeemer of humanity prophesized in Israel. In the vaulting cells the procession of Jesus' Ancestors awaiting His Coming unfolds: from the bottom left are *Zerubbabel and Parents, Azariah and Parents, Rehoboam and Mother* and *Solomon and Mother*. From the top left: *Jesse's Parents, Asa and Parents, Hezekiah and Parents* and *Josiah and Parents*. More of Jesus' ancestors are depicted in the lunettes above the windows.

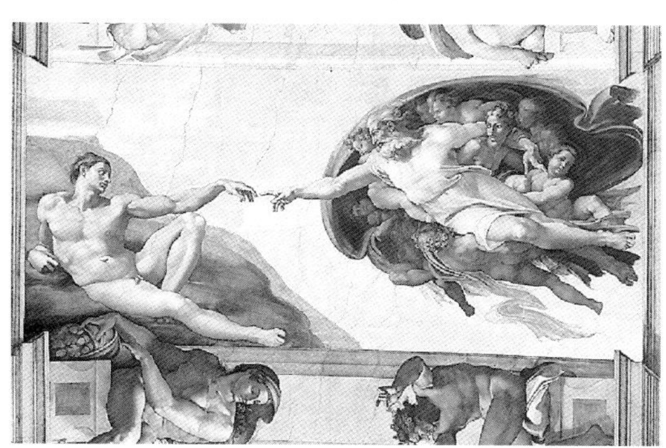

25. The **Creation of Man**, one of the frescoes on the vault of the Sistine Chapel by Michelangelo, perhaps the most beautiful and poetically intense. The significance of the scene is completely concentrated on the two outstretched, almost touching hands. This is the point where Adam receives spritual grace and intellectual strength from God: the Divine finger in drawing closer to his creature's instills in the already formed body the breath of life. Emblematic of Michelangelo's work, this image is much reproduced in engravings by other artists. Often these reproductions are limited to the fingers, to that vital point of the scene which is the extreme expression of an interior state of being of the two characters, the point of contact which apparently does not exist but which in reality takes place despite the Creator's keeping "in pose", gliding in the sky, and His being's remaining stretched out on the ground. That reciprocal gesture is the understanding on an eternal life beyond the limit of time.

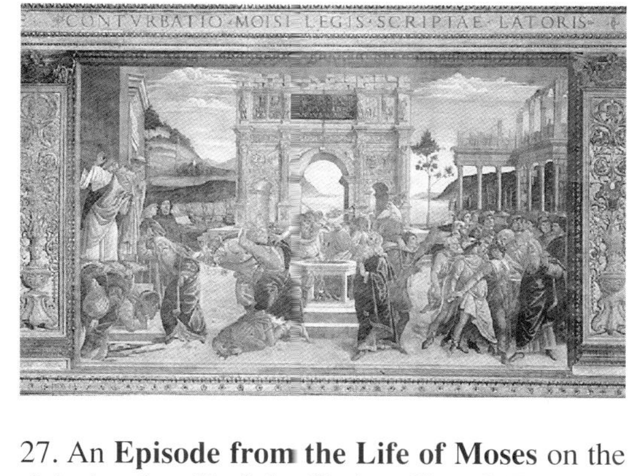

27. An **Episode from the Life of Moses** on the right-hand wall of the Sistine Chapel. Executed in 1483 by Sandro Botticelli, it is the second last painting in the cycle. Represented here, on the right is *The Revolt of Korah, Datan and Abiram* who "rose up against Moses with 250 men" according to the Book of Numbers. In the centre *The Followers of the Rebels Die while Offering Incense to God*, overwhelmed by the perfume from Aaron's incense burner, that same Aaron who was inspired by God to help Moses quell the rebellion. On the left *The Punishment of Korah, Datan and Abiram*, swallowed by the earth which opens up beneath them. In the background Botticelli has depicted two "wonders" of Rome: in the centre is Constantine's Arch and on the right the Septizonium. The latter was still standing at that time, to be destroyed one century later by Sixtus V as part of his urban renewal. At the far left near the house the youthful future Pope Paul III can be seen in profile with Pomponius Leto, his tutor.

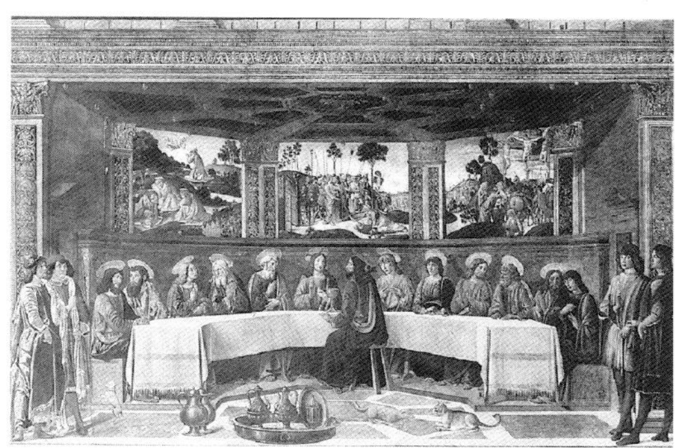

29. **The Last Supper**, a classic theme in religious painting, could not be overlooked in the series dedicated to Jesus. It is the last fresco on the left-hand wall, painted by Cosimo Rosselli in 1483. What distinguishes this fresco is Judas' position. Generally seated with the other Apostles, here he is depicted on our side of the table with his back to us and with a greyish halo and a small devil on his shoulder. The episode is completed by the three background panels painted as if they were three frescoes on the wall in the room of the Last Supper. To be viewed from left to right, they are: *Jesus in the Garden of Olives* praying to the Father while Peter, James and John lie sleeping; the *Arrest of Jesus* betrayed by Judas' kiss while Peter leans over the servant of the high priest whose ear he has cut off; the *Crucifixion* with Peter leaving the scene as if setting off on his mission in the world.

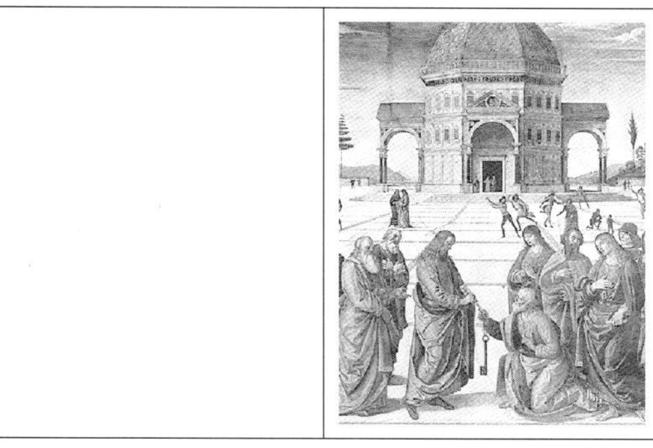

26. **Jesus Handing Over the Keys to Peter**. A fresco of great importance given its symbolic significance in exalting the Church of Rome. Perugino's masterpiece, completed with the assistance of Luca Signorelli, is to be found on the left-hand wall of the Sistine Chapel. The central part of the work seen here has two triumphal arches in the background on the sides of the Temple of Jerusalem, and in the foreground are several characters amongst which Perugino included his self-portrait. The episode is narrated in Matthew's Gospel, when Jesus said "You are Peter and on this rock I will build my Church and the gates of Hell will not prevail against her. I will give you the keys of the Kingdom of Heaven and all that you bind on earth shall be bound in Heaven and all that you loosen on earth shall be loose in Heaven". With these words the Church recognizes the institution of the Papacy. They dictate a role to be exercised until the end of time within a community made up of living "rocks", amongst which Peter is seen as the one that assures the stability of the building. In taking possession of the keys he assumes a doctrinal decision-making power amongst men by the will of God.

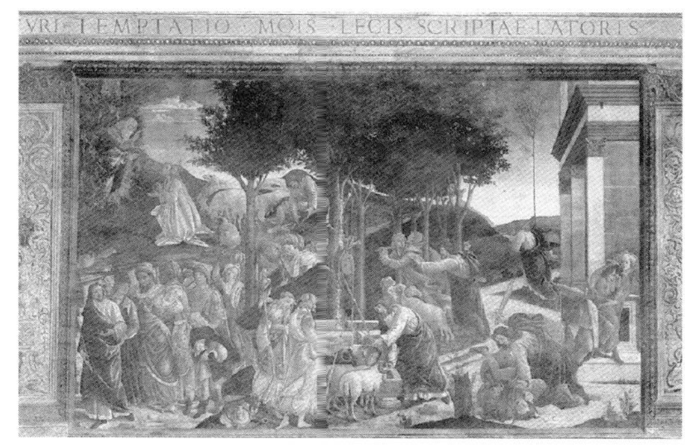

28. Other **episodes from the life of Moses** executed by Sandro Botticelli in 1482 on the right-hand wall of the Sistine Chapel and based on *Exodus*. On the right *Moses Kills an Egyptian* who had struck a Jew, the event which forced him to flee Egypt "and he settled in the town of Madian and stayed near a well". The second episode, represented in the centre, follows on from here: *Moses and the Daughters of Jethro*, priest of Madian. The daughters "came to draw water... and let their father's flock drink. But some shepherds arrived and drove them away. Then Moses rose in their defence and allowed their livestock to drink". As a token of his gratitude, Jethro welcomed him into his home and gave him one of his daughters in marriage, from which was born a son. The third episode is illustrated at the top left and shows *Moses Speaking with God*: "he was grazing Jethro's flock... and arrived at Mount Oreb. The Angel of the Lord appeared to him in a flame in the middle of a bramble bush" and God ordered him to return to Egypt and guide the Jews towards another land.

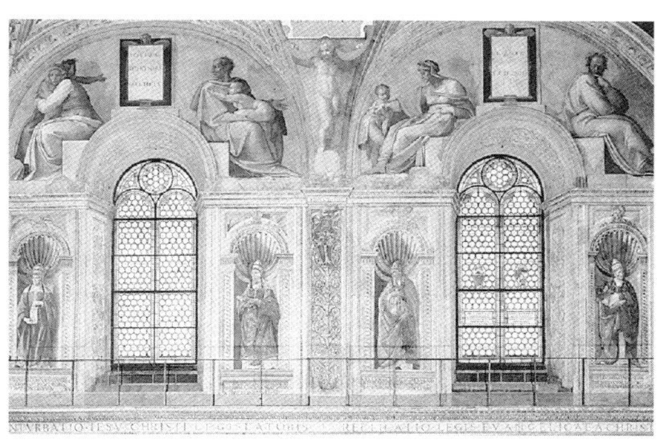

30. The upper part of the Sistine's side walls with some of **Jesus' Ancestors** in the lunettes above the windows. These follow on from the spandrels of the vault, also by Michelangelo. Between the windows is a picture gallery of full-length portraits of 24 **Popes** within grisaille niches, together with the biblical scenes below dating back to the first phase of the Chapel's decoration when they began from the wall behind the altar, later destroyed to make way for Michelangelo's Last Judgement. Reproduced here is a section of the left wall above the stories from the life of Jesus. In the lunettes from left: *Shealtiel and Mother*, and *Josiah with the Little Jeconiah, Zadoch and Mother* and *Azor*. The Pontiffs from left are: *Fabian* (236-250), *Lucius I* (253-254), *Sixtus II* (257-258) and *Felix I* (269-274). The second and third of these are by Botticelli.

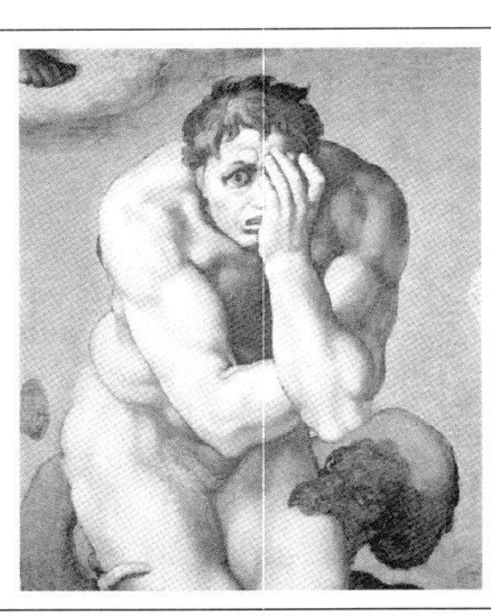

31. The "wretch" in the **Last Judgement**, one of the most dramatic characters in Michelangelo's masterpiece on the wall behind the alter of the Sistine Chapel. Commissioned by Paul III, the work was completed between 1535 and 1541. The huge fresco depicts the souls of the dead preparing themselves to undergo God's dreadful judgement and was requested by the Pope to remind Christians to remain faithful to the Church of Rome, with precise reference to the Council of Trent and the theological questions discussed in the condemnation of the Lutheran Reformation and in exaltation of the Counter-Reformation. This character is in the lower right of the fresco with the damned fallen to Hell despite their resistance which is broken by the Angels. This "wretch", however, does not fight the sentence imposed on him, contemplating the abyss into which he is being dragged. He looks at it as if mad, with only one eye, covering the other with his hand and taking no notice of the devil in the form of a serpent clinging to him and biting his thigh.

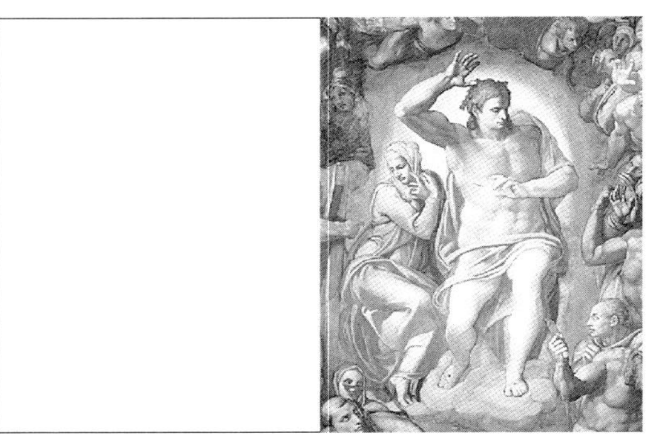

32. **Christ the Judge** in Michelangelo's Last Judgement. The central figure, towering over the whole composition on the clouds in the Christian form of a pagan god (recalling a kind of Apollo-Hercules) in an act of condemnation. His expression, however, is not merciful towards the damned nor benevolent towards the Saints around him; it goes beyond the Judgement itself, the imperturbable face of Eternity in the good and evil of existence. Beside Him is the Madonna, surrounded by His halo, but completely isolated by her immaculate nature and incapable of watching the scene. At His feet to the left we can make out St Lawrence with his gridiron; to the right, part of St Bartholomew's body can be seen with a carving knife, recalling his flaying. The recent restoration has rendered the figure of Christ more imposing on a more intensely lit background within which His athletic divinity is defined as the beginning and end of all the movement of the great scene.

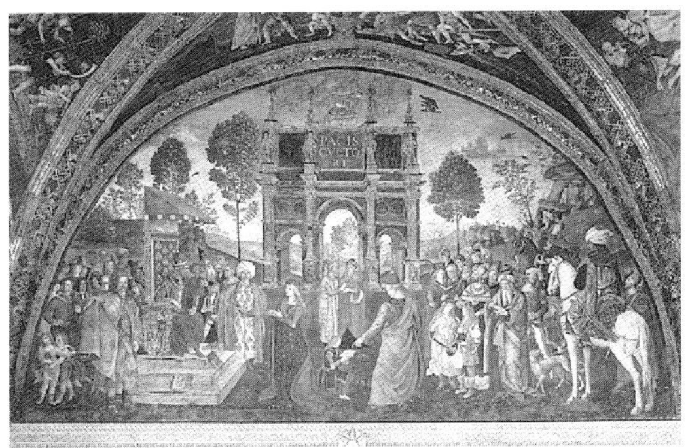

33. **The Debate of St Catherine of Alexandria with the Philosophers before Emperor Maximian**, executed by Pinturicchio in 1494, is the most important fresco in the Borgia Apartment of the Apostolic Palace. The fresco is in the large lunette in the room known as the Hall of the Saints and is particularly important for the historic personages portrayed. The Saint is portrayed in the likeness of Alexander VI's daughter Lucrezia, at that time 14 years old. The youth on horseback in oriental dress is her brother Juan, a lover of colourful costumes, while standing near the Emperor is the Turkish Prince Djem, aspirant to the Ottoman throne in exile in Rome. The Arch of Constantine is in the background, erroneously included by Pinturicchio since Maximian died in 310 and the Arch was only erected in 315 to commemorate the victory over Maxentius.

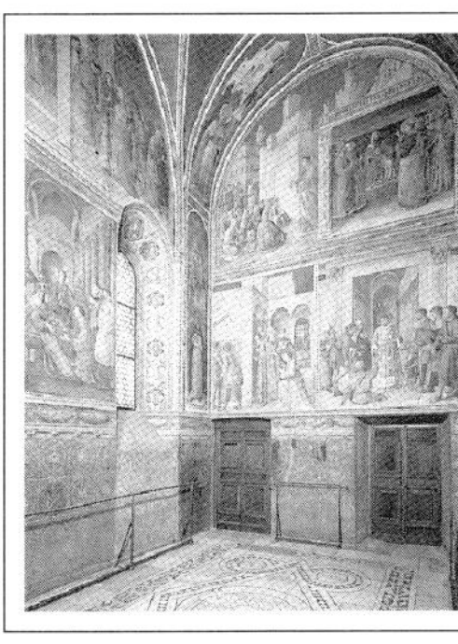

34. A wall of the **Chapel of Nicholas V** (**Cappella Nicolina**) with fresco work by Fra Angelico carried out between 1447 and 1450 for Nicholas V Parentucelli. Here the Florentine artist depicted scenes from the life of St Stephen and St Lawrence. On the wall seen here to the right: in the lunette *The Sermon by St Stephen* and *The Debate in the Sanhedrin*, and below *St Sixtus Hands Over the Treasures of the Church to St Lawrence* and *St Lawrence Distributes Alms to the Poor*. On the wall to the left *St Lawrence is Consecrated Deacon*. In the spandrels of the vault the four Evangelists Luke, Matthew, Mark and John are depicted on a blue background decorated with golden stars. The frescoes are considered a kind of happy junction between the religiously inspired and humanistic movements of the 15th century. The restoration work carried out from 1947 to 1951 have brought back to light Fra Angelico's particular primitive brightness and vivacity, typical of his best years.

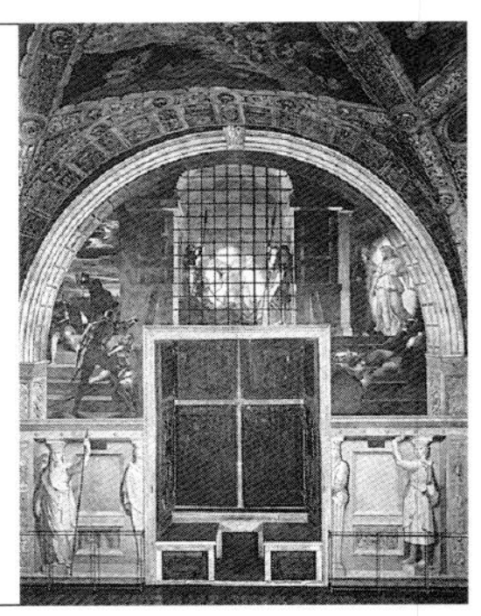

35. The **Liberation of St Peter from Prison**. The fresco is in Raphael's Stanze, on a wall in the Room of Heliodorus (Stanza di Eliodoro) and depicts an episode from the life of St Peter narrated in the *Acts of the Apostles*, which Raphael, assisted by Giulio Romano, followed faithfully. The Apostle had been arrested by Herod who wanted to put him to death and the night before the day fixed for his appearance before the people, Peter was sleeping between two soldiers, bound by two chains, while the guards before the door kept watch. There appeared an Angel, and a light blazed in the cell. Then, touching Peter's side, he woke him saying "get up quickly". And the chains fell away... «Wrap yourself in your cloak and follow me!" Peter followed him... Having passed by the first and second guards, they arrived at the iron gate which leads to the city». The entire fresco is reproduced here and it should be viewed from left to right, in line with the sacred text. In the centre is a detail inside the prison, the black bars in splendid contrast with the Angel's blinding light.

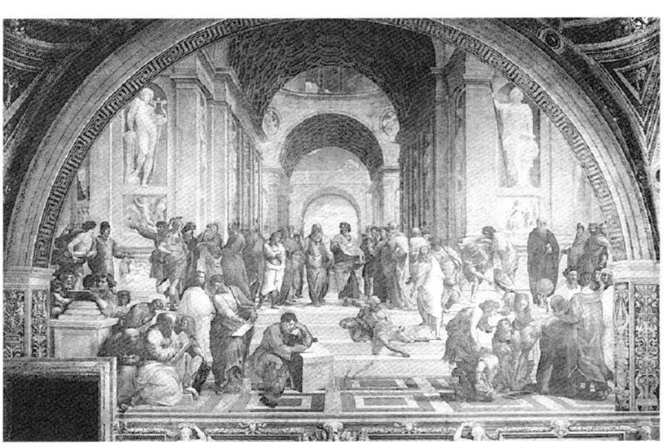

36. **The School of Athens**. This masterpiece by Raphael in the Stanza della Segnatura was begun in 1509 and finished in 1511. It depicts the meeting of ancient and modern thinkers beneath the vaults of a temple with dome, based on a design suggested to the artist by Bramante. Some of the ancients are portrayed in the likeness of Raphael's contemporaries: in the centre Plato holding his book the *Timaeus* is a portrait of Leonardo. Beside him is Aristotle with his book *Ethics*. To the left of Plato is Socrates who is counting off syllogisms on his fingers. In the group listening to him are Aischines and Alcibiades and in the foreground is Epicurus wearing a crown of vine leaves. The curly haired child on his right could be identified as Federico Gonzaga. There is another group around Pythagoras seen in profile: Averroes with the turban at his shoulders and Empedocles seated. Beside the unidentified man pointing to the book, Heraclitus in the likeness of Michelangelo is seated, while in the centre Diogenes reclines on the steps. In the group on the right Euclid in the likeness of Bramante is bending over to

describe a geometrical figure. Ptolomy with the crown and Zoroaster with the stellar globe follow. In profile, Sodoma (with the white cap) and Raphael (with the black cap).

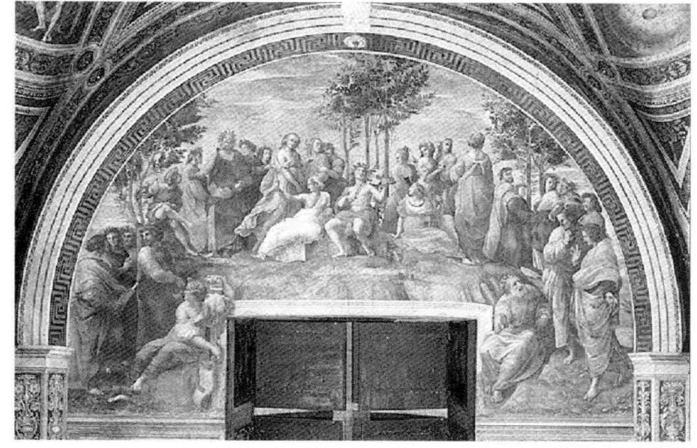

37. **The Parnassus**. This fresco is in the Stanza della Segnatura and dated 1511 on the architrave of the window. On the mythical montain, ancient and modern poets are gathered at the court of Apollo who is seated playing the lyre, surrounded by the Muses. On the left is Calliope, sitting next to the god. Behind her are Euterpe, Clio and Thalia. Seated on the right is Erato and behind her are Urania, Melpomene, Terpsichore and Polyhymnia. Then come the poets: to the left the blind Homer recites the verses that a youthful Aeneas transcribes, with Virgil and Dante at his shoulders. Below from the left are Alceo, Corinne, Petrarch, Anacreon and, seated, Sappho (identified by some as the courtesan Imperia). To the right, other poets whose identities are not certain: Castiglione with the black beard, Boccaccio, Sannazzaro in the yellow robe and Tebaldeo in profile with the white beard; then there is Ovid, Ariosto (with his hand on his chin), Horace and Pindar.

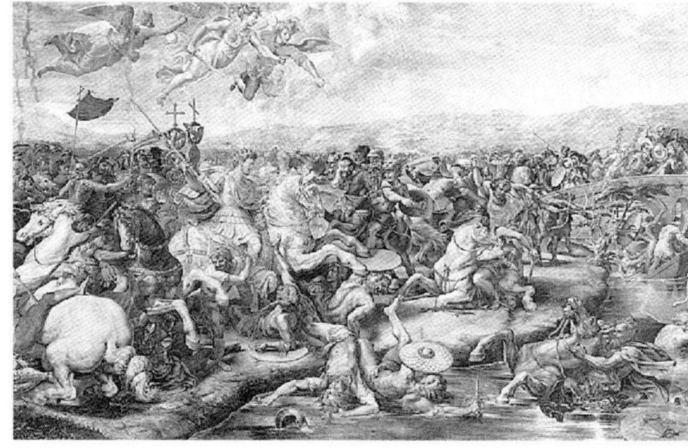

38. **The Battle of the Milvian Bridge**. This fresco is in the only room of the Stanze not painted by the artist from Urbino, namely the Hall of Constantine (Sala di Costantino), decorated after his death almost exclusively by Giulio Romano with the help of Gian Francesco Penni and Raffaellino del Colle. Recalling Constantine's victory over Maxentius in 312, accomplishing God's will symbolized in the cross on top of the Roman eagles and in accordance with an angelic vision immortalized by the motto «In hoc signo vinces». In fact the angels guide the Emperor's army as an expression of the heavenly protection over this event which foreshadows the exaltation of the Christian religion. The famous edict on tolerance resulted a year after the battle, conceding freedom of worship to the Christians as well as all of Constantine's efforts in favour of the Bishop of Rome.

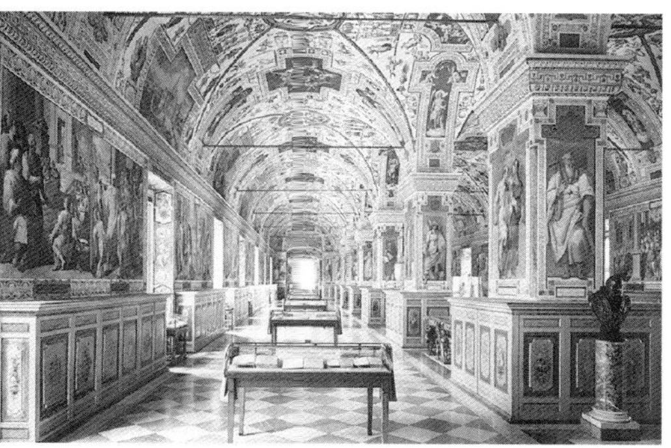

39. **The Sistine Room of the Vatican Library.** Named after Sixtus V who erected the new library between 1587 and 1589 using Domenico Fontana's design. This was to substitute the library on the ground floor of the northern wing of the Palace where Sixtus IV had temporarily arranged it, founding it in 1475. The room, which today is used for the display of books and often houses temporary exhibitions, was originally the reading room. Built around two aisles divided by large pillars and covered by cross-vaults, it is richly decorated by numerous artists, Paul Brill and Ventura Salimbeni amongst them. The decoration is dedicated to episodes from Sixtus V's pontificate, to the great libraries of ancient times (in the left-hand foreground is that of Babylon), to the inventors of the written word, to the Ecumenical Councils and to views of Rome. The vaults are frescoed with grotesques and have cross-shaped panels with allegories at the top and angels below.

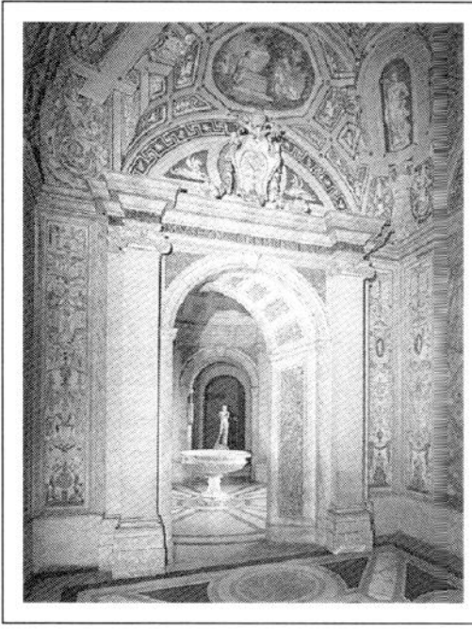

40. Entrance to the **Pio-Clementine Museum** which corresponds to the original entrance to the Clementine Museum. Founded in 1771 by Clement XIV Ganganelli, it was enlarged in 1786 by Pius VI Braschi, in the end being named after them. The coat of arms on the door is in any case that of the Ganganelli family. Beyond the entrance is a round vestibule in the middle of which we can see the large basin. The cabinet of the *Apoxyomenos*, distinguished by its marble whiteness, is in the background. The statue depicts a winning athlete in the act of cleansing himself of the sweat and the powder mixed with oil with which he had covered himself for a bout. Discovered at Trastevere in 1849, it is a Roman copy from the first century A.D. of the original bronze by Lysippus dated 320 B.C.

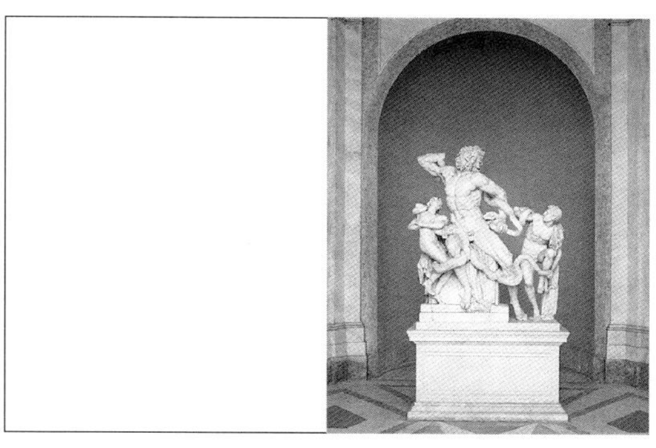

41. The **Laocoön**. The famous sculptural group in marble depicts the priest of Troy who, together with the sons of Athene, was comdemned to death by suffocation by two serpents because he wanted to oppose the entrance of the horse into the city. It is a copy of a bronze original of the late second century B.C. and came to light on 14 January 1506 in the Domus Aurea zone. Its discovery sparked a spirit of emulation amongst the comtemporary artists, especially in Michelangelo. Seeing as the group was damaged, the artist initially wanted to harmonize it and sculpted the priest's arm, later abandoning the idea. That arm is now behind the base. Instead, Montorsoli completed the group in the mid-1500s, adding the right arm of the priest and the youngest son, thereby altering the sculptural outline. These additions were removed in 1960, but later the original fragment of the bent arm, known as the "Pollak arm", was added by the archeologist who proved that the fragment belonged to the sculpture. The statue is in the portico of the Vatican Museums' octagonal courtyard constructed by Simonetti in 1773.

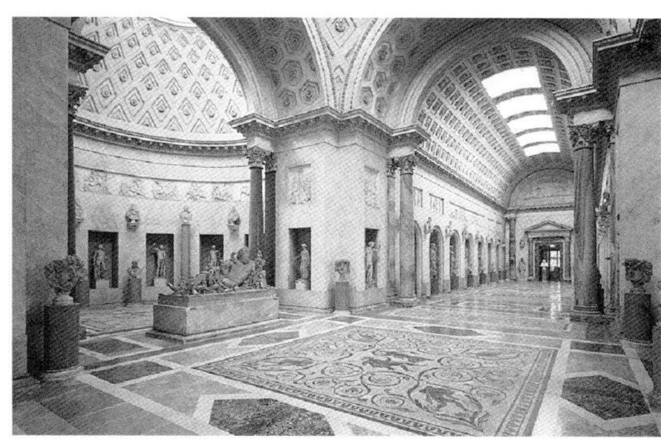

42. The **New Wing** (**Braccio Nuovo**) gallery in the Vatican Museums. It is the last section of the Chiaramonti Museum which Pius VII Chairamonti had constructed between 1817 and 1822 based on Raffaele Stern's plan. The long, barrel-vaulted gallery, flanked by niches with reliefs by Max Laboureur, is paved with mosaics from the Tor Marancia excavations on the Via Ardeatina. In the hemicycle in the foreground is the *Nile*, a Roman work of the first century from a Greek original. It came to light in 1513 in the church of St Mary's above Minerva (Santa Maria sopra Minerva) together with another colossal statue depicting the Tiber. Appropriated by the French, they both ended up in the Louvre, but France returned the work after the Congress of Vienna. The gigantic body of the river is depicted lying near a sphinx and a large cornucopia, with 16 angels climbing over him.

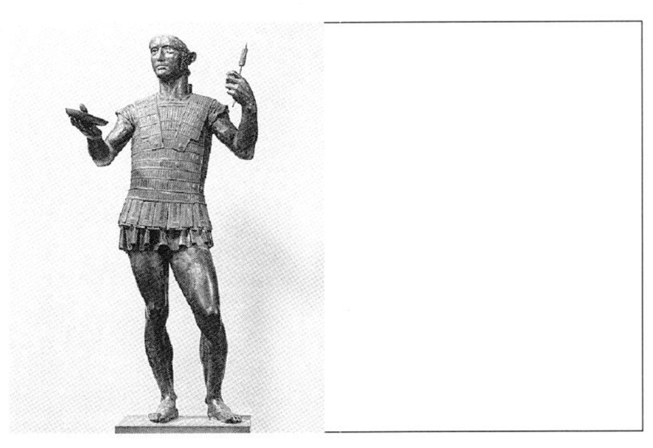

43. The **Todi Mars**. This famous Etruscan bronze from the end of the fifth century B.C. is held at the Etruscan-Gregorian Museum founded by Gregory XVI. It is an extremely rare original of Italic sculpture and depicts an almost life-sized warrior armed with lance and armour captured in the act of carrying out a libation before battle. In fact, it is a votive gift to a sanctuary in Todi, perhaps dedicated to Mars (hence the name of the statue), by a wealthy Celt personage who is recalled in the Umbrian language inscription on the armour's edge: "Ahal Trutitis dunum dede" (donated by Ahal Trutizio). Discovered on 2 June 1835 by a private digger, it entered the Vatican Museum on 6 September 1836.

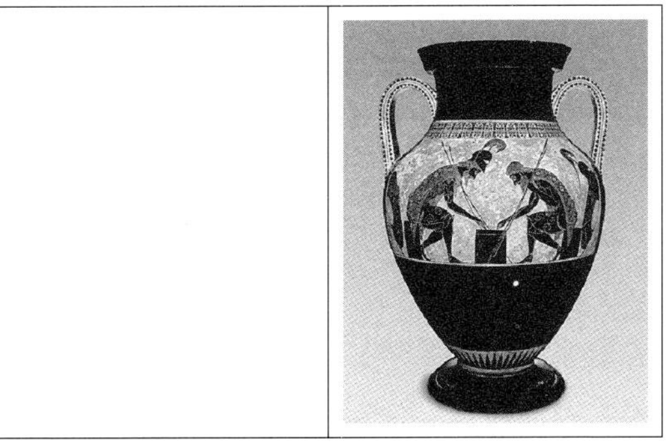

44. **Attic amphora with black figures**. Part of the Etruscan-Gregorian Museum vase collection which is mainly composed of material from southern Etruscan tombs. This, however, is a Greek masterpiece and is on display in the hemicycle of the Museum's last room. It shows Achilles and Ajax playing draughts and is signed by Exekias, the most important Attic black figure artist. The work dates from 530-520 B.C. and is of a splendid and compact form, succeeding in agreeably inserting the designed panel, thanks to its small dimensions, into the framework of the vase. It is an extraordinary piece of evidence of the Attic ceramic artisan's craftsmanship which, in the carving and piercing, black on red effect is capable of giving the figures ample space, as if they were on a canvass.

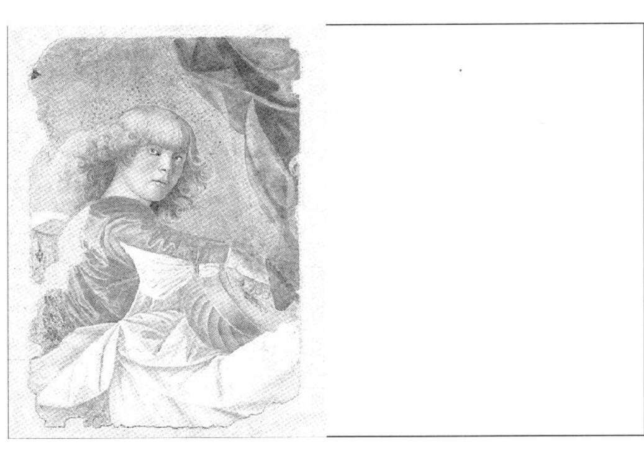

45. **Angel Playing the Lute**. The fragment of a fresco by Melozzo da Forlì (1438-1494) detached from the decoration of the apse in the basilica of the Holy Apostles (Santi Apostoli) in Rome. Here the angel, along with other angels and Apostles, crowned an *Ascension of Christ* painted in 1480. The entire fresco was almost completely destroyed in 1702 because of its instability and several pieces depicting the angels were saved, along with one larger piece with *Christ in Glory*. This last piece found its way to the Quirinal Palace, while the angels, this one included, are conserved at the Vatican Pinacoteca, the painting gallery opened by Pius VI in the present-day Tapestry Gallery (Galleria degli Arazzi). The collection grew after the Congress of Vienna with the recovery of 77 paintings which had ended up in France, further acquisitions and succeeding recoveries. A suitable building was necessary to house the collection, constructed in 1932 and designed by Luca Beltrami.

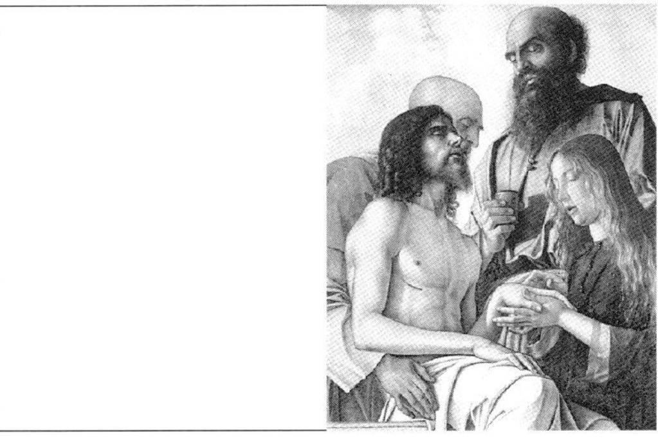

46. **Lamentation Over the Dead Christ.** Oil on panel by Giovanni Bellini held at the Vatican Pinacoteca. Jesus is depicted supported by St John of Arimathea and St Nicodemus, while Mary Magdalen caresses his hand. This is one of the works recovered in France after the Congress of Vienna and is part of a polyptych executed by the artist in Pesaro containing within a single frame: *Coronation of the Virgin with Saints Peter, Paul, Jerome and Francis*, eight saints in the small pillars and stories of saints in the predella. The Vatican panel was the cyma of the main element and is of great pictorial value with a plastic geometrical arrangement of the figures which stand out with features well defined against the light background of the sky.

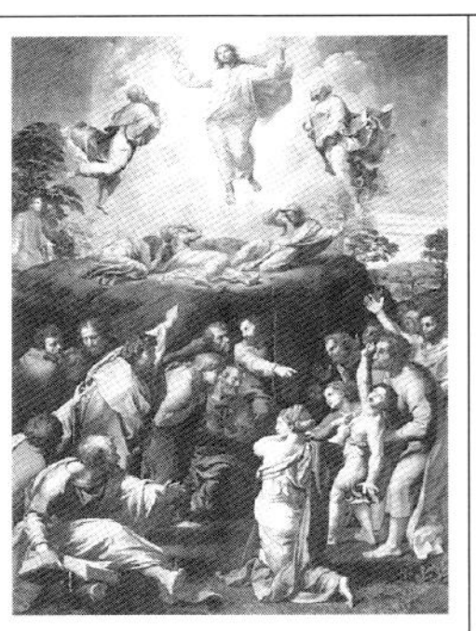

47. **The Transfiguration**. The famous painting by Raphael is housed in a room reserved for the painter from Urbino in the Vatican Pinacoteca. The panel was commissioned in 1517 for the Cathedral in Narbonne by its Bishop, Cardinal Giulio de' Medici, together with a *Resurrection of Lazarus* requested of Sebastiano del Piombo. In the end only this last work went to France because Raphael's painting was left unfinished due to his death in 1520, to be completed by Giulio Romano with the help of Penni. It was placed in the church of St Peter in Montorio (San Pietro in Montorio) in Rome where it remained until 1797 when it was stolen by the French and taken to Paris. It returned after the Congress of Vienna, destined for the Vatican Pinacoteca. Two episodes from St Matthew's Gospel are depicted on the altarpiece: at the top is the Transfiguration with Jesus flanked by Moses and Elijah, all bathed in His light, while Peter, James and John remain lying on Mount Tabor, blinded by the vision. Below are the other Apostles and a person possessed (who Christ will save on his return to the mountain) in a very animated and dramatic scene.

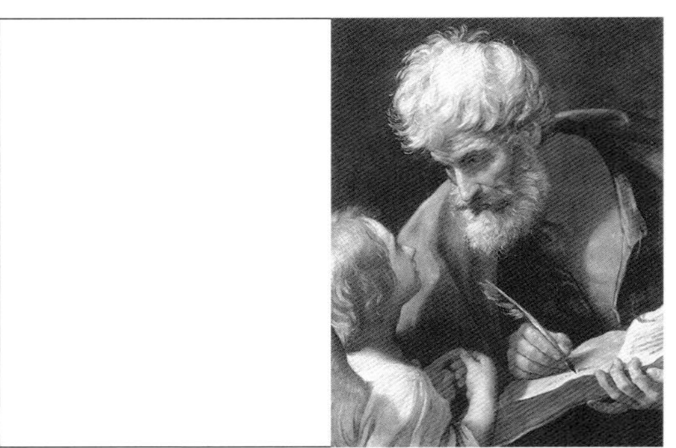

48. **St Matthew the Evangelist**. This oil painting by Guido Reni (1575-1642), which dates from about 1622, belongs to the Vatican Pinacoteca where it arrived as a donation in 1924. The Apostle is shown in three-quarter length and is most intent on writing as an angel dictates to him. Of the four, it is his Gospel which dedicates special attention to the Church founded by Christ in Peter. It follows that the painting has a precise value within the context of the Pontifical See, despite standing alone without the support of the other three Evangelists. It should in fact be part of a series of the four, a theme painted several times by Reni. The most recent critical comments have highlighted its high quality and its pure and formalist design.

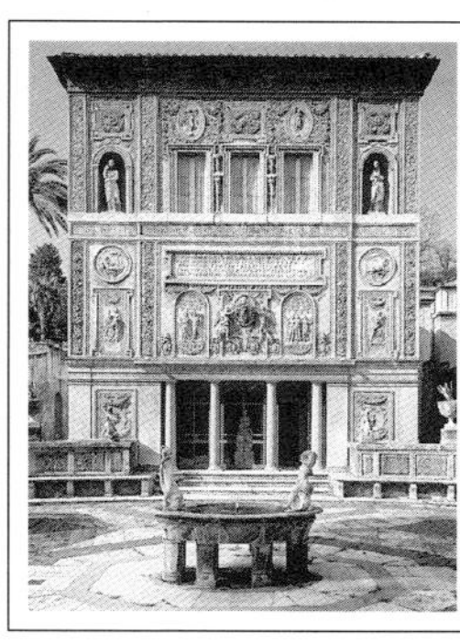

49. The **Casina of Pius IV** in the Vatican Gardens. The construction was commissioned by Pope Paul IV who wanted a place right in the middle of the Gardens for his leisure time. Work on the construction, however, dragged on from 1558 until 1563 under Pius IV, who was the first Pope to benefit from it. Its creator was the architect Pirro Ligorio who put a covered gallery in front of the construction to which it was connected by a courtyard. The result was a complex made up of two buildings which, with the rich stucco work by Paolo Pianetti, Rocco da Montefiascone and Girolamo da Como covering them, constitute an authentic architectural jewel. The construction was restored under Gregory XVI who transformed it into a small museum with marble busts and bass-reliefs. Pius IX chose it as the seat of the Pontifical Academy of Sciences (Pontificia Accademia delle Scienze).

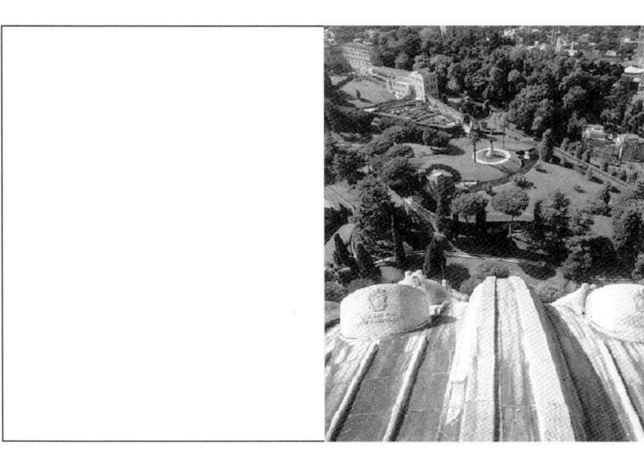

50. The **Vatican Gardens** in a panoramic view taken from the dome. From the bottom, in the foreground we can see the Gardener's House with a medieval tower which was part of the town-walls fortified by Innocent III about 1200. In the centre of the lawn in front of it is the bronze statue of St Peter by Filippo Guaccarini. To the left is the Aquilone (or Eagle) Fountain, constructed in 1612 by Martino Ferrabosco and Giovanni Vasanzio. On the extreme left near the boundary wall is the Tower of Nicholas V, adapted for use as a summer residence by Leo XIII, later the Vatican Observatory from 1906 to 1932 and finally, with the necessary additions, the Vatican Radio's headquarters. On the right is the "Casina" of Pius IV with the Vatican Pinacoteca in the background.

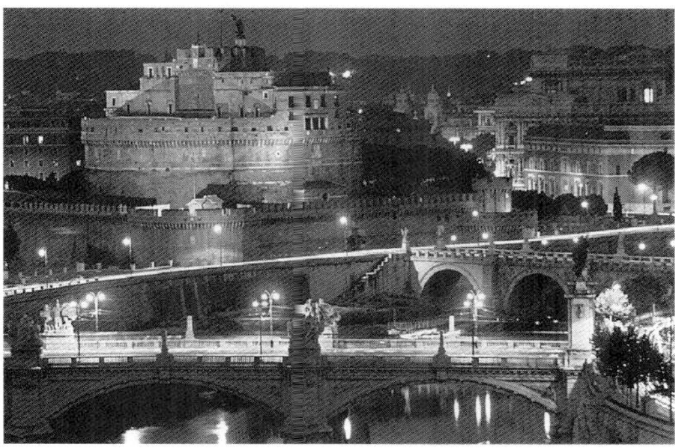

51. A view of **Castel Sant'Angelo**. Located outside the Vatican City, it is connected to it by the Borgo delle mura corridor. Although it does not belong to the Holy See, it nevertheless represents more than eight centuries of Papal history. Constructed as a mausoleum for the Emperor Hadrian in 121 A.D., it became a sacred site in 590 with the miracle of the Archangel Michael sheathing his sword, signifying the end of the plague, at the point where a statue will forever stand in his memory. It becomes a citadel fortified by the walls and the ancient Elio (later Sant'Angelo) Bridge, stronghold of various noble families, before finally becoming a Papal possession from the twelfth century. A fortress in defence of the Vatican Palaces, from the 15th century it was transformed into a Papal residence. Embellished and fortified, it was also a place of justice and imprisonment, as well as the Vatican Treasury's headquarters.

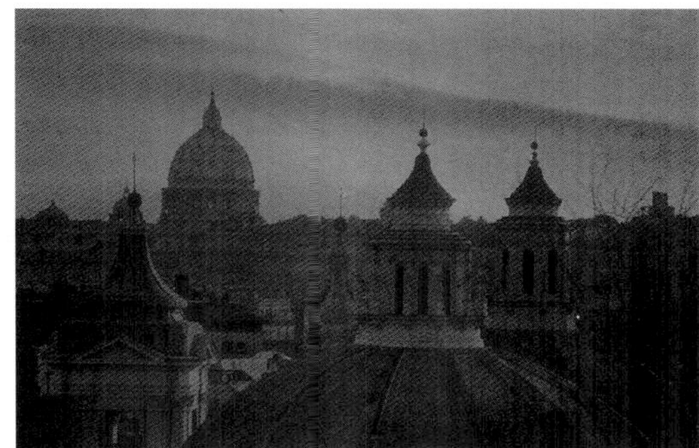

52. **Sunset over the Vatican and Janiculum Hills** from the Trinità dei Monti promenade on the Pincio. The dome of the Vatican soars up in the centre of the photo, dominating, even at a distance, the twin domes of the churches of St Mary's of the People (Santa Maria del Popolo) and St Mary's of Montesanto (Santa Maria di Montesanto) in Piazza del Popolo, seen in the foreground. The others in the background disappear amongst the rooftops and hills where only the antennas seem to signal different heights, picking up transmissions above the palaces and city-walls. The dome is only apparently the highest point of an extensive urban structure which appears compact, obliterating dimensions and boundaries. The Vatican is a city within a city, an *enclave*, but only closed within itself by chance. It is really separated from and united with Rome at the same time, reflected from yesterday to today in its thousand year history, punctuated by a reciprocal exchange of values.

Photo Credits

Pontifical Monuments, Museums and Galleries:
18, 19, 20, 21, 22, 23, 24, 25, 26, 27, 28, 29, 30, 33, 35, 36, 37, 38, 40, 41, 42, 43, 44, 45, 46, 47, 48, 49.

Vatican Apostolic Library: 39.

Nippon Television Network, Tokyo: 31, 32.

Scala Photographic Archive: 11, 13, 14, 15, 34.

The Stock Market / Dimitri-Essel: 51.

I.G.D.A. / G. Cigolini: 12.

Sie / Marcello Bertinetti: 10.

Magnus Photographic Archive / Massimo Mastrorillo:
front and back jacket,
1, 2, 3, 4, 5, 6, 7, 8, 9, 16, 17, 50, 52.